# MIDDLE CHURCH

*Reclaiming the Moral Values of*
*the Faithful Majority*
*from the Religious Right*

# Bob Edgar

*Simon & Schuster*
New York London Toronto Sydney

SIMON & SCHUSTER
Rockefeller Center
1230 Avenue of the Americas
New York, NY 10020

For information about special discounts for bulk purchases,
please contact Simon & Schuster Special Sales at
1-800-456-6798 or business@simonandschuster.com

Designed by Jaime Putorti

Manufactured in the United States of America

10 9 8 7 6 5 4 3 2 1

Library of Congress Cataloging-in-Publication Data
Edgar, Robert, date.
    Middle Church : reclaiming the moral values of the faithful majority from the
religious right / Bob Edgar.
        p.     cm.
    Includes bibliographical references and index.
    1. Christianity and politics—United States. 2. Church and state—United States.
3. United States—Religion. 4. United States—Moral conditions.  5. Progressivism
(United States politics). 6. Religious right—United States. I. Title.
BR516. E43 2006
277.3'083—dc22                    2006047516
ISBN-13: 978-0-7432-8949-8
ISBN-10: 0-7432-8949-8

*This book is dedicated with love and respect
to all those persons who have sought to be courageous
in the face of violence and faithful in the midst of oppression.*

# Contents

*If I speak in the tongues of mortals and of angels, but do not have love, I am a noisy gong or a clanging cymbal. And if I have prophetic powers, and understand all mysteries and all knowledge, and if I have all faith, so as to remove mountains, but do not have love, I am nothing. If I give away all my possessions, and if I hand over my body so that I may boast, but do not have love, I gain nothing.*

—1 CORINTHIANS 13:1–3

# MIDDLE
# CHURCH

# Preface

My purpose in writing this book is to awaken the conscience of average, ordinary, common folks within the United States to do above-average, extraordinary, and uncommon things to insure a future for our fragile planet. I am attempting to give people hope that we still have time to change our attitudes and retool our thinking, to restore and recover what our founders had in mind when they shaped our Constitution and Bill of Rights, calling America to higher moral standards than the rest of the world.

I am especially interested in inspiring and challenging what I call "Middle Church, Middle Synagogue, Middle Mosque"—the many millions of faithful people who do not always connect their spiritual values with political issues and whose voices are, as a result, often drowned out by the far religious right. This faithful majority must have the courage to confront their government when it makes bad decisions and have enough confidence in their own judgment not to believe unquestioningly the "expert" political leaders, who most

Americans assume know more than they do. My goal is to challenge them to read deeply their entire religious texts, to discover God's prophetic call to all of humanity, and to work collaboratively and be faithful stewards of our limited resources.

After forty-five years as pastor and politician, I hope this book helps restore passion for recovering America's moral values. At the same time, I hope it will help move us beyond private piety issues like abortion, homosexuality, and civil marriage to the more important fundamental moral values of ending poverty, healing a broken planet, and seeking nonviolent and peaceful solutions to the world's global conflicts. My pastoral experience calls me to urgently speak a word of hope in the midst of despair. My political experience calls me to urgently confront injustice, insensitivity, and insecurity in the wake of 9/11.

*Fear, fundamentalism, and the Fox Broadcasting Company* must not be allowed to set the agenda for our nation.

To achieve *peace, the end of poverty, and the healing of planet Earth* in America and around the world must be our immediate moral agenda.

This book suggests a framework for rethinking our role as a superpower with integrity and humility. It calls us to a higher sense of morality and helps reaffirm the United States as a model nation, respecting religious pluralism, and civil and human rights. It moves us away from being the nation the terrorists of 9/11 accused us of being. It challenges each of us to accept responsibility for being a part of the solution. And it asks God to remind us all of our common humanity, common values, and common sense on what is *right*.

In this book, I suppose you will find me to be a liberal. But remember what President John F. Kennedy said about being liberal: "If by a liberal they mean someone who looks ahead and not behind, someone who welcomes new ideas without rigid reactions, someone who cares about the welfare of the people—their health, their housing, their schools, their jobs, their civil rights, and their civil liberties . . . If that is what they mean by a 'liberal,' then I'm proud to say I'm a liberal." I own that definition!

# Introduction

One cold February day during my senior year of seminary, I did a controversial and, to some people, even radical thing: I boarded a bus and rode to Washington, D.C., to hear a Baptist preacher deliver a sermon on politics.

Like many others, I had read about his views and activities in the newspaper. I knew he preached against the decay of values in public life, and I knew he was often condemned for mixing politics and religion. His critics believed a clergyman had no business preaching about politics from the pulpit. Some feigned concern about the separation of church and state, but I think they were more opposed to the substance of his message than the fact that a minister was delivering it. He never called on the government to impose his Christian views. He simply spoke from his heart, and his heart and his faith were inseparable. He evaluated public policy according to his beliefs about right and wrong, and those beliefs were grounded in his Christianity. Faith led him to the conclusion that America was a morally sick nation that was ignoring Jesus' teachings, and in calling our society to account, in judging the policies of his country according to the principles of his faith, he threatened the familiarity and ease of the status quo. And, like so many messengers of faith who challenge our comfort too closely, he was denounced and vilified.

I was not troubled by the idea of a minister preaching politics from the pulpit, any more than I would discourage a rabbi or imam from delivering sermons that connect their religious values to public policy. I believe in the separation of church and state, but not in the separation of people of faith and institutions of government. What is politics, if not the highest expression of our moral feelings as a people? If discussion of morality is banished from the pulpit, then where is it permissible to speak about right and wrong? I had been a pastor of my own church since age nineteen, and I always felt the pulpit marked the beginning, not the boundaries, of ministry. So when a friend called and told me there would be a gathering of religious leaders in Washington who were concerned about the detachment between public policy and moral belief, I was intrigued enough to attend.

It was a clear day in Washington, bitterly cold but brilliantly sunny. As I leaned over the balcony rail from the upper level of the New York Avenue Presbyterian Church, the preacher we had come to hear walked up the center aisle. It was one of those profound experiences that imprints itself on one's memory in the form of general feelings rather than specifics. I cannot recall his words, only that his voice seemed to fill every space in the church, that he was earnest and unafraid, and that he was able to challenge America's moral failings without seeming judgmental or alienating. For him, the Gospels formed a seamless tapestry with current events, and he was unafraid to speak of both in terms of right and wrong.

It was a scene that might be repeated in many a church today, with a Jerry Falwell railing against homosexuals, a Pat Robertson endorsing tax cuts, or a Franklin Graham denigrating Islam and proclaiming Christianity to be the one, true American faith. But these were not the voices that called me to ministry or inspired me to political activism. The preacher in the pulpit on that cold but clear February day in 1968 was a thirty-nine-year-old Georgia-raised Baptist named Martin Luther King, Jr.

The occasion was a meeting of Clergy and Laymen Concerned About the Vietnam War. His topics—poverty and peace—may seem somewhat foreign to observers of contemporary politics but should be familiar to any student of scripture. Today those issues have disappeared from too many pulpits, replaced by narrow issues of personal piety.

More than thirty-five years after a Baptist preacher from the Deep South first inspired me to political action, it is time for mainstream Americans—the people I call "Middle Church," "Middle Synagogue," and "Middle Mosque," who may disagree sincerely on questions of personal piety but who can come together on many issues on which our three faiths are so clear—to reclaim our faith and restore it to its proper and historic place in our nation's unfolding story: as a force for justice, peace, the poor, and for the health of our fragile planet.

The Bible mentions abortion not once, homosexuality only twice, and poverty or peace more than two thousand times. Yet somehow abortion and homosexuality have become the litmus tests of faith in public life today. Those with different ideas about them, or even those who simply believe religion is about far more, are routinely dismissed as un-Christian, unfaithful, even un-American. The politics of faith have been co-opted in the service of a political agenda defined by fascination with war, indifference toward poverty, and exploitation of God's creation for the benefit of a relative few.

It is time for Middle Church—an umbrella term I use to refer to mainstream people of all faiths—to stand up to the far religious right and to embrace Christianity no less sincerely. The classic, historical Christianity practiced by Middle Church is far more authentic than the narrow religious expression of most radical right-wing religious leaders. We in Middle Church, Middle Synagogue, and Middle Mosque are not secularists who wish to banish God from the public square. We are people of faith whose traditions lead us to work for peace and care for the poor.

The *far* religious right is fond of condemning homosexuality because they say the Scripture is immutable and its words are literal. I do not mean by this the many good people of faith who espouse conservative political views, but the far right, who are increasingly intolerant of dissent and whose influence in Washington has grown beyond measure. I do not personally believe God stopped talking to us with the final word in the book of Revelation. As a pastor, the services I led always included readings from the Old Testament, the New Testament, and what I call the "Now Testament." I did so because I believe if we listen, we can hear the divine in the words of people like King, Gandhi, or William Sloane Coffin, the mentor who invited me to Washington that day in 1968. But if scriptural literalism is to be the test of morality in public life, then I welcome the discussion that ensues.

I opposed the war in Iraq, for "a harvest of righteousness is sown in peace for those who make peace," according to the Epistle of James (James 3:18). I believe in environmental preservation because God placed Adam in the Garden of Eden "to till it *and keep it,*" Genesis 2:15 reminds us, and I believe God's gift of "dominion" over the land was an invitation to steward God's creation. My faith cannot condone imprisoning suspected terrorists in deplorable conditions for unlimited durations without being charged with a crime or being given access to attorneys, for "justice, and only justice you shall pursue," God commands the Israelites in Deuteronomy 16:20. And most of all, I believe we must end poverty, heal sickness, and embrace the outcasts among us because the essence of faith is contained in Jesus' words in the Gospel of Matthew, words whose lesson is found in similar terms in other traditions, from Judaism to Islam:

> for I was hungry and you gave me food, I was thirsty and you gave me something to drink, I was a stranger and you welcomed me, I was naked and you gave me clothing, I was sick and you took care of me, I was in prison and you visited me. . . . Truly I tell you, just as you did it to one of the least of these who are members of my family, you did it to me. (Matthew 25:35–36, 40—New Revised Standard Version [NRSV])

In these words and similar lessons in other traditions there is common ground on which Middle Church can meet. But to do so, we must broaden what faith means beyond the narrow confines of personal piety to encompass concern for the least of these our brothers and sisters. For *this* is the tradition of faith in public life. Religious leaders led the movement to abolish slavery, to enfranchise women, and to achieve civil rights for all Americans. It is those in the model of Jerry Falwell and Pat Robertson, Tom DeLay and George W. Bush who are the aberration. Those who favor preemptive war and regressive tax cuts, who oppose welfare, and environmental protection.

I do not doubt their sincerity. George W. Bush speaks eloquently of his own conversion, and I deeply respect how he harnessed faith to transform his life. During the 2000 presidential campaign, the intelligentsia ridiculed President Bush when he said his favorite political philosopher was Jesus. I might have given exactly the same answer. But there are times when I wonder whether he read the entire Bible, for his agenda does not square with the faith tradition I have preached as a United Methodist minister, nor is it compatible with Judaism and Islam as I understand them.

Faith and salvation are about more than our individual relationship with God. In the Bible, Jesus' ministry is focused on other people, and it occurs most often in settings of community, not solitude. He is always with the poor and the lepers, always walking among the people, and by defining morality according to how we treat "the least of these," he called us to communal action, not just individual prayer. I deeply respect strains of Christianity that place profound emphasis on salvation and eternity. I admit that I do not give much thought to the afterlife personally, if only because I am keeping plenty busy here on Earth and I trust God to sort out eternity. The promise of heaven and the threat of hell were simply not central themes in the faith tradition I was taught. But all people of faith can agree that there is work to do in this world, no matter what we believe awaits us on the other side. There is too much that is broken in our world to rest our souls on a theology of waiting.

It has become fashionable on the far religious right to describe America as a "Christian nation." But I cannot accept that idea, and neither can my Christian faith. America is a nation founded on the principle of respect for all faith traditions, and Christianity is a tradition rooted in tolerance and respect for those unlike ourselves. "Let mutual love continue. Do not neglect to show hospitality to strangers, for by doing that some have entertained angels without knowing it," we read in Hebrews 13:1–2, and if an angel comes wrapped in a Jew's prayer shawl or kneeling on a Muslim's prayer rug, I do not want to miss his or her message.

Even those who believe in pluralism and tolerance are quick to accept the cliché that God has singled out America for a special mission, a claim increasingly employed to advocate empire. But faith teaches us to walk humbly with God, and there is a tragic arrogance in the belief that America has achieved a superior status conferred from on high. Why would God single out America among the nations? Because we have the most money? Surely not; it was Jesus who said it was easier for a camel to pass through the eye of a needle than for a rich man to enter the gates of heaven. Does God value America more because we are strong enough to impose our will on others, even though we have achieved that strength at the expense of aching human needs? My faith is rooted in the power of example, not the power of arms. How is it possible to reconcile a religion based on turning the other cheek with a doctrine that authorizes preemptive war? I love my country and I believe it is an extraordinary, special place. Patriotism is noble, but it is not divine. I believe God has a special mission for everyone who recognizes God's presence, whether born in America or Africa. And I believe in working collaboratively and with the help of the Holy Spirit to fix what is broken in the world and to care for all our brothers and sisters.

That is not to say I believe personal morality and self-restraint are unimportant. My wife, Merle, whom I married at age twenty-one, has been putting up with me for forty-two years, during which time one of her most important jobs has been keeping me from becoming a stuffed shirt. I'm not especially offended by dirty jokes or cursing, but I prefer not to communicate that way myself. (I'm more partial to puns that evoke groans rather than laughs.) I believe in the First Amendment, but I wish hotels would stop selling in-room pornography. And I'm very decidedly offended by the coarsening of our culture, the growing ease with which we employ epithets and insults, especially of a racial or ethnic character, and I deplore the casual familiarity of sex and violence on television and in the movies.

These are all measures of our morality. But so are hunger, illiteracy, disease, war, and environmental degradation.

In the face of these challenges, how can our faith condone leaders who ignore and even exacerbate such problems simply because they take a hard line on questions of personal piety that merit but a few mentions in the Bible? And even more important, can Middle Church be distracted from these urgent needs and our common concern for them by our narrow disagreements on what the Bible clearly regards, at the very best, as ancillary issues? As one individual Christian, I hope our society ends its discrimination against homosexuals and embraces them with love. I believe abortion should remain each woman's choice. But just as fervently, I hope that the many sincere people of faith who disagree with me on those issues will remember the vast common ground—those two thousand references to poverty and peace—that unites us.

Does that mean I am exhorting people of faith to embrace any particular political agenda? Of course not. As the general secretary of the National Council of the Churches of Christ in the USA, an ecumenical organization representing forty-five million Christians belonging to thirty-five different denominations, I am often asked to provide commentary on the role of faith in American life. As a former Democratic congressman, I tend to be pigeonholed as the "religious liberal." I'm not fond of labels, but I'm not ashamed of that one either, as I said earlier. Interviewers often ask me what Jesus would think of American politics today. I imagine they expect me to say Jesus would be a liberal and caucus with the Democrats. To be sure, I think he'd sooner vote for better child care than punitive welfare reform, and I'm pretty sure he'd be more likely to support more generous Medicaid benefits than to advocate cutting them. And somehow I just can't conjure an image of Jesus pleading for tax cuts at the top income bracket. After all, the only thing I can remember Jesus saying about taxes was to pay them.

But I don't believe Jesus would be a Democrat or a Republican. I suspect he would be as impatient with political labels as he would be with religious denominational ones. When I wonder what Jesus would say about our politics and how we treat the least of these in our community, I simply think of the words in the Gospel of John, chapter 11, verse 35, "Jesus wept."

There is a parable in the Gospel of Luke, chapter 5:1–11, in which Jesus comes upon a group of fishermen who have been casting their nets in a lake but catching nothing. One of the Bible's fascinating mysteries is that we do not know what Jesus says to the gathered crowd when he steps into the boats. We only know what he advises the fishermen to do. "Put out into the deep water," Jesus tells them, "and let down your nets for a catch." Soon, their nets are filled to bursting. The lesson is clear: We need the courage to venture into the deep waters, where the currents are rougher and success is less certain.

Leaders of the radical religious right are fond of saying that Christians are persecuted. This is their answer, it sometimes seems, anytime others disagree with them. The statement itself is somewhere between laughable and absurd, but the problem, I believe, is deeper. Christians like the Beatitudes. "Blessed are the peacemakers" is a favorite. So is "Blessed are the meek." But we tend to omit one of the most important: "Blessed are those who are persecuted for righteousness' sake." I believe the problem with Christianity today is that we are not persecuted enough, we do not risk enough, we do not offend enough. Politicians on the far right treat churches as theaters for applause, not forums for challenge. But Jesus did not change the world by assembling an audience of thousands. He had a staff of twelve, and even one of them didn't work out so well.

I like the story of the bishop whose church was destroyed in a fire. Everywhere he went after the fire, he was known as "the bishop of the church that burned down." One day, he told the story of being given that label and announced from the pulpit, "From now on, I want to be 'the bishop of the church on fire.'" That's what Middle Church, the faithful religious center, needs. We need to venture into the deep waters, into the deep currents, with passionate fire for justice in our hearts!

That trip to Washington was one of the first times I risked going out into the deep water. When we disembarked at the New York Avenue Presbyterian Church, we encountered a group of protestors. Their picket line was led by Reverend Carl McIntyre, the Jerry Falwell of his day, who was waving a placard proclaiming "Kill a Commie for Christ's Sake!" I was shocked and revolted but I felt something else stirring within me, perhaps for the first time as a young man. I felt courage. Courage is what we need for mainstream people of faith to reclaim the political center.

There is only one more thing to say about that day in February 1968. Five weeks after it, Martin Luther King, Jr., was shot dead on a hotel balcony. Among the mixture of emotions I felt when I heard the news, amid the anguish and the anger, was a realization: For so much of the 1960s, we sat around waiting for leaders to arise. Today, many people from the left to the center resort to old excuses for apathy: No one is leading us. The system is impure. Politicians are imperfect. They are excuses we can't afford.

Another one of my life's most powerful lessons came on the day I was sworn into Congress. Little more than a year earlier, I had become disgusted with Watergate and the seemingly never-ending Vietnam War. I looked up "Democratic Party" in the phone book and the next thing I knew I was running for Congress. I called a press conference to announce my candidacy, and one reporter and one photographer showed up. A couple of weeks later, the picture of the event appeared under the headline of the adjoining story: "Youth to Testify at Aunt's Murder Trial."

When I raised the idea of running for Congress with Merle, she laughed at first, then told me I could do whatever I wanted as long as she didn't have to make any speeches and I didn't borrow any money. We were plenty busy with our three young children—Rob, who was eight, five-year-old David, and Andrew, bringing up the rear at two years old. Between family life, my work as a minister, and Merle's job as a nurse, there seemed to be precious little time to campaign. The whole thing was a long shot that would have made Don Quixote proud. I was supposed to lose the primary by a landslide, then I was supposed to lose the general election by even more, and somehow I won by nineteen thousand votes. On election night, Merle's comment to the press was "I don't care who he is, he still has to take out the trash." My high school guidance counselor attended my swearing-in. He was the same man who, having seen my SAT scores and undistinguished high school grades, made the perfectly defensible recommendation that I skip college. "This either says something about you, Bob," he said, "or it says something about Congress." It was the second half of the sentence that was right. As I looked around on the House floor that day—intimidated by the presence of legends who a year earlier I had been watching on television—it suddenly dawned on me that they weren't any smarter than I was. And trust me, I'm not any smarter than you.

In many ways, my life has been a series of "Forrest Gump" moments at which I somehow find myself in the middle of places or events that seem bigger than I am. I met Dr. King just before he died and a decade later, as a member of the House Select Committee on Assassinations, I met James Earl Ray, the man who ended King's life. After serving twelve years in the House—enough for anybody—I made an unsuccessful run for the U.S. Senate from Pennsylvania. Just as I was trying to figure out what to do with my life, the provost of Swarthmore College asked whether I'd like to spend six months as the Visiting Professor for Issues of Social Change. I was wrapping up that adventure when my old colleague Senator Paul Simon asked me to join his presidential campaign as finance director. Paul was a wonderfully down-to-earth man who would have made an extraordinary president, but the people never quite got enough of a glimpse of him to see that. That campaign fizzled, and I signed on as head of the Committee for National Security, an independent organization working for nuclear disarmament.

I was enjoying that job when a Republican businessman from California, Mark Lee, called to say he was coming to Washington and wanted to have lunch. I knew he had supported my Senate campaign in Pennsylvania out of frustration with the increasingly far-right tendencies of his party. What I didn't know was that he was on the board of trustees of a United Methodist seminary called Claremont School of Theology that had just endured a series of financial scandals and was now in serious trouble. Mark was on the search committee looking for a new president. At exactly the same time, I had begun applying to a small handful of religious colleges that were looking for new presidents. I felt too many religious colleges were trying to imitate the exclusivity of Harvard and Yale rather than provide opportunities for young people who possessed what I considered the most important credential, a passionate desire to serve humanity through the ministry. More often, the credentials schools counted most were academic qualifications like GPAs and College Board scores. I felt strongly that test scores rarely tell the whole story of a person's life. After all, Colin Powell and I had the same abysmal College Board scores and we turned out all right. Claremont, whose students were primarily adults turning to the ministry later in life, fit the bill perfectly. I took the job, and Merle and I headed out west.

I managed to stick with that job for a whole decade, during which we stopped Claremont's financial hemorrhaging and launched several innovative educational programs that trained aspiring ministers not simply to contemplate theological questions but to engage actively in their communities. In the fall of 1999, I stepped into my office one day and saw a little pink While You Were Out slip. "Please call Father Leonid Kishkovsky," it said. I had never heard of him, and I have to admit I didn't return the call right away. When we finally connected, he explained that he was a priest of the Orthodox Church in America, one of the member communions of the National Council of Churches, headquartered in New York City.

I knew vaguely what the Council was, but its heyday had been its participation in the civil rights struggles of the 1950s and 1960s, and I, like most people, had not paid much attention to the group since then. Now, Father Kishkovsky explained, the Council was facing a financial crisis of its own, a severe deficit that threatened a revolt among the member communions, and was looking for a new general secretary. My work at Claremont had apparently gotten me a reputation as a turnaround specialist, and he wondered whether I would meet with their search committee.

I felt I had done all I could at Claremont, and Merle and I now had grandchildren back east. Not long after I met with the search committee, I attended a dinner in Colorado for deans and presidents of seminaries. One seminary president who had also been considered for the general secretary's job gave a thirty-minute commentary about the Council's woes, waxing eloquently and lengthily about what a terrible organization it had become. After he finished, I sauntered up to his table.

"I really appreciate this briefing," I said, "because I just said 'yes' to being general secretary." Everyone laughed!

And the rest is history—or ongoing history, because the story of my life is still unfolding. But one moral is already clear: If an ordinary kid like me can stumble into opportunities like these, anyone can. We all have the power to make a difference. God never looks to the rich and powerful. In my tradition, Jesus came to us through a poor and homeless mother, and the disciples he attracted were fishermen, carpenters, and tax collectors. Judaism's prophets were ordinary people. "Woe is me! I am lost, for I am a man of unclean lips," Isaiah protested upon his call, an excuse God rejected for him and will not accept for any of us (Isaiah 6:5). Mohammed was a humble merchant before he became a prophet.

God is calling each of us, I believe, to be modern-day prophets, to care for the least of these, to work for peace, to preserve God's creation. To accomplish those goals, we must reclaim the mantle of faith from those who have co-opted it. For America's faithful majority, the millions of us who are eager to reassert the values of compassion and peace and preservation in public life, *we are the leaders we've been waiting for.* And our moment is now. The year before he died, Reverend King wrote:

> We are now faced with the fact that tomorrow is today. In this
> unfolding conundrum of life and history, there is such a thing as
> being too late. Procrastination is still the thief of time. Life often

16          MIDDLE CHURCH

leaves us bare, naked, and dejected with lost opportunity. The tide in the affairs of humanity does not remain at the flood, it ebbs. We may cry out desperately for time to pause in her passage, but time is deaf to every plea and rushes on. Over the bleached bones and jumbled residues of numerous civilizations, are written the pathetic words "too late." . . . We still have a choice today: nonviolent coexistence or violent co-annihilation. This may well be humankind's last chance to choose between chaos and community.

For the sake of our faiths, our country, our world, we, the faithful majority of Middle Church, Middle Synagogue, and Middle Mosque, must courageously embrace the fierce urgency of now.

CHAPTER 1

# The Two Churches: Faith Based on Love—or Faith Grounded in Fear?

*Beloved, let us love one another, because love is from God;*
*everyone who loves is born of God and knows God.*
—1 JOHN 4:7

*If Christian people work together, they can succeed during*
*this decade in winning back control of the institutions that*
*have been taken from them over the past seventy years. Ex-*
*pect confrontations that will be not only unpleasant but at*
*times physically bloody.*
—PAT ROBERTSON

St. Paul's call to ministry was a lot more dramatic than mine, which might explain why his name is always preceded by "Saint," whereas the nicest thing I've ever been called is "Pastor Bob." "Hey you" and "Bob who?" are a lot more frequent. Well, maybe that's not the only difference between Paul and me, but it's one of them. Paul was traveling to Damascus when the full light and glory of God zapped him right there on the road and called him to a life of ministry and service. Growing up in the Philadelphia suburbs, my call was a little slower and a lot more subtle. In my early childhood, we took the Chester Bus Line from Springfield to Landsdowne, where we went to church on Sunday mornings. This route wasn't exactly the road to Damascus, but it worked for me.

My parents weren't churchgoing people. For a few years after we moved to Springfield, Delaware County, from Yeadon, my mother would take us by bus back to Lansdowne United Methodist Church. Each Sunday, we got off the bus at the corner of Baltimore Pike and Lansdowne Avenue and walked up Lansdowne Avenue to the church. I have a few vague memories of my mother singing in the choir and I recall a few words being spoken from the pulpit, too. It wasn't until much later, however, that I realized the man speaking them, the Reverend Dr. John McKelvey, was a highly educated and prominent preacher. I believe God speaks to each of us in a voice we can hear. For Paul, it was the light and glory on the road to Damascus. For many of the grown-ups in Lansdowne, I'm sure it was Dr. McKelvey's inspiring words. But the Lord sure knows how to speak to first- and second-graders, because my most vivid memories of those early churchgoing days are of fruit juice and cookies. That was enough to get me and my older brother, Ralph, hooked.

Not long after my parents bought their first house in Springfield, the bus ride back to Lansdowne became a burden. We then started attending a new local church that met on Sunday mornings in a nearby elementary school gymnasium. I remember vividly that the pastor, Reverend George Mamourian, preached Sunday after Sunday from a lectern located directly underneath the basketball net. I fantasized every Sunday morning about whether I could sink a basket from wherever I was sitting. Within a year or two, the church moved out of the elementary school and into a new and more modern building of its own. My father worked the 3 P.M.-to-1 A.M. shift for General Electric for thirty-seven years, so Sunday mornings became one of the only times my parents could be together. They woke up Ralph and me each Sunday morning, got us dressed, and we waited for a church leader who lived up the road to come by in her station wagon, honk the horn at the end of our driveway, and give us a ride to church.

I can't identify one moment when I felt called to ministry. Looking back, though, "a still, small voice," the same kind God used to speak to the prophet Elijah, was welling up inside me. Early in life, it took the form of church being my social milieu, the place where Ralph and I hung out on weekends to laugh and play. Gradually, almost imperceptibly, church just became a place that felt like home, like where I was supposed to be, like an extension of home. And I'll let you in on a secret, as long as you close the door, draw the shades and promise *never* to tell another minister that I admitted this: Sometimes, just every once in a while, maybe every other blue moon, church was—and here you have to imagine me whispering like I was sharing a state secret, like a Red Sox fan confessing my undercover loyalty to the New York Yankees—*boring*. Except . . .

Except on those occasions, often in summer camp or Vacation Bible School, when I encountered young, progressive ministers imbued with a passion for changing the world. There was Charlie Lobb, a pastor with a quick wit and a wonderful way of telling stories that brought the needs of real people to life. It was Charlie who first came up to me one day at camp and challenged me to think about a life in the ministry. Reverend Bill Cherry, another camp counselor, once told us a story of heaven and hell that removed those concepts from the frightening tones in which they were typically presented.

"Imagine the most pleasurable place you'd ever want to be," he said in an exaggeratedly flowing voice, "a place where everything is green and the flowers are growing and the water flows and the sun is shining. Think of a place where the birds are chirping and people are walking through a garden. Picture that, picture it. Now picture a dome encapsulating this place, and imagine everything inside that dome being absolutely perfect. That's heaven. Now imagine lying on top of that dome and looking in. That's hell."

These ministers told jokes, they laughed, they made the church come alive in the fabric of who they were, and they opened my eyes to a worldview I had never had before—the possibility of serving others. I had always planned on being a high school football or wrestling coach, and even that seemed like a distant aspiration. But as these young ministers drew the connection for me between the call of personal faith and responsibility to the community and the world, another slow, dripping revelation came to me: With God's help, I could be a coach, so to speak, in the faith community.

I was always the type who learned better by seeing, touching, and feeling than by reading books or hearing lectures. Encountering the true breaches in God's creation, the poor and sick, was how I came to feel my call to ministry, a call to fix what was broken in the world. Once, during a Methodist conference, I remember going on a youth "Come See" tour of sites in Philadelphia where Methodist deaconesses were working with the poor. They demonstrated their love for the children and adults they worked with not with words but with their actions. Over the same period, Chester and other Philadelphia neighborhoods were undergoing a steady transformation from working-class and mostly white, to poor and mostly persons of color. The view out of the bus window evolved from middle-class families and picket fences to shuttered storefronts and dilapidated housing. Witnessing poverty carved a deep and lasting impression in my soul, as did this observation: Poor people under the care and ministry of people of faith lived in a reality totally separate, far safer and more fulfilling, than those left to struggle with poverty alone. And that was when I made the connection. My calling to ministry wasn't to give sermons. It was to make a difference. So I decided to go to college. Drew University turned me down for undergraduate studies, a point of which I was pleased to remind them when, years later, they awarded me an honorary doctorate. Fortunately, Lycoming College in central Pennsylvania had a policy of accepting all students who were committed to a life of ministry, and they liked the fact that I had been a high school wrestler and might wrestle for the school.

My social conscience and religious calling evolved simultaneously, each reinforcing the other. As a young child, my image of God was of an old man with a white beard floating around on clouds. As a young man at Lycoming, I received a letter from Reverend Mamourian, my pastor from back home. "Bob," he wrote, "it's now time for you to lift your sights a little broader and a little wider. It's time for you to see God in the broader context, in the interconnectedness of your spirituality and your social conscience." In part because of that letter, I moved steadily from a view of spirituality grounded in a literal reading of the scriptures to a broader view of God's work in the world. That transformation had taken hold by the time I became an ordained elder in the United Methodist Church, with all the rights and privileges appertaining thereto—one of which, incidentally, is that the Methodist bishop is always obliged to give you a job. It's the best union in the world and a liberating one as well. Often, when I was a member of Congress, my staff would warn me that a controversial vote might cost me the next election. I would simply remind them: "Don't worry, the bishop will give me a job."

One of the most remarkable aspects of my childhood exposure to faith was what never, or at least rarely, occurred, as far as I can recall: the sort of hellfire-and-brimstone warnings that we so commonly associate with faith today. Frankly, I just don't remember hearing all that much about hell or, for that matter, heaven either. We were engaged in the work of the world, and while the afterlife was out there, I developed the general impression that it was, literally and figuratively, God's turf—he'd figure it out. Meanwhile, however brief our journeys in this life might be, we had work to do.

I don't mean to suggest we never talked, learned, or read about the concepts of heaven and hell. Of course we did. They're in the Bible. And yes, we studied the book of Revelation, too. But heaven and hell weren't really an emphasis, much less *the* emphasis, of faith. Faith wasn't transactional; it was never "Do A, B, and C and after you die you'll get X, Y, and Z." Faith was about works, and works were about this world. What was right was just plain right, and that's why you did it—not because you expected a reward or feared a punishment in the next world. Of course, this could all be a case of selective memory, or maybe Reverend McKelvey did rain down a little hellfire and brimstone during his sermons, but I was too busy playing with the other kids in Sunday School to absorb what he was saying. But my wife, Merle, remembers her childhood religious experience the same way, that it had a lot more to do with this world than the next.

For most people of faith—not just in mainline churches but across Middle Church, Middle Synagogue, and Middle Mosque—I believe it remains the same today. But just as former senator and presidential candidate John Edwards spoke of the "two Americas," there are also "two churches" in America today. Middle Church inspires faith through love; the far religious right seeks to instill faith through fear. This latter group speaks in the stark and strident language of the book of Revelation, of a God of violence and vengeance rather than a God of hope and love. Here's how Jerry Falwell once put it:

> You say what's going to happen on this earth when the Rapture occurs? You'll be riding along in an automobile. You'll be the driver, perhaps. You're a Christian. There will be several people in the automobile with you, maybe someone who is not a Christian. When the trumpet sounds, you and the other born-again Christians in that automobile will be instantly caught away . . . Other cars on the highway driven by believers will suddenly be out of control. Stark pandemonium will occur on that highway and on every highway in the world where Christians are caught away from the world.

To be sure, Jerry didn't create that vision from whole cloth, with the possible exception of what I guess every frustrated commuter could now literally call the traffic jam from hell. The book of Revelation does speak of the Rapture, and the portrait it paints is in fact quite fierce. But it's equally important to understand that the books of the New Testament are the works of human beings. That does not diminish the divinity of Jesus' ministry or the beauty of the apostles' words. Still, theologians have spent centuries interpreting the differing records the apostles give of Jesus' life, which ought to give us a pretty good clue that not every single word can be taken as literal historical fact. I am not prescribing moral relativism here; the Bible holds us to some pretty high standards, and it's our job to live up to them. My point is that to understand the Bible's message, we need to take the whole book into consideration. Once we do, there is ample room to debate the afterlife, but there can't be any disagreement on this: The central message of Jesus' ministry was the imperative to love one's neighbor. Know that, he said, and you understand every other commandment.

Now, I need to be very clear on this next point: The fact that my own faith doesn't emphasize the afterlife doesn't mean I condemn the opinions of people who believe differently. I have many, many friends and colleagues who are evangelical Christians and in whose faith the Rapture and its aftermath play a central role. I respect Jerry Falwell's right to believe as he does, which is not to say I simply tolerate his practice of a faith with which I disagree. I respect, very deeply, his interpretation of faith itself. The last thing I want to be guilty of is doing to the far religious right what they do to the religious left: dismissing them with overbroad labels and personal attacks.

The problem arises when that faith becomes political rather than personal, when it is co-opted for the sake of legislation rather than love. Today, we call the intersection of evangelical Christianity and political conservatism the "religious right." I reject applying that term to all evangelicals, because I know many whom I would characterize as highly conservative personally but who are nonetheless passionate about, for example, poverty and the environment. But there is a strain of thought that, for lack of a better term, I call the "far religious right." And somewhere back in the 1970s, not long after I started serving in Congress, the far religious right underwent a civil marriage with political conservatives. People with conservative agendas began bankrolling religious organizations. The Institute for Religion and

Democracy, for example, was founded for the express purpose of attacking the organization I now lead, the National Council of Churches. Its fundraising list reads like a Who's Who of contemporary conservatism, from Peter Coors, the far-right heir to the Coors Brewing fortune, to Richard Mellon Scaife, the billionaire publisher who financed the witch hunts against President Bill Clinton. Nor was this solely a matter of political conservatives co-opting religious leaders. Preachers like Jerry Falwell and Pat Robertson made the quiet but critical shift from their personal beliefs in, for example, cutting taxes to the suggestion that faith somehow *compelled* these positions.

While I served in Congress, for example, Falwell's Moral Majority began rating public officials, presumably on how their votes accorded with his conception of faith. That's fair enough. But the criteria, on which, again, I'm proud to have scored a flat zero every time, had to do with matters like tax cuts and defense spending. Falwell was therefore in the odd position of trying to square his very literal interpretation of the Bible (which, as I recall, says something about turning the other cheek) with, for example, his zeal for nuclear arms. He once tried to explain away this zeal by teaching that true believers would be spared the devastation of nuclear Armageddon when, as he fully expected, it occurred. As for me, my faith shaped how I viewed political issues, but I no more believe that God endorses my political agenda than I think he would vote for anyone else's. I've never believed that people should agree with me because of my vocation. And given recent political history, I can't help but recall with a smile that, during my first campaign for Congress, the Republicans began a telephone attack campaign against me. "Did you know," they would ask in hushed and sinister tones, "that Bob Edgar is a *minister?*" Evidently, they saw it as an insult. The voters, fortunately, decided it was an asset. Still, I never wore a clerical collar on the floor of Congress because I felt it was inappropriate to do so. I simply tried to do what I thought was right based on a set of beliefs that were, in my own case, indelibly shaped by the influence of spirituality in my life.

But in the case of the radical religious right, that intersection has become far more explicit. Rather than simply informing one's political belief, the clear implication is that people of faith can believe no other way. The marriage of political conservatism and a particular strain of evangelical Christian thought grounded in a vengeful God has spawned several philosophical implications that remain highly influential in American politics. Evangelical Christianity, for example, strongly emphasizes one's personal relationship with God as a means of eternal salvation. As I've explained, my own conception of our personal relationship with God is different, but that's not my point here. After all, who am I to say my own interpretation of faith is any more or less valid than anyone else's? My concern is that when this interpretation of the Bible is exploited for political purposes, it tends—contrary to many evangelicals' personal beliefs—to emphasize one's relationship with God at the expense of one's relationship with other human beings. The result is rampant individualism rather than group responsibility. As my friend Rabbi Jack Moline puts it, the far right tends to see life as a web of personal relationships, a person's relationship with his property, his gun, and so forth. But it doesn't place enough value on the character of the community as a whole.

Often—and again, I'm speaking of political leaders who co-opt evangelical Christianity, not its individual adherents—the quality of life in the next world seems more important than the conditions against which individuals are struggling in this one. Jesus' promise that the meek will inherit the earth somehow becomes a subtle assurance that the reward of the meek will come in the next world, but in this one, they should keep quiet and quit agitating so much. Moreover, if our individual relationship with God matters most, issues of personal piety can eclipse interpersonal responsibilities. And, the reasoning goes, if God is vengeful, then surely America, his anointed nation in the eyes of the far religious right, has the right to inflict his vengeance on the world, even if it requires preemptive military action that is obviously contrary to everything Jesus taught.

The marriage of radical-right Christianity and radical-right political conservatism has given birth to another offspring: human beings who are almost granted a license for bringing about God's prophecies. Jesus' teaching, "You always have the poor with you, but you do not always have me" (John 12:8), becomes a sort of fatalistic excuse for ignoring poverty. After all, some on the far right seem to say, God said poverty would always be around, so what do you want me to do about it? (By the way, that teaching about the poor from the Gospel of John is reported similarly by Matthew. But I prefer Mark's version: "For you always have the poor with you, *and you can show kindness to them whenever you wish*; but you will not always have me" [Mark 14:7]. The middle clause is, in my view, the essence of the verse.) In a similar way, global warming becomes a fulfillment of the book of Revelation's prophecy of environmental destruction in the End of Days.

Again, we can interpret those verses differently, but one thing is quite clear to me: Prophecy and its fulfillment are God's business, not ours. If God has some purpose in inflicting suffering on the world (that's pretty hard for me to accept, but we can have that theological debate another time), that doesn't grant humanity permission to ignore the suffering of our brothers and sisters or to not be good stewards of this fragile planet Earth. The saying Lincoln invoked when he spoke of slavery is just as true of these other evils: "Woe unto the world because of offenses; for it must needs be that offenses come, but woe to that man by whom the offense cometh."

The question we face today is not whether to banish religion from public life. America never has done this, nor should we. Each of us brings our personal values, whether spiritual or secular, to bear on our political beliefs. Rather, the questions are whether the call we hear will be grounded in hellfire or hope, in the rewards we expect or the responsibilities we feel, and, most of all, whether our conception of what is right will be based on personal piety or morality-in-community. It is the latter vision to which Dr. King's "Beloved Community" calls us. The Beloved Community gathered together the elements of Dr. King's vision—racial equality, peace, economic justice, and more—into an interwoven tapestry of love. It was a dream rooted in spiritual faith, one that recognized that God's love is realized most powerfully in our relationships with one another.

My church, my faith, is the one grounded in love, not fear, in hope, not hellfire. For me, God is a God of love. God isn't telling us to love one another in exchange for a reward. God is telling us to do so because it's right. I believe in God as a creator, but a creator who was smart enough not to undertake such an awesome task alone, who instead invited each of us to join in the ongoing call to renew the world. God has given us the gift of life, and God wants us to use it to figure out how to live together on this little sandbox called Earth.

And my God *is* a personal God. This much I have learned, for although I have offered prayers all my life, it was not until 1998 that I fully understood the power of prayers—my own and others'. That fall, I was attending a meeting in Pittsburgh, where our son David, a local radio broadcaster, lived. Our oldest son, Rob, delivered on-air traffic reports for a Washington, D.C., radio station, riding in a single-engine plane each rush hour. I was in my meeting when David called with a combination of urgency, fear, and matter-of-fact directness in his voice.

"Rob's plane crashed. The pilot was killed. Rob's still alive. He was sitting in the flames, and they got him out. That's all I know."

Rob's plane had crashed into a house while the pilot attempted to land in heavy fog at an unfamiliar airport. No one in the house was hurt, thank God, but the pilot died when the plane burst into flames on impact. Rob sat in a fireball of burning fuel until he somehow freed himself from his seat belt, climbed out of the plane, and rolled on the ground until the flames were out.

A four-hour car ride later, David and I were at the burn unit of Washington Hospital Medical Center. As we rushed in, I remembered my days as a part-time chaplain at the University of Pennsylvania hospital in the late 1960s, when the rooms I most dreaded to enter were those in which patients had suffered burns or undergone tracheotomies, each of which entailed horrible suffering. Now our son had both. The sight of him was beyond anything I can describe. He was scorched literally from his shoulders to his ankles, his back was broken, and he needed a tube in his throat because he had inhaled super-heated air in the cockpit.

Merle flew in from California—this happened during my tenure as president of the Claremont School of Theology—and arrived that night. The moment she saw him, years of experience as an operating room nurse told her Rob's situation was grave, but her brave face and calm demeanor shielded me from knowing the worst. It would take a miracle for our son to survive and an even greater one for him to walk again. Each day brought horrifically painful changes in his bandages. He underwent repeated operations as surgeons repaired the burn damage with grafts from his scalp, the only area of his body that was not severely burned. His broken body was forged back together with a series of metal rods.

Merle and I moved into a hotel room and spent fifty-five days by Rob's bed, packing his body with ice to fight fevers that spiked to 105 degrees as his body fended off infections. And we prayed. We prayed for Rob to survive and to heal and for God to give us the strength to endure this ordeal. Not only did Rob survive, his body healed so completely that the doctors were stunned. Today, he installs TV satellite dishes, making his living by climbing up on roofs. And he still gets a kick from setting off airplane metal detectors with the rods that hold him together.

God gave us another gift as well: For the first time in more than three decades as a minister, I fully understood what prayer can mean. I do not believe God plays tricks, inflicts tragedy, or dispenses the miracle of healing on the basis of who offers the most fervent prayers. But Merle and I did learn the strength people can draw from their personal prayers and from one another. Friends and colleagues from around the country told us they were praying for Rob and for us, and in a physical way that defies description we could *feel*, tangibly and meaningfully and literally *feel*, the force of their prayers. They were a cloud of witnesses who blanketed us with love, who reminded us that God's spirit and theirs were with us, that we had to endure a great deal, but that we did not have to do so alone.

Another minister whose son died of AIDS once told me, "This is going to sound strange, but if this had to happen, I wish it had happened earlier in my ministry. I have been comforting mourners for years, but I never appreciated what they were going through." Rob's accident was a learning experience for me just as the death of my friend's son was for him. I had been counseling people to pray for all those years, but it was not until my own family was coping with tragedy that I understood what prayer really meant.

The greatest lesson was that the power of prayer is its force in *this* world, not another. And that is the kind of spirituality we must feel and practice to heal our world today. My faith is not one of waiting for future rewards. It is a call to act *today*, to feed the hungry and clothe the naked and visit the prisoner with the fierce urgency of now. My God hears prayers, but I believe the prayers God answers are the ones we precede with the words so wonderfully formulated by Marian Wright Edelman, president of the Children's Defense Fund: "I take responsibility for . . ." It is not enough to ask God to heal the sick; we must provide for their health care. It is not enough to pray for relief for the poor; it is up to us to provide it. It is not enough to pray for our fragile planet; we must take personal responsibility for its future. I believe in moral absolutes, none more so than those Paul identified in a letter he wrote in prison: faith, hope, and love. But these are not mere feelings. They are actions. They are ways of life.

Above all, and here is the most important point, the truest measure of morality occurs in community. For morality-in-community is God's calling. This is the church I follow, the church of Dr. King's Beloved Community, the church whose work is felt in the world around us, not simply the world to come. All we can know, and all we can act upon, is the imperative to love one another. We are admonished in the first book of John, "those who do not love a brother or sister whom they have seen, cannot love God whom they have not seen" (1 John 4:20). I have not seen God, but I have seen children go hungry because the social supports on which they depended for nourishment were pulled out from under them in the name of faith. I have not seen God, but I know our earth is getting warmer, our schools are crumbling, our people are sick. I entertain no notions that God is speaking to me about politics; I believe God would rather I listen to the voice of a single mother or a child holding up an empty bowl and asking for food. For in those voices, God's call can be heard.

And more than ever before, whether the cause is poverty or peace or the healing of our planet, those voices are crying to us for help.

# In the Beginning, God Created the Heavens and the Earth ... So Stop Messing Them Up!

*A generation goes, and a generation comes, but the earth remains forever.*
—ECCLESIASTES 1:4

*The fact is that there is no global warming. . . . I urge everyone to go out and buy an SUV . . . today.*
—JERRY FALWELL

## Dominion as Stewardship

Merle loves the antique mahogany table in our living room. I think it looks pretty neat. I guess you'd call it Empire style, and it dates at least to the middle of the nineteenth century and maybe even earlier. But its emotional significance is what matters most to Merle. It belonged to her great-great-grandmother, who was born in Philadelphia in 1842. In fact, pretend you're doing a logic problem on the SAT and see if you can follow this one: Merle's great-grandmother died in childbirth, so Merle's great-great-grandmother raised Merle's grandmother, and in her ripe old age, which lasted into the 1920s, lived with Merle's mother.

Anyway, the table has been passed down through the generations from her great-great-grandmother to her grandmother to her mother. In the early 1980s, Merle and I started collecting antiques, and her mother decided it was time to pass along the table to a new generation. It was a family heirloom, her mother said, something truly special, a connection to the past and a bridge to the future. And she loved Merle so much she wanted her to have it. Merle remembered the table from growing up. As a teenager, she used to sit by it as she spent long evenings on the telephone chatting up a dashing, handsome young suitor named "Bob." But that's another story.

The point of the table is this: When her mother passed it along, suppose Merle had said thank you, then carelessly scratched the table and kicked it around before hauling it out to the curb for the garbage crew to cart away.

There's a word for that kind of behavior: ingratitude. No decent person believes a gift should be treated so callously, especially not one that was given as a token of real and personal love. And least of all would you tell the parent who gave that gift, "Well, you said you wanted me to have it, and I thought that meant you wanted me to do whatever I wanted with it."

That's exactly how we're treating a precious gift from a loving parent: God's creation. This is an issue that must unite those on the religious left and the religious right *and*, just as important, mobilize the many in Middle Church, Middle Synagogue, and Middle Mosque who are concerned about the environment but have not yet been active. Not only are we ignoring the clear teachings of faith, but many leaders on the far religious right are actually twisting those teachings and either openly advocating or tacitly tolerating the destruction of our earth. For some, the issue is capitalism. Some see environmentalism as a threat to free markets, and they believe free markets are ordained by God. It's a belief built on myths. The idea of Jesus as the prophet of capitalism, a would-be corporate raider ready to trade his robes for a pin-striped suit, is one myth; the supposed enormous cost of environmental protection, which the radical right tends to inflate wildly, is another. We'll get to those. But I'm more concerned about another line of argument: the belief, often stated right out in the open, that God wants us to exploit the earth.

One commonly invoked theme is that human beings were created in God's image, so God surely intended for our interests to outrank the rest of creation's. But that's a false choice. The environmentalist of faith wants human beings to live in harmony, not competition, with God's creation. The fact that we were created with reason and free will is precisely why we have a special responsibility to protect the earth. The radical religious right also bases its opposition to environmental protection on Genesis 1:28, in which God gives humanity "dominion" over the earth. That's interpreted as a license, sometimes even a command, to use up all we see for our own purposes.

If so, the Bible must be a tangle of contradictions. Seeing dominion as a license for exploitation flies in the face of everything we know about God's view of creation. "As for me," God tells Noah, "I am establishing my covenant with you and your descendants after you, and with every living creature that is with you, the birds, the domestic animals, and every animal of the earth with you, as many as came out of the ark" (Gen. 9:9). Mark painted a beautiful literary portrait of Jesus walking through the fields on the Sabbath, putting his hands down in the wheat, communing with the land. "The earth is the Lord's," the psalmist wrote (Ps. 24), a powerful reminder that we are but temporary inhabitants of this fragile place, this little spaceship called Earth, custodians on whom all future generations depend. In Leviticus, the Israelites are commanded to let the earth rest every seven years, hardly what you'd expect if "dominion" meant open season on creation. Psalm 104 is one of many beautiful songs of praise for God's creation and, specifically, a lyrical expression of gratitude to God for engaging in what today we'd call "sustainable development":

*You make springs gush forth in the valleys;*
   *They flow between the hills,*
*Giving drink to every wild animal;*
   *The wild asses quench their thirst.*
*By the streams the birds of the air have their habitation;*
   *They sing among the branches.*
*From your lofty abode you water the mountains;*
   *The earth is satisfied with the fruit of your work.*

"Dominion" to me means something entirely different from what it apparently means to many on the far religious right. I believe that it means "stewardship." I think God invited us and challenged us to help in the work of Creation. We have dominion over the earth the same way a parent has dominion over a child, as a mandate to protect and nourish, not to consume or exploit. How can we believe dominion gave us the right to treat the earth differently from the sustainable, care-taking stewardship for which we praise God? How can we believe that a God who takes personal responsibility for protecting the creatures of the earth condones—even encourages—their senseless destruction by human hands? The reasoning seems impossible, yet it's routinely employed, and it has an even more disturbing strain: the idea that environmental destruction is a sign of the End of Days and that it therefore should be tolerated or even encouraged. I know that sounds far-fetched, yet that belief is pervasive. Several far-right web sites actually track environmental destruction, along with disease, wars, and political developments, and hail them as fulfillments of Biblical prophecies about the Rapture. And here's Pat Robertson reacting to the deadly hurricane season of 2005, just after Hurricane Katrina destroyed New Orleans and much of the Gulf Coast as part of a pattern of intensifying storms that many scientists attribute to global warming:

If you read back in the Bible, the letter of the apostle Paul to the church of Thessalonia, he said that in the latter days before the end of the age that the earth would be caught up in what he called the birth pangs of a new order. And for anybody who knows what it's like to have a wife going into labor, you know how these labor pains begin to hit. I don't have any special word that says this is that, but it could be suspiciously like that.

If you think that sounds like a far-right theological strain on the fringes of political discourse, consider this: Armageddon theology—or, more to the point, Armageddon politics—is shared today by many of the foremost political leaders in the United States, including former House Majority Leader Tom DeLay as well as Senator Jim Inhofe of Oklahoma, a leading opponent of environmental protection. Journalist Glenn Scherer noted in *Grist* magazine:

> Forty-five senators and 186 representatives in 2003 earned 80-to 100-percent approval ratings from the nation's three most influential Christian right advocacy groups—the Christian Coalition, Eagle Forum, and Family Resource Council. Many of those same lawmakers also got flunking grades—less than 10 percent, on average—from the League of Conservation Voters last year.

That's more than coincidence. Not only are some of the most conservative leaders in politics indifferent to the environment, many of them openly associate their actively anti-environmental beliefs with their faith. For the sake of argument, let's assume these politicians are genuinely impelled by religious principle to oppose environmental protection. And let's set aside the rather stunning consistency with which the "faithful" views of politicians on the far religious right happen to coincide with the interests of wealthy corporations. (*Mother Jones* revealed that one of the major contributors to the "Acton Institute for the Study of Religion and Liberty," a self-described promoter of "a free and virtuous society characterized by individual liberty and sustained by religious prin-

ciples" and a frequent doubter of global warming, is—surprise—
ExxonMobil.)

Before we go on, let's be clear on one point: These are views held
by one particular strain of religious and political leaders. It is a powerful one, to be sure, but it would be a mistake to attribute hostility
or indifference toward the environment to evangelicals generally. If
there was ever an issue that could unite people of faith across the political spectrum from left to right to the vast but silent faithful center,
the environment is it. Recent years have seen a flourishing commitment to the environment on the part of many evangelicals. Consider
my friend Richard Cizik of the National Association of Evangelicals.
I bet if we took a random sampling of political issues, I'd disagree
with Rich on at least six out of ten—if not nine. But it's that tenth
issue, the environment, that makes our partnership important.

A few years ago, Rich was born again on the importance of what
he describes as "Creation Care," mobilizing a coalition of faith groups
called the "Noah Alliance" to address issues like global warming. He
explained the effort to the *New York Times* by quoting Genesis 2:15:
"The Lord God took the man and put him in the garden of Eden to
till it and keep it." As you can imagine, Rich has come in for some serious criticism from the far right. Senator Inhofe replied to the campaign this way: "You can always find in Scriptures a passage to
misquote for almost anything."

Well, that's true, and it brings us back to the radical religious
right and its misreading, and sometimes outright misuse, of Scripture to justify environmental exploitation. As I've said before, I don't
want to disrespect Tom DeLay's or Pat Robertson's faith. Even to the
extent that I wonder whether their spiritual claims are sometimes
clouded by political and economic interests, I certainly do not dismiss the beliefs of the many millions of Christians who take the
warnings of the Rapture to be the literal truth. The fact that my own
theological views are different isn't really relevant here. The critical
point is that no matter how you interpret the Bible, there isn't a

word—not a chapter, not a verse, not a solitary clause of a single sentence—that suggests humanity's job is to nudge Armageddon along
by hastening its dire predictions. Some prophecies in the New Testament do in fact predict earthquakes, disease, and war. But nowhere
in the Old or New Testament or in any faith tradition of which I'm
aware are human beings asked to start wars or infect people with diseases or pollute the land to make those prophecies come true. If
those events are necessary (again, I have my doubts), surely God can
handle it without our help.

What the Scriptures do tell us, over and over, is to steward the
earth and care for God's creation. In fact, if we're going to base our
environmental views on prophecy, I prefer the passages in which Isaiah and Jeremiah cry out against the destruction of the earth. If Revelation is our guide, we should remember the beautiful verses that
predict the renewal of the earth. The last chapter of Revelation begins this way:

> Then the angel showed me the river of the water of life, bright
> as crystal, flowing from the throne of God and of the Lamb
> through the middle of the street of the city. On either side of the
> river is the tree of life with its twelve kinds of fruit, producing its
> fruit each month; and the leaves of the tree are for the healing of
> the nations.

If we want to help prophecy along, the challenge of making the
rivers as clear as crystal and the trees blossom with fruit seems like a
far better place to start than filling the air with greenhouse gasses
and the waters with toxic chemicals.

This isn't a Christian value alone. Stewardship is a theme in
nearly every faith tradition from Judaism to Christianity to Islam to
Native American belief systems and beyond. The most poignant
statement of those beliefs I have ever heard was spoken on a Palm
Sunday in 1990 when I went to Nevada as part of a worship service

to protest nuclear proliferation. I was asked to give the sermon. As we walked along the road to the worship service, I asked everyone to pick up a stone. I was going to speak on the text found in chapter 19, verse 40, of the Gospel of Luke, in which Jesus explained that if the people were silent, "the stones would cry out."

When we arrived at the site of the service, the leader asked all of us to sit down. I was wearing a black suit, so naturally I wound up covered in sand. Then I stood up to give my sermon. It was titled "Building Pyramids of Peace." I invoked that passage in Luke and said God was calling us to be courageous, speak out, and stand up when others were telling us to sit down. I was at the top of my form. And boy, did I ever think I was good. I was pretty sure I had just established myself as the best orator since Lincoln at Gettysburg. Then I asked everyone who had picked up a stone to stand, place their stone in a pile, and say what they believed their stone was crying out. And that's when I learned what a good sermon really was.

The first woman to stand was carrying a child on her hip. "As I passed this stone, it cried out to me to care for the environment and make sure my child has a future," she said. An elderly woman rose to say "I never thought I would live to see the Berlin Wall come down and peace break out. I'm so pleased that I have lived to see peace as a possibility, and my stone cried out, 'Peace! Peace! Peace!'" Several more people spoke of their stones. Then the last woman to speak stood, but she had no stone to place on the pile. Her name was Ruth, and she was wrapped in a Native American blanket.

"As a Native American," she said through tears, "I was taught to wake up in the morning and breathe out to the north, to the east, and to the south, and to the west, and to breathe new life onto the planet. A fundamental teaching for me was to leave the planet just as I found it. As I passed my stone, it cried out, 'Leave me alone, leave me where I am.'"

That woman was challenging us not simply to preserve the earth as we find it but to regenerate the land, to restore the beauty of creation as God gave it to us. This is a moral and spiritual challenge of which we are falling scandalously short.

## Sharing Our Sandbox:
## A Small Planet with Limited Resources

*The good leave an inheritance to their children's children ...*
—PROVERBS 13:22

*A secular society will lack faith in God's providence and consequently men will find fewer natural resources. The secular or socialist has a limited resource mentality and views the world as a pie (there is only so much) that needs to be cut up so that everyone can get a piece. In contrast, the Christian knows that the potential in God is unlimited and that there is no shortage of resources in God's earth. The resources are waiting to be tapped.*
—AMERICA'S PROVIDENTIAL HISTORY, *A HISTORY TEXT-BOOK WHOSE SELF-DESCRIBED PURPOSE IS "TO EQUIP CHRISTIANS TO BE ABLE TO INTRODUCE BIBLICAL PRINCIPLES INTO THE PUBLIC AFFAIRS OF AMERICA."*

I remember when the Soviet Union launched Sputnik in 1957, inaugurating the space race and a thrilling era of exploration that captured the imagination of many adventurous teenagers, including me. Like every young boy of my generation, I entertained wild dreams of being an astronaut and zooming into the great beyond. Today, space exploration allows me, and indeed all of us, to imagine something else. It empowers us to see the world from the outside, a place far smaller and closer together than the infinite vastness of everything we see around us in our daily lives. Once you look at the world from that perspective, the conclusion is inescapable: This little sandbox we share is small, its resources are limited, and the demands on them are growing.

Just how quickly are the demands on our fragile planet escalating? Consider the astonishing rate of population growth over the last century. By the best scientific estimates, the world is approximately

5 billion years old, give or take a billion. (I know there are biblical literalists who place the age of the earth at less than six thousand years. That's a topic for another book. Let me just say here that I believe God is an "intelligent designer," and that's why God "intelligently designed" the theory of evolution.) Demographers estimate that it took almost all of that time—until around 1830—for the world population to reach 1 billion for the first time. Then it was off to the races: Within one hundred years, by 1930, the population was 2 billion people, all wanting access to clean air and clean water. In 1960, within just thirty years, when John F. Kennedy and Richard Nixon were vying for the presidency and I was wrestling for Springfield High, we hit 3 billion people. Fifteen years later, when I was a freshman member of Congress, there were 4 billion of us sharing this sandbox. In 1987, I left Congress, having won the silver medal in a campaign for the U.S. Senate. That was just twelve years, and the world population had already reached 5 billion. The United Nations estimates that we reached 6 billion on or about October 15, 1999, not long before I became general secretary of the National Council of Churches. Today, the world's population stands at more than 6.5 billion people. What those statistics tell us is remarkable: *more than half of all the people who ever lived on planet Earth are alive today*, increasingly competing for land, food, air, water, and other life sustaining gifts.

Does that mean we have too many people? Of course not. People of faith welcome each life that is brought into the world. The combination of soaring population and dwindling resources simply means we must begin to plan and conserve. Yet we are doing precisely the opposite. Listen to the words of David Orr in his book *Earth In Mind*:

> If today is a typical day on planet Earth, we will lose 116 square
> miles of rainforest, or about an acre a second. We will lose another
> 72 square miles to encroaching deserts, as a result of human mis-

management and overpopulation. We will lose 40 to 100 species, and no one knows whether the number is 40 or 100. Today the human population will increase by 250,000. And today we will add 2,700 tons of chlorofluorocarbons to the atmosphere and 15 million tons of carbon. Tonight the earth will be a little hotter, its waters more acidic, and the fabric of life more threadbare.

The truth is that many things on which your future health and prosperity depend are in dire jeopardy: climate stability, the resilience and productivity of natural systems, the beauty of the natural world, and biological diversity.

It is worth noting that this is not the work of ignorant people. It is, rather, largely the result of work by people with BAs, BSs, LLBs, MBAs, and PhDs. Elie Wiesel made a similar point to the Global Forum in Moscow last winter when he said that the designers and perpetrators of the Holocaust were the heirs of Kant and Goethe. In most respects the Germans were the best educated people on Earth, but their education did not serve as an adequate barrier to barbarity.

The math is as disturbing as it is direct: Barring a miracle, this finite planet cannot forever sustain us at current rates of consumption. According to the far religious right perspective, reflected in *America's Providential History*, a miracle is exactly what we should depend on. The reasoning essentially proclaims that God would not have created more people than the earth had the ability to support, and consequently, we simply need to have faith that what we need to survive will be there. To which my response is: Yes, God did give us wonderful natural gifts, among which are common sense, reason, and the ability to think ahead. Remember the story of Joseph in the Old Testament. He received a prophecy that a famine was coming in Egypt. That was a memo direct from God, so if anyone ever had a good excuse to place his faith in God's provenance rather than his own common sense, I'd have to say it was Joseph. But what was his response?

It was *human action* and *common-sense planning*. Joseph began rationing grain so some would be left for lean times. He never said, "Hey, God wouldn't have put us here without enough grain, so have faith in next year's crop and eat up." God told Joseph what was coming, and Joseph responded by taking personal responsibility.

The idea that God will provide all the resources we need and that human beings need exert no responsibility for our own future reminds me of the old joke about the preacher who's in the middle of a sermon when his church begins to flood. As the water rises above his ankles, his parishioners pull up a car and say, "Reverend, we'd better get out of here." "Don't worry," the preacher responds, "God will save me." When the water begins to rise above his neck, rescuers come in a boat. "Don't worry," he insists, "God will save me." Eventually, the entire building is submerged, and a helicopter arrives to lift the preacher from the roof, but he refuses again. "Don't worry, God will save me." Naturally, he drowns, and upon his arrival in Heaven, he demands: "Dear God, I was a man of faith. Why did you not save me?" To which God responds, "Reverend, I sent you a car, a boat, and a helicopter. What are you doing here?"

God has sent us all the resources we need, scientific warnings, technological know-how, and a sense of compassion toward our fellow human beings and generations unborn. Yet what we are doing today, at an increasing and alarming pace, is consuming nonrenewable resources that, once used, vanish from the earth forever. Faith calls on us to use the foresight God gave us to steward the planet and preserve creation, not to cling to an unseeing and unthinking belief that what we consume today will be miraculously replaced tomorrow. And I regret to say that faith often has less to do with these practices than finances. The idea that oil companies can stick a straw in the ground, drink up all the oil in the earth for the sake of profit and never ask what right generations five hundred years hence might have to those resources is breathtakingly arrogant and morally abhorrent.

Even today, as evidence gathers that we are rapidly depleting nonrenewable resources, our response is simply to assume we can find more of them. When Congress was given an opportunity to address the energy crisis in 2005, the far-right majority pushed through a bill that provided $14.5 billion in tax breaks and a few token dollars for renewable energy sources, most of which, however, went to finance production of more fossil fuels like oil, natural gas, and coal. Rather than seize an opportunity to make energy affordable and cleaner, Congress chose to make both problems worse. President Bush and his allies continue to push for oil drilling in the pristine Alaskan wilderness, a shortsighted (and, at least as of this writing, thankfully failed) policy whose very best hope is simply to extend, for a very short time, our lease on nonrenewable resources.

My own awakening to the environment as a moral cause came from my father, a man with an abiding love for the wilderness. My father never owned a car, never owned much of anything but the very small plot of green land on which our house was built. Well before I ever considered entering politics, back in the late 1960s or early 1970s, a real estate developer offered him a large payout to bulldoze the house and make way for a shopping center. He refused. "I'd rather have green grass than green money," he said. It was remarkable to see him, a blue-collar working person who could have used all the money he could get, stand up to such powerful people. His neighbors, who stood to make a nice profit by selling their homes, were infuriated. The pressure from the developer mounted, but my father was resolute. And he prevailed. He kept his little piece of God's creation and the shopping center was built up the road. My father is gone now, but his house is still standing. Around the time of that fight, he read a book called *The Greening of America*, an analysis of the youth movement that also addressed threats to the environment. "That guy's got it right," I remember him saying of the author, Charles Reich. "The corporations are going to cement over the world."

It was my dad who first introduced me to fishing. My father, my brother Ralph, and I often took the trolley to beautiful fishing holes in pastoral rural settings. As a boy, I sometimes found the day-long outings mind-numbingly boring. I was a workaholic adult before I understood that the peace and inactivity of these outings were precisely the point. Fishing to me provides a connection with nature, an opportunity to steep myself in creation, to appreciate the beauty of all that God made. Today, I take fishing vacations every year, often with Ralph. Not long ago, I took my twelve-year-old grandson, Benjamin, fishing for bass in Connecticut (put your arms about three feet apart and say it with me: I caught a fish *this big*).

Yet I wonder if that is a legacy my grandson's grandchildren will be denied. The fishing holes along the Delaware River that we frequented with my father have long since been poisoned by paper mills, industrial pollution, and agricultural runoff. Ninety percent of the world's great fisheries are depleted. Extinction is wiping out the great species of the sea, each of them created by God, and once they are gone they will never be seen on Earth again. But when Congress last considered the Endangered Species Act, it was the Christian Coalition that signed a letter saying "private property rights" were more important than protecting creation. They were one among many groups on the radical religious right who have discovered an implicit endorsement of capitalism in the Bible that, for them, outweighs the many explicit scriptural commands to steward the earth.

As a member of Congress, I joined the Public Works Committee and made a lot of enemies by opposing pork-barrel water projects, like dams that wasted money and despoiled nature. Then as now, members of Congress routinely squirreled away federal funds for such urgent public needs as catfish farms and marinas for huge yachts, simply hoping no one would call them on it. If I had been a smarter politician rather than a minister who stumbled into Congress, I might have gone along. The opportunities were certainly there. One of the first things that happens when you get elected to

Congress is that the old-boy network comes calling. "You want a water project for your district?" they offer. "We'll take care of you." But I didn't want a water project. I simply wanted those old fishing holes and creeks along the Delaware River to be left alone. So I started demanding explanations for water projects, and the wrath of the old boys came down. "You're the meanest Methodist minister I ever met!" Ray Roberts, one of the senior members of the Public Works Committee, once exploded in a fit of frustration. Eventually I was able to persuade my colleagues to demand that communities that wanted water projects pay for part of their cost, which went a long way, but by no means all the way, toward curbing Congress's appetite for pork.

My relative inexperience—some might say naiveté—was also useful during the late 1970s when a toxic waste storage facility along the Delaware River in Chester, Pennsylvania, caught fire. When the firefighters went in, the chemicals that were spilled on the floor were so foul and toxic that their boots literally melted off. It seemed to me that the people we ask to deal with these messes have a right to know what they're getting into, and that if polluters had to disclose what they were up to, maybe they would be shamed into cleaning up their acts. A more experienced politician would have known this was a hopeless cause, but I was still pretty new around Capitol Hill, so I wrote an amendment called "The Community Right to Know Provision" and attached it to the Resource Recovery Act.

Miraculously, it passed by a single vote, and corporate interests sprang into action. Congressman John Dingell of Michigan, a long-standing ally of the automakers, used a parliamentary maneuver to call for a re-vote the following week and used the intervening time to exert all his considerable muscle on members. He prowled the floor of the House and worked the phones, offering deals where he could and using his political clout when the enticements didn't work. I didn't have a vote-counting apparatus, much less any clout to offer, so all I could do was walk around and try to persuade people that I was right.

Surprisingly enough, that worked. Once again, the bill passed by a single vote, a compelling reminder that what we do as individuals can make a difference, and that political battles are worth fighting no matter how long the odds. Those are two lessons we must heed if we are to have any hope of confronting the greatest ecological and moral challenge of our time, global warming.

## Global Warming: The Moral Challenge of Our Time

Sometimes God sends us subtle signals, and sometimes God pulls out a celestial sledgehammer, hits us right over the head, and tells us exactly what's going on. When it comes to global warming, I can't imagine how the signals could be any more obvious. Never before in the history of humanity has a problem of such dire proportions been so completely predictable. And fixable. Global warming has happened gradually, and while we're rapidly approaching a disastrous point of no return, the tipping point hasn't yet arrived. We can still avert this crisis, but to recall Dr. King's phrase, "procrastination is the thief of time." Climate change is *the* moral issue of our day, and no other challenge more powerfully illustrates his call to heed "the fierce urgency of now." On this issue above all others, the faithful center must rise up, speak, and act. This issue will rise or fall—and the earth with it—based on the action or apathy of the mainstream.

Here's what we know: Greenhouse gasses like carbon dioxide, which is produced by human processes ranging from manufacturing to driving to power production, trap heat in the atmosphere and result in rising temperatures that imperil the earth's fragile ecological balance. Right now, there are around *one trillion* tons of carbon in the atmosphere. Even if the most serious curbs on emissions are imposed, that number will rise to 1.2 trillion by the end of the century, and if we do nothing, it will nearly triple to 2.8 trillion tons. Remember that as you think about this issue: Not even the most aggressive plans out there would reduce the amount of carbon in the atmosphere. Today we're talking about *reducing the rate at which the problem is getting worse.* The real challenge, beginning to turn environmental degradation around and actually starting to clean up the damage we've inflicted, still awaits.

Even at current levels of carbon, the results are devastating: Over the last century, average annual temperatures in the United States alone have risen by nearly one degree Fahrenheit. In case that doesn't sound like much, keep in mind that a few degrees is all that separates our thriving, modern age from the last ice age. And the United Nations predicts that global temperatures will rise as much as ten degrees in this century. The slightest changes trigger cascades of ecological reactions, from melting ice caps to fiercer storms. Entire species could be wiped out. Tropical diseases are sure to intensify. Far more study needs to be done to understand the impact of climate change on the weather, but many scientists believe warmer ocean temperatures are helping to feed powerful storms like Hurricane Katrina. Melting ice caps means rising oceans and lowland flooding that could imperil tens of millions of people. Remember that minister who ignored the water around his ankles?

Global warming is also about global justice. Industrialized nations produce the vast majority of greenhouses gasses, yet those who live in the areas most likely to be devastated by sea levels are among the poorest and most vulnerable people in the world, a point that the Asian tsunami of December 2004 brought home. The tsunami wasn't caused by global warming—the wave was generated by a cataclysmic earthquake deep under the ocean—but it did provide a harrowing warning of what the consequences of catastrophic flooding in these areas might be. If global warming floods the same kinds of areas flooded by the tsunami, which scientists say is likely, what we saw in December 2004 is a haunting preview of what may lie in store.

I visited Indonesia with a delegation of American Christians one hundred days after the tsunami. I had been to war zones from the

Middle East to Central America and I had visited many a crime
scene as a young minister in Philadelphia, but nothing prepared me
for the sheer scale of devastation we saw in Indonesia. We flew into
Banda Aceh, where the airport was functioning and, for the most
part, the environs looked normal. But as we wound down a small
road toward the coast, we began to see, even several miles inland, a
landscape of sheer desolation and misery unlike anything I had witnessed before. The destructive power of water is difficult to comprehend until one sees what a wall of water that rises up from the ocean
can do in a single day. The countryside was dotted by field after field
of slabs where houses had been washed away. In one field, an enormous oil tanker that had been carried more than a mile inland by the
tsunami sat atop several crushed houses. The local people had con-
verted it into an electric generator. A huge coal barge also sat on dry
ground as though it had sailed right over the now-dry fields.

A Lutheran pastor told us how he survived by clinging to a tree
and hanging on for five hours. At a Methodist church, we met a minister who could barely speak because his lungs filled with floodwater
during the tsunami. Twenty-two people had died in his church.
Every pew was slicked with mud, and the yellow-brownish waterline
was visible on the wall well above our heads. One Muslim university
we visited had more than six thousand students enrolled in classes
on the morning before the tsunami hit. Twenty-four hours later, the
student body had shrunk to around four thousand. Every surviving
student had lost relatives and much of the campus had been washed
away.

We spent the night at a hotel on the edge of the damaged area.
There was neither toilet paper nor a toilet seat. We filled up a bucket
to flush the toilet, and slept on a mat, a difficult night made all the
more disturbing by the knowledge that what was for us a temporary
inconvenience was for millions now a way of life. The next day we
visited the Indonesian island of Nias, which had suffered a massive
earthquake just three months after being hit by the tsunami. The

population was a literal island of Christianity in a predominantly Muslim nation, and aid had been slow to arrive. The island's churches were pancaked into the ground. We sat with a Lutheran pastor whose church had been flattened. He spoke calmly and rationally of the deaths of many of his parishioners and the emotional and physical exhaustion of caring for the survivors. When he paused, I asked if we could pray for him. He nodded quietly. I asked everyone to hold hands, which is my custom during prayer. It's a small but, for me, meaningful act that reminds us of the power of human community. I had barely spoken two words when he erupted in an awful, wailing cry, rivers of tears rolling down his cheeks, his chest heaving with sobs. There was little we could do but put our arms around him and let him grieve.

But there is a great deal humanity can do to prevent such suffering in the future. Global warming is one of many silent tsunamis in our world, tragedies whose toll is terrible yet gradual enough to escape our notice in the daily news. If the ocean rises up and consumes these islands and coastal areas, the devastation will be less sudden than that caused by the tsunami, but every bit as destructive. We have a responsibility as people of faith and members of the human community to prevent that now, while we still can. And it is our special responsibility as Americans to act. We must do so first and foremost because we are the leading producer of greenhouse gases, but also because we have the wealth and power to make a difference, and our impoverished brothers and sisters around the world do not.

I'm not given to alarmism, but I don't believe in mincing words, either. Global warming is threatening God's creation. If that's not a direct challenge for all people of faith, it's hard to imagine what might be. I'm convinced that global warming is to our generation what civil rights and the Vietnam War were to the 1960s: the defining moral challenge of our age. How we respond will define our place in history. Future generations will look back at this time with either gratitude for our foresight or the most profound regret for our apathy. This is a moral challenge. And if we believe, as I do, that creation was God's gift, that God challenged us to be co-creators, stewards of creation, to take good care of this earth so that future generations might have it, too, then global warming is an urgent religious issue that we must act upon *now!*

Yet the problem is being ignored and exacerbated by the very leaders who tell us their political beliefs are guided by God's word. Leaders of the far religious right from Pat Robertson to James Dobson of Focus on the Family routinely deride the overwhelming science on global warming as inconclusive or flawed. (By the way, if you figure out what protecting polluters has to do with focusing on families, let me know.) Ironically enough, religious leaders who deny the clear, consistent, and proven conclusions of objective scientists are the same people who routinely decry American society for our moral relativism and our supposed reluctance to recognize absolute truth. Yet when science fails to conform to their political agenda, the truth suddenly seems malleable and the fact that it concerns a religious and moral imperative as urgent as preserving our earth makes the double standard all the more tragic. Meanwhile, their denial of science has been aided by journalists who, in the name of objectivity and fairness, feel a need to balance every bit of evidence for global warming, no matter how rigorously proven, with a denial, no matter how flimsy its basis. It reminds me of what some wit recently said about the media's he-said-she-said equivocating about the truth: If President Bush said the world was flat, the headlines the next day would proclaim, "Controversy About Shape of Earth."

President Bush, too, has treated the truth like clay to be molded to the convenience of corporate interests. In 2001, shortly after taking office, he abruptly and unilaterally withdrew the United States from participation in the Kyoto Protocol, an international effort to curb greenhouse gas emissions that his own father helped to launch. To place events in perspective, Kyoto simply hoped to curb a bare fraction of greenhouse gas emissions.

Yet the United States, a nation that has been and should always be a light of inspiration to the world, was not present. We abandoned our responsibility at precisely the moment the world needed us most. That stunning announcement may very well have been one of the most important foreign policy decisions of the Bush presidency. It was a tragic proclamation to the world that we were so consumed by our own greed that we were unwilling to join the community of nations and do our part to steward this fragile planet.

And the widespread concern over this move raised by leaders of several American faith traditions was compelling evidence that global warming is a spiritual issue. I was one of several religious leaders— Jewish and Christian alike—who wrote to President Bush urging him, on the religious grounds he routinely invoked on issues of personal piety, to reconsider:

March 29, 2001
President George W. Bush
The White House
1600 Pennsylvania Avenue
Washington, DC 20500

Dear Mr. President:
We reach out as senior leaders of major American faith communities eager to discuss with you a challenge of paramount religious significance: the condition of God's creation at the hands of God's children, the climate of planet Earth as being altered by the activity of the Earth's people. . . .

Projected impacts of global warming on the most poor and vulnerable are ethically unacceptable. Domestic and international action is urgently required. The United States has a moral responsibility to lead the world's nations and to serve its people. In recent days, we have been reading reports of what the administration is not prepared to do to address climate change. We are eager to learn what our government will enact here: in a credible, binding program to honor international commitments, successfully prevent destructive impacts on humankind and habitat, and embody equity.

Our Scriptures are plain about the religious dimension of this challenge. When it is all creation on Earth that is being affected, we freshly appreciate the principle that, "The Earth is the Lord's." (Ps. 24:1) Our climate and seasons are God's handicraft. "Yours is the day. Yours is also the night . . . You made summer and winter." (Ps. 74:16–17) All life is embraced by God's covenant and with particular instructions regarding our children and children's children. "This is the token of the covenant which I make between me and you and every living creature that is with you, for perpetual generations." (Gen. 9:12) . . .

We in the faith community are in a process of open dialogue and inquiry here. We are heartened by your early commitment to civil, moderate, bipartisan dialogue, and, particularly, by your willingness to hear the voice of the faith community. We hope you will follow this path on the issue of climate change. We are eager to meet with you for further reflection, perhaps in a small gathering in June.

Meanwhile, we believe an historic challenge is before us all here, foreseen by our scriptures, and freshly vivid in these signs of the times, "I have set before you life or death, blessings or curse. Choose life, therefore, that you and your descendants may live." (Deut. 30:19)

Ismar Schorsch
Chancellor, Jewish Theological Seminary

Dr. Bob Edgar
General Secretary, National Council of the Churches of Christ in the USA

The Reverend Clifton Kirkpatrick
Stated Clerk, Presbyterian Church (USA)

Bishop Melvin G. Talbert
Senior Ecumenical Officer, United Methodist Church

The Reverend Richard L. Hamm
General Minister and President, Christian Church (Disciples of Christ)

Bishop McKinley Young
Bishop of the Tenth Episcopal District, African Methodist Episcopal Church

Unsurprisingly, the White House never granted our request as Jewish and Christian leaders to meet with the man who had promised to govern on the basis of his religious values. Nor did President Bush ever relent in his unyielding opposition to addressing global warming. Then as now, President Bush, like other opponents of reducing carbon dioxide emissions, was blunt about his reasons. When he pulled the United States from the Kyoto Protocol negotiations, he said the accord would cost American jobs, and he asserted his frequent claim that global warming is based on faulty science, a claim that has become a right-wing mantra, along with the assertion that international treaties like Kyoto deprive the United States of sovereignty.

I do not believe that dealing with global warming would cause economic problems. On the contrary, many experts believe that mitigating global warming would create economic opportunity. But let's imagine, just for a moment, that curbing greenhouse gases would require us to tighten our belts a bit. Are we actually willing to risk catastrophic ecological consequences just to make a few extra dollars? Who among us is willing to look our grandchildren in the eyes and say, "We would have saved the earth for you, but it cost too much money"? I'm not aware of any biblical verses that provide exceptions to God's commandments when the cost seems too high. On the contrary, we are called to God's work in the face of threats and sacrifices far more serious than a moderate diminishment of material consumption. The psalm says, "Be strong and let your heart take courage, all you who wait for the Lord" (Ps. 31:24)—not, "be strong, unless it imperils your disposable income." "Be not afraid," the angel says in Luke. The Bible is filled with stories of martyrs who endured horrific deaths rather than violate God's teachings. Is it too much to ask that we accept a little less income?

Well, depending on who you ask, the answer might very well be "yes." Consider Phyllis Schlafly, the founder of Eagle Forum, a far-right organization that describes itself as "pro-family" and often appeals for "Christian" values. Schlafly railed against the Kyoto Protocol. Writing in one of her many newsletter columns on the topic she said that global warming united several "anti-American" interests, including (by the way, check for yourself on this list) "socialists," "leftist radicals," "foreign dictators," and, lest we forget, "Democrats." But it's the following "anti-American" interest that catches my attention: "the cult of radical environmentalists who believe we should subordinate our standard of living to the supremacy of global ecology . . ."

More often than not, the far religious right distorts and caricatures the beliefs of those with whom they disagree, but in this case, Schlafly might just have a point: If the choice is between global ecology and our standard of living, count me among those who believe the planet's survival matters more. I don't think that makes me (or you, if you agree) either a radical or a cultist. Nor do I believe environmental protection and material prosperity are inherently opposed to one another. But I do know this: No reasonable reading of Scripture, which takes a rather dim view of wealth, can support the destruction of God's earth in the name of material comfort.

So even if you accept what the far right says about the economic costs of curbing global warming, the possibility of sacrifice does not relieve us of moral responsibility. Similarly, even if you accept what they say about science, that the evidence about global warming is "mixed," you still can't avoid the moral imperative to care for the earth. Now, for the record, I can't help but notice that the only science the far right calls junk or unproven is the science that happens to contradict their political agenda. But again, let's just accept that premise that we're not totally sure about global warming and explore the implications. Do we actually want to be wrong? Is it morally acceptable to take such a gigantic risk with our children's future, with their very lives, at stake? I don't think so and neither should conservatives. After all, those on the far right who oppose action on global warming are the same conservative leaders who are always preaching to us about prudence and responsibility.

In 2005, I attended a meeting with British Prime Minister Tony Blair in Washington. I recall how he characterized the disagreement about science: "For those of us who believe in the science and understand the facts, we must urgently work to address the issue of climate change and global warming before it is too late. For those of you who don't believe the science and think it is wrong or misguided, you too must act urgently just in case you are wrong."

And if science won't convince the far right about global warming, that common sense they're always telling us about should come in handy too. Do you remember the old Bob Newhart routine where Sir Walter Raleigh calls England to tell them he's discovered tobacco? "What do you do to it?" they respond incredulously. "You set fire to it! Then what do you do, Walt? You inhale the smoke! Walt, we've been worried about you . . . you're gonna have a tough time getting people to stick burning leaves in their mouth." Well, pumping poisonous chemicals into the atmosphere makes about as much sense to me as sticking a dried leaf in your mouth and setting it on fire. The overwhelming scientific evidence for global warming helps clarify the issue, but the fact remains that you don't need a PhD or a pile of studies to figure out that putting a trillion tons of black carbon into the once-clear blue sky isn't a good idea. Somehow, I can't help but imagine future generations responding to President Bush like Bob Newhart: "What was that, Mr. President? What do you do? You put a bunch of gas-guzzling cars on the highway and fire up coal-burning factories and let them cough a trillion tons of black smoke into the sky just to make a few extra bucks? And that's good for the earth? Mr. President, we've been worried about you . . ."

You don't need much common sense to know that we're poisoning the earth. For that matter, we don't need common sense at all.

Scientists on this topic are nearly unanimous. The National Academy of Sciences, the Environmental Protection Agency, NASA, the United Nations, as well as researchers from many of the world's leading universities tell us global warming is a real, persistent, and worsening problem.

As for the idea that an international treaty somehow diminishes America's independence or power, making a treaty *is* an act of independence and power. The ability to agree, voluntarily, to an international agreement is a compelling sign of autonomy and sovereignty. Countries agree to treaties because they see benefits in doing so. It's what mature, self-assured nations do; it's also the only way to control global warming. We're all on this planet together, and what one nation pumps into the skies affects every other nation.

Opponents of international action also tried to claim the treaty exempted some polluters in the developing world. But regardless of what others do, we are responsible for adhering to our own values. The idea that we can behave immorally as long as we believe other nations are doing so is both abhorrent and dangerous. Any parent will recognize that strain of logic—come on, everyone else was doing it—as childish, too. We must do what we can and we must do so together. Atmospheres and oceans don't recognize borders, and I daresay God doesn't, either. Each of us is called to care for God's creation.

Of course, problems of this magnitude can be intimidating. Often, we don't know where to start, or we're overwhelmed by a sense of futility. An excellent guide is to think globally and work locally, to have an eagle-eyed view of the world, but an ant-eyed view of your community. Thinking globally means we have to demand—not ask, not cajole, but outright demand—that our political leaders get serious about global warming. Reentering the community of nations by enlisting in the Kyoto Protocol would be a modest but important start. There's also a great deal our government can do here at home. But timid half-measures won't do the job. This is a big problem, and it requires dramatic measures. Some people say government can't step in and mandate lower emissions. I say: Why not? I'll tell you an irrefutable truth that too few politicians in today's market-obsessed government are willing to admit: *Regulation works.*

In 1977, when I was a member of Congress, I attended the White House ceremony where President Carter signed the first major energy bill of his administration. America had recently endured the Arab oil embargo, gas lines, and soaring fuel prices, and the nation's conscience was awakening to the fact that we faced an energy crisis and a fast-dwindling supply of natural resources. One of the most controversial provisions in that bill was a mandatory fuel efficiency standard for cars. No incentives, no asking nicely, we just told automakers to get the job done. I supported that law, and I remember the fight well. The lobbyists for the Big Three car manufacturers jumped up and down and insisted that there was no way they could meet the law's requirement of more than doubling fuel efficiency. They said jobs would disappear and plants would close. We passed the law anyway and a miracle ensued: The car companies did exactly what Congress required. They developed new technologies, and soon cars were getting an average of twenty-seven miles per gallon. The economic apocalypse never came. Then Congress let that requirement lapse. It became voluntary—the classic free-market strategy—and, sadly but predictably, the rapid improvement in fuel efficiency came to a halt.

Having said that, I don't have any illusions about Washington suddenly freeing itself from the grip of the auto and energy lobbies, but promising avenues of action are available to us at the state and local levels. The National Council of Churches has worked with Catholics, evangelicals, and Jews to push for policies in eighteen states that address global warming. And even though we aren't getting as far as we'd like in Washington, we've made some very impressive progress in state capitals.

While we wait for government to act, the most effective strategy left to us is moral persuasion. That challenge must come from our faith communities. The radical religious right may be making the most noise, but the faithful religious center holds the balance. Fortunately, many religious leaders from all faiths and across the political spectrum are accepting care for the earth as a spiritual imperative. In 2002, I joined a group of leaders from several faiths in a campaign to promote more fuel efficient cars. Jim Ball, a Baptist minister with a quick wit, a wonderful sense of humor, and deeply impassioned convictions, came up with an ingenious slogan: "What would Jesus drive?" That formed the basis of a widespread advertising campaign, and Jim took a tour across America in a hybrid car to promote his vision. He and his wife, Kara, took turns at the wheel of their Toyota Prius, equipped with Jim's signature bumper sticker, "What would Jesus drive?" They traveled the country, preaching in churches, meeting policymakers, and urging other clergy to think about transportation choices as a moral issue. As Jim notes on his web site (www.whatwouldjesusdrive.org):

> Jesus is concerned about what we drive because pollution from vehicles has a major impact on human health and the rest of God's creation. It contributes significantly to the threat of global warming. And our reliance on imported oil from unstable regions threatens peace and security. Making transportation choices that threaten millions of human beings violates Jesus' Great Commandments to "Love the Lord your God with all your heart and with all your soul, and with all your mind and with all your strength" and "Love your neighbor as yourself" (Mark 12:30–31), as well as the Golden Rule to "Do to others as you would have them do to you." (Luke 6:31)

That November, Jim helped lead a group of religious leaders to Detroit to meet with William Clay Ford, the young chairman of

Ford Motor Company, as well as autoworkers and other car manufacturers to discuss the campaign. At the time, automakers were
spending around $13 billion a year encouraging people to drive gas-
guzzling vehicles like SUVs and light trucks, then turning around
and claiming, in wide-eyed innocence, that they made them only because consumers wanted them. Rabbi David Saperstein of the Religious Action Center for Reform Judaism, an old friend with whom
I've worked for years and whom I knew back when I was in Congress, was there. So was Ron Sider, an evangelical who holds conservative views on many social issues but is passionate about caring for
God's creation. Ron heads up a group called Evangelicals for Social
Action. Among the four of us, we had enemies on just about every
side of the political spectrum, a powerful testament to the coalitions
we can build for environmental progress if we're willing to set aside
other disagreements.

William Clay Ford impressed me with what seemed to be a sincere commitment to the environment. I was less convinced by his
pledge that hydrogen-cell technology might be ready for the market within ten to fifteen years—if only because I had heard the
very same promise well over twenty years earlier. I heard it when I
served in Congress and automakers were begging off environmental regulation with an eternal promise that a clean, miracle technology was just around the corner. But he did assure us that the Ford
Escape, a hybrid SUV, was in the final stages of development and
would hit the market soon. Almost two years to the day after our
meeting, it did.

Our institutions of faith must also set their own examples of environmental preservation. One start would be every synagogue,
church, and mosque pledging to build energy- and water-efficient facilities with healthy building materials. My inspiration in that project
was a man named John Lyle, a California professor of landscape ar-
chitecture who pioneered the idea of "regenerative development."
This is development that actually regenerates the environment rather

than simply refrains from damaging it. I had met John when I became president of the Claremont School of Theology in Southern California.

When you land at Ontario airport outside Los Angeles, you're struck by the desert landscape, but when I visited Claremont for the first time, I couldn't help but notice that it looked like a campus in a quaint New England town. Right in the middle of the desert, ivy hung from the walls and the ground was covered in lush grass, extravagances purchased at the price of massive use of water, fertilizers, and chemicals, to say nothing of the fact that ivy in the desert is a perfect hiding place for rats. It was John who first suggested that we tear down the ivy and replace it with indigenous plants. "You can go from rats to rabbits," he said, which is exactly what we did. We began teaching courses in regenerative theological studies as well.

It's a challenge many other religious institutions have taken up. During our visit to Detroit for the "What Would Jesus Drive?" tour, we met an order of nuns, the Servants of the Immaculate Heart of Mary, who had renovated their campus and made it one of the most environmentally sound facilities in the country. They cleanse and recycle water from the showers to flush toilets. Large portions of their campus were reserved for holding ponds, so rainwater runs off and percolates back into their water supply. The facility was designed to maximize daylight, minimizing the use of electrical appliances, all of which are highly energy-efficient. The sisters utilize geothermal heating and cooling, piping water deep below the earth, where the temperature is static. It's a fantastic example of how the faith community could respond to the challenge of stewarding creation.

What if every church, synagogue, and mosque built green and worked toward the healing of the planet? Would it solve every problem? Of course not, and neither will putting more hybrid cars on the road. Nor can any of us hope to purify the atmosphere through the relatively small difference we can make in daily life. But all of us acting together with both the ant-eyed perspective of changes in our daily lives and the eagle-eyed view of working with our government on national and international action can turn this problem around. As serious as global warming has already become, the most important thing to know is that it is not yet out of control. Renewal of the earth is still within our grasp, if we embrace the fierce urgency of now. Those who claim to espouse faith in public life cannot dodge responsibility for this grave moral challenge, and least of all can they credibly claim that God has given humanity an unfettered license to pollute and ultimately destroy creation. Nor can the faithful millions in the middle be silent.

We must all take up the challenge expressed in an open letter to church and society that many faith leaders released in 2005: "Join us in restoring God's Earth—the greatest healing work and moral assignment of our time." It is not too late. But a moment will come when it is, when the crisis has slipped from our control and ecological processes we can neither restrain nor survive are unleashed. When that moment arrives, the marginal economic sacrifices of which George W. Bush and other self-described politicians of faith warned in such apocalyptic terms will seem like a small price to have paid for preserving a wonderful gift from God. The "standard of living" that radical religious right leaders like Phyllis Schlafly sought to preserve will be exposed for what it was, a momentary desire hardly worthy of poisoning the earth.

If global warming and other forms of environmental degradation are a sign of the End of Days as some on the far religious right would have us believe, it is an end brought about by our own sin, not God's salvation. God is calling us to this moment as the Old Testament prophets were called. We have been to the mountaintop and discovered the glaciers melting. We have been to the valley of the shadow of death and seen our fish floating poisoned on the water. The prophetic voice we must hear is not the one that welcomes the squandering of God's creation. It is the still, small prophetic voice calling each of us to do our part to steward and safeguard the planet.

CHAPTER 3

# What Part of "Blessed Are the Peacemakers" Don't They Understand?

*Blessed are the peacemakers, for they will be called children of God.*
—Matthew 5:9

*We should invade their countries, kill their leaders and convert them to Christianity. We weren't punctilious about locating and punishing only Hitler and his top officers. We carpet-bombed German cities; we killed civilians. That's war. And this is war.*
—Ann Coulter

Caroline was a typical four-year-old girl, innocent, playful, and a touch flirtatious. When I met her at a New Year's Eve service in a Presbyterian church, she was outfitted in bright red, a squat Santa-type cap perched atop her head, and LET IT SNOW, every child's winter wish, emblazoned across the seat of her pants. Throughout the service, she darted out of her seat to tease the grown-ups in the front pew, holding a cookie up to our mouths, beckoning us to take a bite, only to pull it back the moment our lips parted. It might have been a scene from any church in America. But the location that New Year's Eve was decidedly different. It was a Presbyterian church in central Baghdad on December 31, 2002—less than ninety days before the

63

United States launched preemptive war over the protests of most other nations in the civilized world.

Back home, the voices for war were escalating, Republicans and Democrats marched in lockstep with encouragement from the far religious right, and the few of us pleading for peace were increasingly being marginalized as unpatriotic, un-American, even unfaithful. In an e-mail to his supporters, moralizer Gary Bauer asked:

> In the long run, who most harms the United States? Is it clueless UN bureaucrats like [weapons inspector] Hans Blix, feckless French leaders like Jacques Chirac, or radical Islamic terrorists? They all make a contribution, but at the end of the day I believe we have more to fear from the anti-American crowd right here at home.

Strong stuff. Not only was it apparently anti-American to oppose the war and question the president, it was worse than terrorism, too. D. James Kennedy, the prominent conservative and head of Coral Ridge Ministries, seemed to have little doubt about who the anti-American crowd was when he wondered aloud "why any churchman would choose to support [Saddam Hussein] rather than to support our own president." Never mind the fact that nobody ever stood with Saddam Hussein. Or that opposing killing and urging peaceful diplomacy had nothing to do with choosing for or against geopolitical leaders. All a Christian minister had to do was choose the rather clear and consistent message of Jesus. So if Pastor Kennedy is still curious why a Christian would oppose the war, Matthew 5:9 would be a pretty good place to start his research. For his part, Pat Robertson would later accuse then Senate Minority Leader Tom Daschle of lack of patriotism for daring to speak out against President Bush's policy in Iraq. "Now, when people like Sen. Daschle stand up in the Senate and attack the president one day before the war starts, then that, to me, borders on lack of patriotism and I think it is wrong."

Five leaders of the far religious right, corralled by Richard Land of the Southern Baptist Convention, wrote the president to tell him they believed the war was compatible with Christian doctrine.

Three years have passed since then. Looking back, it's hard to say exactly what disturbs me most about the Iraq war—the lies that led to it, the tens of thousands of our fellow human beings who have been killed, or the insistence, still stubbornly clung to in the face of all available facts, that the war is going well. Even the administration now calls for a gradually phased withdraw. But if I had to pick what's most offensive, using the name of Jesus Christ to support the waging of preemptive war that has shed the blood of innocents would have to be near the top of the list.

Still, on that New Year's Eve in Baghdad, domestic politics were the furthest thing from my mind. And from Caroline's. As I looked into the face of this four-year-old Iraqi girl, who was distinguished from any one of my grandchildren only by her olive-toned skin and her Arabic heritage, all I could think was: This is the face of those who may die if my country goes to war. When the bombs begin to fall, they will be equipped with the most advanced military technology in the history of humankind, but not one of them will bear a sensor telling it how to avoid Caroline. And she was a Lamb of God, no less so than any four-year-old who, by coincidence alone, was born in the United States rather than Iraq.

I was in Baghdad with a thirteen-member delegation of American clergy sent by the National Council of Churches to make a humanitarian inspection of Iraq. While we supported the weapons inspections the United Nations was conducting at the time and, indeed, prayed fervently that the inspectors, our last and still-active hope for a peaceful solution, would be permitted to continue their work, we thought that an examination of the lives of ordinary, innocent people in Iraq was equally important. All that Americans saw was the image of Saddam Hussein, whose justly deserved reputation as an evil dictator seemed to have turned our impression of every

Iraqi into that of the faceless and ugly foreigner. Our television sets bore Saddam's face daily; Caroline's or her mother's or that of any other Iraqi of any faith was rarely seen. Within moments of our arrival in Iraq, I rankled organizers of the trip, who had booked face-to-face meetings with Iraqi government officials, by insisting that we visit everyday people so we, and by extension *all* Americans, could see their faces and hear their voices.

For more than a decade, the people of Iraq had endured a regime of severe sanctions imposed by the United Nations and maintained at the insistence of the United States and Great Britain. Sanctions are the tool of choice in foreign policy for those who are reluctant to employ force; they are surely better than bombs, but they are rarely effective and can be as deadly as munitions. The Iraqi people endured a more than decade-long embargo on every essential commodity except for food and water. Schoolchildren could not have lead pencils lest the metal they contained (graphite) be diverted to make weapons of mass destruction. Repair equipment for incubators needed by premature babies was off-limits too, as were materials for rebuilding the water and sewer systems we obliterated in the Gulf War of 1991. By conservative estimates, as many as one million Iraqi children died of waterborne diseases as a result, and countless people were suffering from cancer and other lingering effects from our use of radiated munitions. And all this was for naught: Saddam did not slow construction of his palaces, his henchmen continued to stash wealth in secret accounts, and only the innocent were left to bear the burden.

We met many of the innocent as we visited Iraqi hospitals. The stench was horrific. We saw emaciated babies dying of diarrhea and other conditions caused by the poor water quality. Mothers were bringing in food for their newborn babies because the hospitals did not have enough to feed them. Doctors showed us pictures of people dying of diseases that might have been treated had medical supplies been available. In nearly every medical setting we visited, the conditions in this once-modern country were primitive. Some, no doubt, will say all we saw was propaganda orchestrated by the Iraqi regime. Maybe they tried, and perhaps they even succeeded in exaggerating the sanctions' effect. But the dying babies, so fragile they looked as though the simple caress of a loving adult might break them in two, the children dying of conditions Americans think of as nuisances to be cured with over-the-counter remedies, the mothers weeping for the waste of young lives—all these were real. All these people I saw with my eyes and touched with my hands, and the sight of their suffering, the senseless destruction of our brothers and sisters who were being treated as pawns in a geopolitical game, would scorch the conscience of any person of faith.

What I saw reminded me of the time I visited North Korea as part of a humanitarian mission delivering food during a horrific famine.

"Don't bring them food," one U.S. official told me. "They'll feed it to their soldiers."

"Well," I replied, "I didn't see any fat soldiers." All I saw in both countries was suffering. There are moments when the real suffering of real human beings, every one of them a reflection of God's image, must trump the larger questions of world politics and bring us together as people of faith. A hungry North Korean needs food; a sick Iraqi child needs medicine. And I cannot imagine Jesus or the prophets of Judaism or Islam or any faith having any question about these things.

On our visit to Baghdad, my heart was with the innocents, not the leaders of Saddam's regime. I have no sympathy for dictators. Fidel Castro, the only one with whom I have ever dealt, despises me because I once went to Cuba on a humanitarian mission and refused to go to his palace so he could use an American church delegation for propaganda. Yet any avenue for peace, any opportunity to spare the Carolines of Iraq the random and undiscriminating destruction of another war, was worth pursuing, no matter how distasteful. And the

Iraqi leaders with whom we met were certainly distasteful. Deputy Prime Minister Tariq Aziz, a Chaldean Catholic, was arrogant and belligerent. When we pressed him on why his government had played games with weapons inspectors, he was defiant. When we explained that Saddam's atrocious human rights record made it more difficult for us to preach peace, he was defensive. Our attempts to convince him that the threat of war was as real as our prayers for peace seemed only to fuel his hostility. That was the public posturing, the face of the Iraqi regime that had so often taunted Americans.

Yet in a subsequent meeting conducted in secret, Aziz was neither brash nor argumentative. All we could sense were desperation and fear, but there was nothing constructive he could offer. A meeting with Saddam's defense minister, with whom we discussed the option of the regime's leaders going into exile to avert war, was similarly unproductive. It seemed to me that the leaders feared the wrath of Saddam himself more than a U.S. invasion. The only remaining hope was that Bush would see what the weapons inspectors were saying, that despite the antics of the Iraqi regime, the inspectors were making progress. War was premature, unjustified, unnecessary.

It was a distant hope, but we carried it in our hearts on New Year's Eve. Early in the evening, around 6 P.M., we visited a Syrian Orthodox church. The bishop led us in prayer, showed us a model of a center he was building for elderly parishioners, and offered a quiet plea that was not in our power to fulfill.

"I hope," he said, "it won't be bombed."

Two hours later, we arrived at the Chaldean Catholic church. Aziz's wife was known to attend it daily. A choir and congregation sang with enthusiasm, especially when the organist played a version of "Jingle Bells" with religious Christian lyrics substituted for the traditional secular ones. The sermon was delivered by a member of our delegation, United Methodist Bishop Mel Talbert, and was very moving—a powerful message, delivered by a Protestant bishop, in a Catholic church, in a foreign country, on New Year's Eve. It was made even more special when Bishop Talbert, an African-American, ended the sermon by singing "We Shall Overcome." We were all in tears when the congregation joined in and sang that historic civil rights song, some in English, others in Arabic.

At 10 P.M., we arrived at the Presbyterian church in downtown Baghdad, whose congregation, despite the ominous prospect of war, was upholding an age-old tradition: welcoming the New Year with a celebration in their fellowship hall, complete with carols, a band, and a New Year's birthday cake. As we moved through the crowds, several Iraqis leaned forward and whispered that they did not like Saddam any more than we did. "But," ran the near-unanimous refrain, "we want to govern our country. We don't want to be occupied."

We came away with the distinct impression, an impression easily available to anyone walking the streets of Baghdad, that any American occupation would be fiercely resisted. And then there was the highlight of the evening, indeed, of the entire trip, Caroline. On January 2, as we prepared to leave Baghdad, we issued this statement expressing the hope for peace to which our visit had given added urgency:

> We are a delegation of thirteen religious leaders and experts visiting Iraq under the auspices of the National Council of Churches (USA). Ours is a religious and not a political delegation. We came to see the faces of the Iraqi people so that the American people can see the faces of children laughing and singing and also hurting and suffering. We brought with us dozens of pictures drawn by American children. We shared these pictures with Iraqi children who, in turn, gave us messages to take back to children in the United States.
>
> We are called by God to be peacemakers. War is not inevitable and can be averted, even at this moment. President Bush reiterated, on New Year's Eve, his desire to reach a peaceful conclusion to this crisis and we are grateful for his words.

We came as humanitarian inspectors, not weapons inspectors. We visited schools and hospitals and saw for ourselves the devastating impact of twelve years of sanctions on the people of Iraq. We touched babies suffering illnesses that can be prevented by proper medication currently unavailable to the people of Iraq. We held the cold hands of children in unheated schools with broken windows and underpaid teachers, nurses, and doctors.

UNICEF officials shared heartbreaking statistics of malnutrition, disease, and hunger with us. We are concerned by the increasing reliance of Iraqi people on the food basket provided through the Oil-for-Food Program, a program not intended to be the primary source of nutrition or a balanced diet. We intend to advocate to our government for changes in the Oil-for-Food Program that will allow for humanitarian, educational, and medical needs to be better met. We understand the cruelty embedded in the Oil-for-Food Program as it affects ordinary Iraqis.

We worshiped with Iraqi Christians and in the presence of Muslims, and we prayed with both. This is the birthplace of Abraham, the father of Judaism, Christianity, and Islam. We acknowledged and celebrated our oneness in God. We attended a New Year's Eve Mass at a Catholic church and a potluck dinner at a Presbyterian church—a potluck that would be intimately familiar to American Christians. On the street and in informal settings we experienced the spontaneous warmth, hospitality, and openness of the Iraqi people. We feel privileged and honored by these human relationships.

We asked pointed questions of Deputy Prime Minister Tariq Aziz regarding the human rights situation in Iraq, the opportunities for dissent and criticism of the government, and choices made by the government with the resources available to it. We want to be clear with the American people and the Iraqi government that we do not support authoritarian governments.

We came with "what?" questions—"what's going on?" "what can

we discover?" but we were met with "why?" questions—"why us?" "why now?" We have concluded that we are opposed to this war because:

+ a war against Iraq will make the U.S. less secure, not more secure. All wars have unintended consequences. We believe the entire region, including Israel and the United States, will be at greater risk of terrorism if war takes place.

+ widespread suffering and death will result for innocent people. So-called smart bombs do dumb things like missing their targets and destroying homes, water and sewage treatment plants, schools, churches, and mosques.

+ preemptive war is immoral and illegal. It is theologically illegitimate and profoundly violates our Christian beliefs and religious principles. As disciples of Jesus Christ, the Prince of Peace, we know this war is completely antithetical to his teachings. Jesus Christ taught peace, justice, hope, and reconciliation and rejected revenge, war, death, and violence.

When we return to the United States:

1. We pledge support for the "All Our Children" campaign, a project of the Church World Service and other partners.

2. We will continue to build constructive, positive relationships between our nations and peoples through our ecumenical and interfaith relationships.

3. We will meet with U.S. administration and Congressional leaders to urge them to turn away from war. We will ask U.S. government and military leaders to take the time to learn the names and faces of average, ordinary Iraqi people.

4. We will meet with the permanent members of the U.N. Security Council to seek a revamped and more humane "oil-for-food" program.

5. We will share our photographs and our stories with the people in our one hundred forty thousand congregations so that they may see that, like us, our Iraqi brothers and sisters are children of God.

The weapons inspectors need to be allowed to do their work. Now, it is time for the humanitarian inspectors to do theirs.

In closing, we affirm the words shared with us by the Metropolitan of the Syrian Orthodox Church: "Together, we must sow the seeds of peace and let God water and nurture the seeds."

Yet despite the White House's constant claim that the president was reluctant to go to war, few leaders would listen to our message of peace. Vice President Cheney was roaming the talk-show circuit linking Saddam with the 9/11 attacks. Images of Saddam detonating a nuclear device in an American city—the now-infamous mushroom cloud as smoking-gun metaphor—were being used to stoke fears. In late January, President Bush announced in his State of the Union Address that Iraqi agents had attempted to purchase yellow-cake uranium in Africa. The propaganda was unshakeable: Saddam Hussein was poised to unleash as-yet-unimagined nightmares inside America. And President Bush, somehow portrayed as a reluctant warrior when all evidence suggests he was eagerly hunting up excuses for war with Iraq at least from the very first days after 9/11, said war was all that could save us.

There was nothing left but prayer and pleas. On January 30, I joined forty-six religious leaders in asking the president, who was still claiming to be hoping for peace, to meet with us to discuss the moral consequences of the war. We wrote:

January 30, 2003
President George W. Bush
The White House
1600 Pennsylvania Avenue NW
Washington, DC 20500

Dear Mr. President:

We greet you—our president, our nation's highest military leader, and a member of the community of faith—in the name of Jesus Christ our Lord.

At a time when our nation, and you as its leader, face unprecedented challenges affecting the security of the United States and of the entire world, we wish to bring to you the insights and perspective of one of the largest segments of the Christian community of our country.

Because you are weighing the prospect of war on Iraq and all the terrible consequences that war involves, you will have faced firsthand the truth that war is not only—or even primarily—a military matter. It is a moral and ethical matter of the highest order, one that we have made a priority for many months as the possibility of war has loomed on our national horizon.

As leaders of tens of millions of Protestant and Orthodox Christians across the United States, we are in touch with our clergy, with lay leaders, and with church members everywhere on this issue. We are also in communication with our counterparts in Europe and elsewhere around the globe. Several of us have traveled to Iraq in recent years, and even in recent days, to speak with Iraqi people of faith. We draw on the tenets of our Christian faith in all these encounters, seeking a way toward peace that is both prophetic and practical.

It is with the utmost urgency that we seek a meeting with you to convey face-to-face the message of the religious community that we represent on the moral choices that confront this nation and your Administration. You are no doubt well aware of our activities to slow the rush to war and our continuing uneasiness about the moral justification for war on Iraq. What we ask now, as fellow believers and as the spiritual leaders of Americans in congregations in every community of our great nation, is a pastoral opportunity to bring this message to you in person.

Be assured of our prayers always for you and the members of your Administration, that God may keep and guide you.

A form letter denying our request arrived in short order. Meanwhile, I flew to Berlin to stand with European church leaders who were expressing their opposition to war. Shortly after our press conference, a few of us watched on television in dismay as Colin Powell laid out a methodical case before the UN Security Council detailing Iraq's purportedly massive program to develop weapons of mass destruction. If anyone could stop the war, we had thought it would be Powell, yet now his credibility was being co-opted not as a voice for moderation, but simply to validate the administration's most outlandish claims about Iraq. With each word, we could feel the gates of hope swinging shut.

We now know that all these charges, from the mushroom cloud to the 9/11 connection to Powell's case before the UN, were absolute hokum. The imminent threat of Iraqi nuclear weapons was a myth. The yellow-cake claim was based on forged documents peddled by a hustler. The 9/11 connection had been pure fiction from the very beginning. And Powell now calls his presentation before the UN a blot on his otherwise distinguished record. But fear clouds the judgment, and panic can override even the most closely held moral values, never more so than when it is foisted on an entire society through the mass media. Even in the face of fear-mongering, millions of people in cities around the world from New York to Europe and beyond walked the streets in the largest single day of protest in human history. I was proud to be one of the protestors, and it was deeply moving to see so many people from so many places and of such different backgrounds unite in the one prayer that can draw all humanity together: peace. Yet our voices were not heard; President Bush had long since stopped listening. He had predetermined the path of war, and in March 2003, it began. When I heard the news that the bombs were falling, there was no surprise, only sorrow—and the thought of that little four-year-old girl in Baghdad.

I keep Caroline's picture on my office wall, near the door. I see it almost every day. She is on her mother's lap in church that New Year's Eve, her body arched backward in a joyful, exuberant pose, her eyes showing no trace of the tension that gripped her country. Every time I see that snapshot, it is a heart-breaking reminder that, as of this writing, a minimum of more than thirty thousand Iraqi civilians have been killed in the war, not because our military is vicious or reckless, but because modern wars cannot be confined to soldiers alone. I have never been able to discover whether Caroline was one of them. But one thing I know for certain: There is no defensible reading of Scripture that could possibly defend this war as a "just war" in the name of Jesus Christ.

## The Bible's Message: War or Peace?

That I would even need to raise the question of whether Jesus was a holy warrior or a preacher of peace tells us that something has gone drastically wrong in America's conversation on faith. For of course there is no question at all. We can count well into the hundreds the Bible's references to peace. Yet more than that, we can simply read the New Testament with anything approaching open hearts and minds and see that Jesus was a gentle person who repeatedly, no matter how extreme the circumstances, chose love over vengeance and forgiveness over violence. Here is a man who, on the night he was arrested by the Romans for what he knew would be a terrible ordeal, rebuked his own disciple for attacking one of the captors and then reached out in love and healed the man's wounds. "Love is patient; love is kind; love is not envious or boastful or arrogant or rude," we read in 1 Corinthians 13:4. "It does not insist on its own way; it is not irritable or resentful; it does not rejoice in wrongdoing, but rejoices in the truth. It bears all things, believes all things, hopes all things, endures all things."

Yet where is love in our foreign policy? Love does not insist on its own way, Paul wrote, yet America did insist against the overwhelming opposition of the world. Love is patient, he counseled, yet we rushed to war when inspectors were still on the ground, still insisting they were making progress. Love is not boastful or arrogant, yet

President Bush taunted Iraqi insurgents, daring them to attack our troops, with his blustery declaration, "Bring 'em on." "And now faith, hope, and love abide," Paul wrote, "these three; and the greatest of these is love" (1 Cor. 13:13). Instead, our foreign policy has become a matter of pure expediency. We did not attack Saddam because he was a terrorist. There were Saudi Arabian hijackers on 9/11 but no Iraqis. We did not invade Iraq to rid the world of a terrible dictator; our country regularly does business with regimes with atrocious human rights records. The simple truth of the matter is that Iraq had something we wanted. Our foreign policy isn't based on love. In Iraq, it was based in larger measure on oil.

Of course, love is a convenient concept if we interpret it narrowly. To love our spouses and our children, our friends and our allies is easy most of the time. But Jesus tells us in some of the Bible's starkest and most challenging language that this is not what love means. Listen to Jesus in Luke 6:27–32 and 35–36:

> But I say to you that listen, Love your enemies, do good to those who hate you, bless those who curse you, pray for those who abuse you. If anyone strikes you on the cheek, offer the other also; and from anyone who takes away your coat do not withhold even your shirt. Give to everyone who begs from you; and if anyone takes away your goods, do not ask for them again. Do to others as you would have them do to you.

> If you love those who love you, what credit is that to you? For even sinners love those who love them. . . . But love your enemies, do good, and lend, expecting nothing in return. Your reward will be great, and you will be children of the Most High; for he is kind to the ungrateful and the wicked. Be merciful, just as your Father is merciful.

This is a difficult commandment, perhaps the hardest in all of

Scripture. It challenges us all, me included, because it calls on us to rise above our basest yet most innate human instincts for revenge. Yet the literalists, those who tell us that every word of the Bible is to be taken exactly as it was handed down, are the very first to tell us, right out in the open, that Jesus didn't really mean what he said. Pat Robertson, for example, says the commandment to turn the other cheek applies to individual Christians, but not necessarily to governments. But we don't bomb governments; we bomb people. Of course, even many mainstream Christians would likely say "turn the other cheek" is no basis for a foreign policy. Of course it isn't, not by itself. But I would more readily accept that argument had we ever tried a foreign policy that actually reflected biblical ideals: love and goodwill to one another, feeding the hungry and clothing the naked, patience and humility, and that wonderful challenge of Isaiah to become "repairers of the breach." Perhaps if we tried, there would be fewer occasions on which our cheek would have to be turned.

Against the Bible's overwhelming message of peace, those on the far religious right who supported the Iraq war, who, sadly, have endorsed military buildups on every possible occasion since Vietnam, turn repeatedly to one verse, Matthew 10:34, which seems to be one of Jerry Falwell's favorites: "Do not think that I have come to bring peace to the earth; I have not come to bring peace, but a sword." That, too, is a challenging verse, one with which many people of faith and conscience have struggled. One was my friend the late Reverend William Sloane Coffin. "Years ago, while still in seminary, I used to wonder what Jesus meant" Bill wrote about this verse. "Finally, I concluded that the sword Jesus must have had in mind was the sword of truth, the only sword that heals the wounds it inflicts." I share Bill's conclusion. For the only alternative is to say that Jesus contradicted himself, that in this one verse and (in some interpretations) in the book of Revelation, he meant to repeal everything else he said and lived. There is no way of reading the Gospels and concluding that Jesus yearned for anything but peace.

That does not mean we must never draw our swords. As one person of faith, I deplore war, but that is not to say I am a complete and unthinking pacifist. The world is a dangerous place, and there are times when humanity has no resort but to violence. Yet what Martin Luther King, Jr. said about two kinds of laws is also true of wars: there are the just and the unjust. And just wars are the only ones we should fight.

## Just and Unjust Wars: Finding the Difference

Dietrich Bonhoeffer was a German theologian whose early writings reflect the powerful and inspirational words of a pacifist. Although an opponent of Hitler from the beginning, Bonhoeffer attempted to resist the Nazi regime through moral persuasion, standing courageously with a select and brave few church leaders, and eventually teaching in an underground seminary. After earning his doctoral degree, he spent a postdoctoral year at Union Theological Seminary in New York City, not far from where my office is today. He loved attending church in Harlem, where African-American spiritual music stirred his soul. A rich and safe career in academia and the pulpit awaited him in America, perhaps in England, anywhere in the world he chose to go. But he felt a call to stand with his fellow Germans in their moment of spiritual need and, under those extraordinary circumstances, to do what he could to stop Hitler's inhumanity. He joined an assassination plot, was discovered, and died on the gallows a month before the German surrender.

I first discovered Bonhoeffer's writings as a seminary student in 1967 and 1968, when I was trying to figure out whether to oppose the Vietnam War. Bonhoeffer became a just war theorist who understood the rare but unavoidable circumstances under which violence is the only means of preserving humanity. There are such circumstances, times when I believe Christ himself would say fighting is the only choice. Christianity can accommodate a doctrine of just war. But there is simply no way I can see—absolutely no way at all—for Christianity as I understand it to conclude that the war in Iraq is just. Just war theory is a complicated field, and I make no claims to being a theological scholar, but it returns often to some common themes: war must be *defensive*, it must be the *last possible option*, and it must *confine violence to the minimum necessary and avoid the deaths of noncombatants.* The war in Iraq very plainly flunks each of those tests.

This was not a war of self-defense. We now know that Saddam Hussein's Iraq posed no threat to the United States. The claims that he was training terrorists were false, and the lies are made all the more tragic by the fact that Iraq was turned into a breeding ground for terrorists only after our invasion. There were no weapons of mass destruction. There was no imminent threat to our safety. Nor did we exhaust the many peaceful, diplomatic solutions available to us—most obviously the weapons inspections that could have continued up until the moment the invasion began. The violence we used was overwhelming. Bombs rained down over crowded cities where the deaths of civilians and the destruction of civilian infrastructure were inevitable.

This war was not just in any conceivable sense. Preemptive wars almost never are; there is no reconciling the pure eagerness and fervor for war that swept Washington in 2002 and 2003 with the message of love and peace that Jesus brought to Earth. The fact that Democrats went along is no excuse for them or for President Bush. Democrats, like Republicans, made a tragic mistake. Though they tragically did not insist on it, Democrats did call for an international effort, and this, too, must become a criterion for just wars in an age in which any war inevitably involves broad regions of the earth and touches upon the conscience of all humanity. And surely this is a criterion too: If there are times when we go to war, sorrow rather than bravado is the only feeling appropriate to the moment.

There are, of course, just wars. World War II was one. The war in Afghanistan after 9/11 was far more defensible than the war in Iraq. Even the first Gulf War, which was a response to territorial aggression that had already occurred and not a preemptive strike, could be called just. But what would be the most just wars of our time are those that—with the most awful consequences—we choose not to fight. In one hundred gruesome and terrible days in the spring of 1994, nearly one million Rwandans were slaughtered like lambs in a systematic campaign of genocide. The United States—and most of the world— did nothing. If ever there was a just cause for war, for sending in overwhelming military force and occupying another land, surely this was it. Yet there were no threats, no buildup, nothing but absolute and lethal silence while at least eight hundred thousand of our brothers and sisters were hacked to death with machetes. Stopping genocide is a just cause; such a mission in Rwanda would have been a just war. But our country lacked the moral courage even to admit that genocide was happening until the bodies were already piled high, the nation had been laid in ruins, and the conflict was over.

The journalist Samantha Powers, with whom I have had the privilege to work, noted in her book *A Problem from Hell: America and the Age of Genocide* that no western nation has ever admitted genocide was occurring during an actual genocide. Only in hindsight, when there are no longer sacrifices to be made, no longer lives to be saved, do we state what had been obvious for all to see. That shameful precedent changed when the Bush Administration labeled the slaughter in Darfur a genocide. But even after that courageous declaration—for which this administration, with which I have disagreed so often on so much, deserves credit—the world has done far too little. The people of Sudan are still being mutilated and raped and killed while we sit by. As I write, some estimates put the death toll at four hundred thousand. By the time you read these words, it will surely have grown.

This, too, would be a just war. Yet it is not being fought. Why? After all, when the lies about the Iraq invasion were exposed as fiction, the White House claimed to have fought to free the people of Iraq from the horrific suffering they endured. Does a black child in Sudan or Rwanda deserve any less? There is no avoiding the uncomfortable truth that our brothers and sisters in Africa seem to have been abandoned because their skin is black and they do not have any resources we want. If Rwanda or Sudan sat atop an oil field, it is difficult for me to imagine we would not have found a pretense to save them.

If it sounds as though I feel strongly, well, I do. In fact, I'd have to admit I'm angry. But it doesn't do much good and, in fact, it's contrary to all the values I've espoused for those of us who opposed the war in Iraq to become bitter toward those who waged it. I was deeply moved by the prayer one grassroots activist submitted to www.faithfulamerica.org, an organization we helped start at the National Council of Churches to mobilize mainstream people of faith around issues like peace, poverty, and planet Earth: "Almighty God, bring peace to my nation and the world. Help me not to be at war, even with those who believe war to be an honorable course. Let your perfect peace dwell in the hearts of so many women and men that the next time the war drums sound, their noise will be drowned by love's irresistible music." That is our challenge—to turn our anger into love. And now that war has begun and is being waged, love must guide us as we ask the very difficult question: What should our nation do now?

## Iraq: Where Do We Go From Here?

There's something that bothers me deeply about the way we talk about wars. Okay, there are a lot of things that bother me about the way we talk about wars, starting with dragging Jesus into the discussion on the side of violence and vengeance. But there's one thing in particular that's on my mind right now. We talk about wars like football games. "Winning" matters most; showing weakness is what we can least afford to do. Yet even if we set aside the obvious strategic questions such as the fact that the White House has never been willing to tell us what exactly would constitute victory in Iraq, the issue confronting people of faith is: What victory could be more important than stopping the killing?

In November 2005, my friend Jack Murtha, a career Marine, combat veteran, and fellow Pennsylvanian with whom I served in Congress, called for an immediate plan to end the war and withdraw our troops from Iraq. His courage was extraordinary, and so was the impact of what he said. On military matters, Jack has always been about as far to the right as people say I am to the left. If I'm a dove, he's a hawk. He supported the invasion of Iraq. As the war went on, he spent more and more time visiting with wounded soldiers at Walter Reed Army Hospital—not for the publicity, not with the news media in tow, but as a simple act of quiet duty. And in time, he looked at those young men and women—limbless, lives blown apart—and at the growing insurgency in Iraq, and Jack Murtha spoke the one word many politicians were thinking but so few had the courage to say: "Enough."

The condemnation was swift. A few on the extreme right called him a coward. From those with the good sense not to attack him personally came the "strategic" warnings. We have to stay in Iraq until we "win," they said, never defining what exactly winning meant. Leaving now would encourage our enemies and damage our reputation, they warned. Abandoning the mission would dishonor the brave troops who gave their lives, the story goes, and even discussing the idea demoralizes the troops.

Those arguments sound familiar to me. I heard them all in two decisive days on the floor of Congress in April 1975 when finally, after more than a decade of folly and more than fifty-eight thousand lives were destroyed for a mistake, we brought the Vietnam War to a close.

## From Vietnam to Iraq: Real Courage Is Doing What's Right

In early 1975, I was a minister by vocation and a congressman by surprise. I was elected to the House of Representatives in the "Watergate baby" class of 1974, and nobody ever told me I was supposed to sit back and keep my mouth shut. I was perfectly happy to set up shop in my first-floor office, whose previous occupant left an old couch and a dead mouse behind, and set to work. I assembled a staff so young and green it took us a few weeks just to figure out where to get our paychecks. When the paycheck came, I realized I was paying more taxes on my $42,500 Congressional salary than I had ever made in an entire year as a minister. So I irritated my new colleagues by wondering aloud whether we were being paid too much. My first resolution in the *Congressional Record* called for Congress to stop taking recesses until we had finished our business. A grand total of seven other members signed on.

I wasn't, suffice it to say, a legislative powerhouse. So on April 22, 1975, when Saigon was rapidly falling and President Ford wanted Congress to give him the authority to prolong the war, I didn't know I was supposed to stay quiet. And I didn't. Ford cloaked his request in humanitarian language, claiming all he wanted was the authority to rescue refugees, but he was actually seeking far broader authority that would have dragged out a tragedy. My staff and I pulled an all-nighter, and the next day I offered what was called a "substitute amendment" denying Ford the troops.

By a fortunate twist of fate, Congressman Tip O'Neill, who was then the House majority leader and supported my proposal, happened to be presiding over the House at the time. When Republicans mounted a legislative revolt against me, Tip came down and started whispering strategy in my ear. A ferocious debate erupted. Alternative proposals were announced. Votes were taken. I lost almost every last one of them. But by the time it was over, the situation in Saigon had resolved itself, and the troops Ford wanted would have been futile. The war, finally, was over.

There was no joy in that for me. It had been a painful chapter in our history, and it was especially difficult to know of the suffering that many people would endure under the North Vietnamese regime. But the overriding and undeniable fact was clear for all to see, however difficult it was to admit: Dragging out a futile cause would have meant more suffering, more bloodshed, more death than finally admitting what Jack Murtha would say about Iraq almost thirty years later: Enough. There comes a time when the killing has to end.

In Iraq, that time has come. We are in Iraq today where we were in Vietnam in 1964 and 1965—at a moment of profound loss, but before the count of body bags has begun to multiply by new orders of magnitude. This war was a mistake, and it is time for it to end. There is nothing to celebrate in that fact, no cause for smugness, only sorrow. But sacrificing more lives will not somehow redeem the more than two thousand five hundred we have already lost. Continuing a mission that has been exposed as fraudulent will not make the world respect us. I am glad Saddam is gone, but launching preemptive wars against all the tyrants on the planet will make for a very bloody world. Young men and women are dying, and so are innocent Iraqi civilians, and we cannot continue killing simply to "win." The fourth quarter is not going to come, a buzzer is not going to go off, there is no trophy to be presented before screaming fans on the fifty-yard line. And there is a terrible perversity in saying the only way to support the troops is to risk their lives in a cause that was hollow and a mission that is not working.

The decision to go to war was wrong, and it is plain for all to see. We cannot confuse stubbornness with courage. Few acts are more courageous than what Jack Murtha did for our country. If President Bush is simply afraid of having been wrong, I hope he will find solace in a faith built on the premise that we are all fallen, we all make mistakes, and grace is there for all of us to seize. Peter denied Jesus three times on the night he was arrested, and yet Peter became the rock on which a church was built. "Each one helps the other," Isaiah wrote, "saying to one another, 'Take courage!'" (Isa. 41:6). There would be no shame in President Bush's stopping the killing. On the contrary, nothing could be more courageous.

# CHAPTER 4

# Deny Them Their Victory: Faith in the Age of Terrorism

*The Spirit of the Lord is upon me, because he has anointed me to bring good news to the poor. He has sent me to proclaim release to the captives and recovery of sight to the blind, to let the oppressed go free, to proclaim the year of the Lord's favor.*

—LUKE 4:18

*If it takes ten years, blow them all away in the name of the Lord.*

—JERRY FALWELL

It was a community of strangers in a small and contained space who became brothers and sisters, a source of love, support, and sustenance in one horrific moment. The Amtrak train I was riding between New York and Washington, D.C., on the morning of September 11, 2001, was, in short, everything our world must be, and all we can still become, if we are to have any hope of defeating terrorism. I boarded the train in suburban New Jersey before dawn, heading to Washington for a routine day of meetings at the National Council of Church's Capitol Hill offices. I don't recall exactly what time I overheard someone say, "A plane hit the World Trade Center." Around 9:15 perhaps. That was a tragedy. News of the second crash swept through the train like wildfire and made clear that it was a catastrophe beyond our capacity to imagine. Instantly, cell phones were shared, loved ones were called, words of support were exchanged, and in that small little world, as in so many places that awful morning, strangers became brothers and sisters.

By the time the train arrived at Washington's Union Station around 9:30 A.M., word of the Pentagon attack had already arrived, rumors of a fourth plane were spreading, and there was no way of knowing whether what was obviously a full-fledged attack on our country involved five, six, or seven aircraft more. As I stepped outside, thousands of staffers were streaming out of the Senate office buildings, walking away toward Union Station in an evacuation of the Capitol area. After a quick call to confirm that Merle, who was in our New Jersey home just across from the George Washington Bridge, was safe, I stepped into the crowd and began walking against the current, toward our offices just next to the Supreme Court. In those first hours, and in the ensuing days, I was thinking less as a political figure than as a pastor, for a tragedy of this magnitude would create an enormous need for pastoral care. Some staffers in our New York headquarters were initially unable to locate their families, and they needed the love and support of their colleagues. Our churches would be, and soon were, overloaded with funerals.

And there was the most difficult challenge members of the clergy face after tragedy—how to help our brothers and sisters understand it, to cope with their anger and grief, to comprehend a world in which a loving God could allow such a horrific event to occur. It was a question I had asked myself before, when our son Rob had barely survived the fiery airplane crash and spent sixty-six days in a burn unit, second and third degree burns from his shoulders down. During day after day of prayer, not just mine and Merle's, but those of a vast community of loved ones and friends, I came to the conclusion at which America would have to arrive to cope with this tragedy: that God gave us the opportunity to live in a world with both free will and chance, that God does not cause human tragedies, but God's love is available to help us endure them. I do not know all of God's purposes. All I know is what we can do on this earth: love one another. And in those first hours after 9/11, I was gravely concerned that love would be the first casualty of what would soon become known as the "War on Terror."

I sent most of our staff home when I arrived at our offices that morning, but one of our colleagues, Gaby Habib, insisted on staying to help. Gaby is a Lebanese-born minister of the Antiochian Orthodox Christian Church, a former general secretary of the Middle East Council of Churches and a passionate peace activist with an expansive heart and an even bigger smile. "I want to help you," he explained. Most people wondered whether Capitol Hill was safe that morning, but for Gaby the worry was whether it was safe to leave, whether a man with his Middle Eastern features would be safe from either the immediate crackdown of law enforcement or the vengeful feelings welling up in Americans' hearts. All our hearts are susceptible to dark and impulsive thoughts, of course, but I also knew Americans had the capacity to overcome them with love. I spent that afternoon on the phone with other religious leaders like Reverend Wes Granberg-Michaelson, Rabbi David Saperstein, and Reverend Jim Wallis, preparing a statement attempting to provide comfort to the hearts of the faithful while appealing to Americans' better natures. The next morning, we released it under the headline, "Deny Them Their Victory."

**We, American religious leaders, share the broken hearts of our fellow citizens.** The worst terrorist attack in history that assaulted New York City, Washington, D.C., and Pennsylvania, has been felt in every American community. Each life lost was of unique and sacred value in the eyes of God, and the connections Americans feel to those lives run very deep. In the face of such a cruel catastrophe, it is a time to look to God and to each other for the strength we need and the response we will make. We must dig deep to the roots of our faith for sustenance, solace, and wisdom.

**First, we must find a word of consolation for the untold pain and suffering of our people.** Our congregations will offer their practical and pastoral resources to bind up the wounds of the nation. We can become safe places to weep and secure places to begin rebuilding our shattered lives and communities. Our houses of worship should become public arenas for common prayer, community discussion, eventual healing, and forgiveness.

**Second, we offer a word of sober restraint as our nation discerns what its response will be.** We share the deep anger toward those who so callously and massively destroy innocent lives, no matter what the grievances or injustices invoked. In the name of God, we too demand that those responsible for these utterly evil acts be found and brought to justice. Those culpable must not escape accountability. But we must not, out of anger and vengeance, indiscriminately retaliate in ways that bring on even more loss of innocent life. We pray that President Bush and members of Congress will seek the wisdom of God as they decide upon the appropriate response.

**Third, we face deep and profound questions of what this attack on America will do to us as a nation.** The terrorists have offered us a stark view of the world they would create, where the remedy to every human grievance and injustice is a resort to the random and cowardly violence of revenge—even against the most innocent. Having taken thousands of our lives, attacked our national symbols, forced our political leaders to flee their chambers of governance, disrupted our work and families, and struck fear into the hearts of our children, the terrorists must feel victorious.

**But we can deny them their victory by refusing to submit to a world created in their image.** Terrorism inflicts not only death and destruction but also emotional oppression to further its aims. We must not allow this terror to drive us away from being the people God has called us to be. We assert the vision of community, tolerance, compassion, justice, and the sacredness of human life, which lies at the heart of all our religious traditions. America must be a safe place for all our citizens in all their diversity. It is especially important that our citizens who share national origins, ethnicity, or religion with whoever attacked us are, themselves, protected among us.

**Our American illusion of invulnerability has been shattered.** From now on, we will look at the world in a different way, and this attack on our life as a nation will become a test of our national character. Let us make the right choices in this crisis—to pray, act, and unite against the bitter fruits of division, hatred, and violence. Let us rededicate ourselves to global peace, human dignity, and the eradication of injustice that breeds rage and vengeance.

**As we gather in our houses of worship, let us begin a process of seeking the healing and grace of God.**

We invited Americans of all faiths to sign the statement online. Within hours, nearly four thousand of them had. It was a clear moment when our hearts as a people were one and the hearts of the world were reaching out to us. And it was a moment of choice: to embrace the world or to push it away, to become the nation we were capable of being or the nation the terrorists were trying to tell the world we were, to embrace God's message of brotherhood and sisterhood or to turn away from humanity with arrogance and fury.

In those first days and weeks, there was hope. There still is; there always is. But to reclaim it, we must reclaim the prophetic values so often rejected by the very political leaders who claim to speak for people of faith. We need a prophetic strategy for overcoming terrorism, not a war strategy.

Our spiritual values compel us to recognize first and foremost that Christians and Jews are not at war with Islam. Our Muslim brothers and sisters are, like Moses, aliens residing in a foreign land, strangers who deserve to be welcomed into our communities, not ostracized from them. America's dispute with terrorists is political, not spiritual, a point that many on the far religious right refuse to acknowledge. Not long after 9/11, Franklin Graham cast the conflict in the stark language of a holy war:

"We're not attacking Islam but Islam has attacked us," he proclaimed. "The God of Islam is not the same God. . . . It's a different God, and I believe it [Islam] is a very evil and wicked religion." Never mind the fact that Graham's statement was factually wrong. "Islam" did not attack us; individual terrorists did. And the God of Islam is very decidedly the same God as ours, a fact Graham might verify by consulting Genesis 17:20, in which God promises Abraham: "As for Ishmael, . . . I will make him a great nation." Chapter 22:21 of Exodus provides an equally relevant command: "You shall not wrong or oppress a resident alien, for you were aliens in the land of Egypt."

We must certainly defend ourselves against those radical few Muslims who engage in terrorist acts. I cannot arrive at Jerry Falwell's enthusiasm to "blow [the terrorists] all away in the name of the Lord," for my faith teaches that every life, no matter how blameworthy, is sacred, and that taking life, no matter how necessary, must always be an occasion for sorrow. I nonetheless believed our war in Afghanistan was a defensible act—not of retribution, but of self-defense because the Taliban regime was openly harboring terrorists. But if the Bush Administration is to be believed, there are terrorist cells in dozens of countries. There are not enough bombs, not enough soldiers, not, thank God, enough tolerance for bloodshed to destroy them all. So we must ask ourselves: Are we simply out for blood and revenge, or are we serious about stopping terrorism? Because if our choice is the latter, then we must stand ready to rejoin the community of nations, bring good news to the poor, and set free the oppressed. We must, in the formulation of former Secretary of Labor Robert Reich, be equally tough on terrorism and on the causes of terrorism.

This is the vision that Karl Rove has derisively called the "liberal" approach. Here's how he put it: "Conservatives saw the savagery of

9/11 in the attacks and prepared for war; liberals saw the savagery of the 9/11 attacks and wanted to prepare indictments and offer therapy and understanding for our attackers. . . . I don't know about you, but moderation and restraint is not what I felt when I watched the twin towers crumble to the ground, a side of the Pentagon destroyed, and almost three thousand of our fellow citizens perish in flames and rubble."

There's a lot I could say in reply. One point is that moderation and restraint were not what I was feeling on the morning of September 11, either. But God calls us, and our leaders, to appeal to our better angels, not our basest ones. Another is that while I wish we had taken greater care to spare civilian lives, I supported the war in Afghanistan. Nor do I offer "understanding" for our attackers, much less therapy: Love can accomplish a great deal, but love alone cannot always reach the hearts of those so incomprehensibly desperate to kill that they are willing to forfeit their own lives just for the chance of taking another. But perhaps the most important response to Karl Rove is this: The anti-terrorism strategy he derides is neither liberal nor Democratic. It originated in the heart of someone else, someone whom the White House, on many an occasion, has invoked: Jesus Christ.

I love the story in the Gospel of Luke when Jesus attends services at a synagogue in Nazareth and is called to read from the Torah. He arose, unrolled the scroll to those powerful words of Isaiah, and read them. *The Spirit of the Lord is upon me, because he has anointed me to bring good news to the poor. He has sent me to proclaim release to the captives and recovery of sight to the blind, to let the oppressed go free, to proclaim the year of the Lord's favor.* He then rolled up the scroll and sat down. The poignant and powerful simplicity was, I think, Jesus' way of teaching that all we need to live by is contained in those words. And there is a great deal of wisdom within them for overcoming terrorism, too.

Let me be clear: I don't for a moment believe we can end terrorism simply by reading from Isaiah. The very same yearning for peace that caused me to speak out against the war in Iraq compels me to speak with infinitely greater force against anyone who would slaughter innocents in an act of terror. I might add that I served in Congress for twelve years. I fought repeatedly to do away with outdated weapons systems that were older than I was precisely so we could modernize the military and make it more effective. I supported hundreds of billions of dollars in military spending. I know we live in a big and dangerous world and that we must have both the weapons and the will to defend ourselves.

That's exactly why I would ask every faithful American to look carefully at two very different visions for fighting terrorism and ask: Which one is naïve? One vision says we should prowl the world, hunting down everyone who hates us, that it is realistic to roam this vast planet and uncover every place where a terrorist might hide, that we should rain down bombs from above, that the deaths of bystanders is the price we must pay for our safety, and that doing so will make people respect us rather than resent us. It is a vision that says it never matters what the world thinks, that it is irrelevant whether we follow our own rules or respect our own values, that we have the might and the power to force everyone everywhere to fall into line and do our will, and that doing so will somehow transform hatred into respect.

The other vision—the prophetic vision—recognizes that the world is dangerous, that violence is sometimes a sad necessity, but one to which we must resort only with sorrow and humility rather than eagerness and pride. It says we must defend ourselves against violence, but the world is vast, and to kill everyone we dislike or who dislikes us will place an unacceptable strain on our resources and an unbearable burden on our souls. The prophetic vision knows liberties are always taken away in the name of defending them, and that it is as perilous as it is absurd to behave undemocratically to further the cause of democracy. The prophetic antiterrorism strategy does not entertain baseless hopes of reaching the hearts of the most hateful, but it *does* recognize a truth unavoidable for anyone who confronts terrorism realistically: The terrorists cannot succeed if they cannot recruit, and some of their most fruitful recruiting grounds are the places on earth most bereft of hope and most filled with frustration.

Neither of these visions—the militaristic vision or the prophetic vision—is capable of eradicating evil, for evil is an inescapable element of a world with free will. But if our goal is to minimize it, to do all we can to be safe while being moral, then we must ask which is more naïve: the vision that plans to kill every terrorist on earth, or the vision that says we can dry up the recruiting grounds by cultivating freedom in hope? This is one of those questions on which the most passionate people of faith and the most hard-thinking realists can come to the same conclusion: Realistically and spiritually, our only hope *is* hope.

If we are to act in accordance with our own values, the first step must be to change how we think and even how we talk about our antiterrorism efforts. Terrorism is a horrific and inexcusable crime whose perpetrators should be locked up forever and never permitted to harm another person again. When it is impossible to stop terrorists because sovereign states are openly harboring and encouraging them, as the Taliban was in Afghanistan, it may be necessary to use military force. But here I am going to say something of which three things can be said for certain. First, that it will get me into trouble, second, that I've been in worse trouble before, and, third, that it is the truth: The war on terror is not a war. It is, or should be, a global law enforcement campaign.

That doesn't mean it should be a weak-willed effort. As a young, urban minister who worked with the Police Clergy Unit in Philadelphia, I spent dozens upon dozens of hours riding in the back of squad cars. I saw officers run at full pace and without the slightest hesitation into situations more dangerous than most of us can comprehend. I saw them employ the most ingenious investigative techniques to flush out criminals and capture them. And I have yet to meet a weak-willed police officer. The notion that a law enforcement strategy is the weaker approach is an insult to everyone in law enforcement. The FBI and other authorities should be given every power permissible under the Constitution to find terrorists wherever they are. When they need it and where it is appropriate, they should have the military's support. But they, not the national defense apparatus, should lead the effort. And there are several reasons why.

Most important, treating antiterrorism efforts as a war clouds our thinking and impedes our success. The military is trained to inflict widespread violence on sovereign states. Terrorists are isolated individuals hiding in some of the remotest places on earth. We dropped enough bombs on Afghanistan to kill several thousand civilians, and Osama bin Laden still vanished into the mountains. Militaries work when nations fight nations. But military force is a blunt instrument, and terrorism is a surgical problem, except where states are giving open support to terrorists. Militaries plan and fight on the basis of "we have/they have" calculations. They have tanks, so we need airplanes; they have one kind of missile, so we need another that can intercept it.

All this has its place. But if there are terrorists in sixty countries, heaven forbid that we entertain the belief that we can bomb every one of their capitals, invade every one of their borders, and start wars on all fronts. A false belief has taken hold that if we simply spend enough money on defense, we can destroy all the terrorists. Yet we could triple our defense budget and quadruple enlistment in our military, and a single terrorist, one safe from our bombs because he or she is hiding in a cave or a basement unbeknownst to us, could still destroy an entire building with a backpack. Overwhelming military force is sometimes necessary, but it cannot destroy terrorism.

Moreover, the rhetorical treatment of antiterrorism efforts as a war has resulted in what amounts to a permanent suspension of civil liberties. Wars involve territory. They begin and end. Yet can anyone say when, indeed, if ever, the war on terror will be won? There are no capitals to capture, no hills to overrun. The Bush Administration has set up a standard by which it and its successors will always be able to justify any use of wartime powers simply by saying terrorists might exist, somewhere, sometime.

It is bad enough that terrorist suspects are treated as though they deserve no rights. "Remember those who are in prison, as though you were in prison with them," Paul writes in Hebrews 13:3, "those who are being tortured, as though you yourselves were being tortured." Neither should we be deluded into believing that only a mysterious and ill-defined "other" is at risk. The USA Patriot Act, conceived in an atmosphere of crisis and fear, never a good combination for the preservation of liberty, gave the FBI powers it has not wielded since the heyday of J. Edgar Hoover. I am old enough to remember the days when Hoover ran roughshod over Martin Luther King, Jr., and as a member of the House Select Committee on Assassinations, I read confidential material that showed the reckless and invasive tactics the FBI used to discredit both King personally and the civil rights movement generally. The revelation that President Bush authorized domestic wiretapping with no warrants or other judicial controls, wiretapping that reportedly included sifting through millions of telephone conversations, not all of which could have involved terrorist suspects, makes the picture all the more alarming. The White House has responded to these reports by blaming the media for daring to tell the public that they were being spied upon, and by returning to the implied defense: Trust us, we're good people.

I actually do believe they're good people who are doing their best to do what they believe is right, no matter how strongly I may disagree. But we're not a nation of good people, we're a nation of good laws. Consider it from this point of view: I think I'm a pretty nice person, or at least I try to be, and I also believe, as President Bush does, that I have some insights into the kinds of policies Jesus might support. Would you trust me to wield the powers he does? Would you feel comfortable with me signing a secret order to tap your telephone? How about dispatching agents to search your house without telling you? Or worse yet, what if I ordered foreign nationals to be kidnapped and tortured, tried to dissuade the news media from telling you about it, and then said that even though I don't trust you to know what I'm doing, you have to trust me that everyone I'm after is guilty?

Well, no need to worry, that's not going to happen. I'm not interested in being president, and I've probably got too big a mouth to get elected even if I wanted to. What's more, if my ego ever got more than about two inches off the ground, Merle would grab me by the ankles and yank me back down to earth. But that's not the point. *Nobody* should be trusted with these kinds of powers, and there are several reasons why. The most important is spiritual: My own religion, like so many others, is founded on the dignity of each individual, and that means everyone has a right, morally as well as constitutionally, to be free of the kind of guilt by association or degrading treatment that domestic spying and invasive searches involve.

Here's another reason not to trust me with those kinds of powers: Promise not to tell Merle, but *sometimes I'm wrong.* We do not have to impugn the good motives of the Bush Administration to ask whether the same people who called Saddam Hussein's possession of weapons of mass destruction a "slam dunk" should be trusted never to target the wrong suspect. Nor should we assume—again, however pure their motives when the Patriot Act was passed—that either the administration or the authorities will confine themselves to investigating suspected terrorists. In 2004, an Episcopal church in California was threatened by the IRS because its minister gave an antiwar sermon. The ACLU forced the FBI to reveal that law enforcement officers have actually gone so far as to consider infiltrating environmental and animal-rights groups, all under color of combating terrorism. Federal authorities have compiled some three thousand five hundred pages of information on progressive groups, including nearly one thousand two hundred on the ACLU.

Can anyone seriously argue this monitoring has anything to do with fighting terrorism? I doubt it. And I doubt equally strongly that a group as strong-willed and courageous as the ACLU would ever be deterred by it. For that matter, I can only assume, or hope, I have made a few government enemies lists in my time, and I haven't slowed down yet. But what such figures can never show is the number of ordinary Americans who never bother to speak out—not because they are consciously frightened, but because this harassment seems to add another layer of hassle to activism. We do not have to fear imprisonment or even tax audits for domestic spying to exert a chilling effect. Government simply needs to make activism, something to which most Americans were already disinclined, more of a bother. But even apart from its practical consequences, this invasion of privacy and usurpation of law violates the innate dignity of human beings engaged in the loving work of trying to make their world a better place. The best way to deny terrorists their victory is to refuse to become, or to act like, the nation they want the world to believe we are. We should live up to our standards, not down to theirs.

One of our standards, and perhaps the single best hope for overcoming terrorism, must be investing in hope around the world. In defending preemptive action against terrorists, neoconservatives are fond of saying we must "drain the swamp they live in." But the deepest and most fertile swamp they live in is despair, the pervasive feeling of hopelessness that leads young men and women to choose suicide and fanaticism because they expect nothing better from life. To be sure, the leaders of terrorist organizations are often middle-class professionals or, in the case of Osama bin Ladin, fabulously rich. But they depend much more on poverty than they do on wealth. The youth they recruit are desperately poor and utterly without hope for a better life, and the terrorists cannot survive without their discontent and despair. Nor can the terrorists escape detention without at least the tacit support of civilian populations whose poverty stokes deep-seated resentments toward wealthier nations.

None of this excuses terrorism or explains religious fanaticism. But if we want a preemptive strategy for defeating the terrorists, we will not find a more effective one than investing in hope across the developing world. The Pentagon's budget for 2006 alone exceeded $500 billion. Consider the words of Dick Bell and Michael Renner of the Worldwatch Institute:

A 1998 report by the United Nations Development Programme estimated the annual cost to achieve universal access to a number of basic social services in all developing countries: $9 billion would provide water and sanitation for all; $12 billion would cover reproductive health for all women; $13 billion would give every person on Earth basic health and nutrition; and $6 billion would provide basic education for all.

These sums are substantial, but they are still only a fraction of the tens of billions of dollars we are already spending. And these social and health expenditures pale in comparison with what is being spent on the military by all nations—some $780 billion each year.

There is a sad irony in watching the Bush Administration's strenuous efforts to build an international coalition. There is no such muscular effort under way in the United States, or in any of the other rich nations, to build a coalition to eradicate hunger, to immunize all children, to provide clean water, to eradicate infectious disease, to provide adequate jobs, to combat illiteracy, or to build decent housing.

The cost of failing to advance human security and to eliminate the fertile ground upon which terrorism thrives is already escalating. Since September 11, we know that sophisticated weapons offer little protection against those who are out to seek vengeance, at any cost, for real and perceived wrongs. Unless our priorities change, the threat is certain to keep rising in coming years.

By choosing to mobilize adequate resources to address human suffering around the world, President Bush has a unique opportunity to seize the terrible moment of September 11 and earn a truly exalted place in human history. But first, we must all understand that in the end, weapons alone cannot buy us a lasting peace in a world of extreme inequality, injustice, and deprivation for billions of our fellow human beings.

Those words were written in 2001. Years have passed, promises have been made, hundreds and hundreds of billions more have been spent on weapons, yet there is still no concerted investment in the most potent weapon of all: hope. That is not to say hope alone can dissuade fanatical murderers. But it can drain the swamp of misery and despair in which they live and on which they thrive.

One reason our national priorities have not changed is that Middle Church, the faithful religious center, has not spoken. For many, there is a subtle form of self-censorship: the fear that any honest look at ourselves will be seen as making excuses for terrorists. I have neither comfort nor apologies to offer to terrorists; all I counsel is that we act in accordance with our own values and, it must be said, our own interests. There are no weapons strong enough to protect us in a world consumed by despair and fueled by resentment. By all means, our military defense must be strong, but our moral defenses must be stronger.

If we are to defeat terrorism, if we are to be true to our faith, we must love America enough to challenge and criticize her with aching honesty. A few years ago, Bill Coffin was honored at the Union Theological Seminary in New York. He was bent over a cane, slowed in body by a few strokes—"old football injury," he joked after being helped to the microphone—but his mind and soul were as powerful as ever. He explained then what I passionately feel: that it was precisely because of his patriotism that he was engaging in a "lover's quarrel with America":

I think the insecurity produced by 9/11 is responsible largely for the fresh militancy of the country. I'm worried that we have a self-righteousness now that comes from feeling unfairly hurt. Now, when we felt unfairly hurt we could have expanded our horizons, widened our hearts to understand that a lot of people in the world are being unfairly hurt. But we've closed in on ourselves, and the most powerful nation in the world became the victim of victimhood. And that's been exploited mercilessly by Karl Rove, Cheney, Bush, and the Administration, so the conventional wisdom says whatever we want to do is right now. It's very scary—*very* scary. St. Augustine [said]: "Yea, my pride-swollen face has closed up my eyes." . . . What is immoral finally is not politically expedient. The world swings on an ethical hinge. You mess with that hinge and history—and nature, too, now—are going to feel the shock.

Perhaps it seems like I am blaming America for terrorism. I blame the terrorists. It may sound as though I naïvely believe if we feed the world the terrorists will go away. I think nothing of the sort. It is with a sad but a resolute heart that I know there will be moments when we have no choice but violence, and others when justice and security must preclude mercy. But what I reject, emphatically, is the idea that to question America is un-American. Bill put it best, and Middle Church must heed his words: "We know that dissent is not disloyal. What is unpatriotic is subservience."

We are not responsible for the actions of terrorists. We are responsible for the actions of our own government. And that is why it is time for Middle Church, Middle Synagogue, and Middle Mosque to join in a lover's quarrel with America. Here it might be helpful to hear from two of my heroes, Dr. King and Archbishop Desmond Tutu:

> *"We will have to repent in this generation not merely for the hateful words and actions of the bad people, but for the appalling silence of the good people."*
> —Dr. Martin Luther King, Jr.

> *"To be neutral in a situation of injustice is to have chosen sides already. It is to support the status quo."*
> —Archbishop Desmond Tutu

# CHAPTER 5

---

# We're the Good Guys—
# Let's Act Like It!

*The United States condemns unequivocally the despicable
practice of torture. We have fought to eliminate it around the
world.*
　　—U.S. DEPARTMENT OF STATE, 2002, CRITICIZING OTHER
　　　　　COUNTRIES FOR USING TORTURE

*[Torture] must be equivalent in intensity to the pain accom-
panying serious physical injury, such as organ failure, im-
pairment of bodily function, or even death.*
　　—U.S. DEPARTMENT OF JUSTICE, 2002, APPROVING THE USE
　　　　　OF TORTURE BY THE UNITED STATES

*Why do you see the speck in your neighbor's eye, but do not
notice the log in your own eye?*
　　　　　　　—MATTHEW: 7:3

In 1630, a Puritan leader named John Winthrop, invoking the
words of Matthew 5:14, called on America to become a shining
"city upon a hill," a moral example to the rest of humanity. Like Jesus'
in Matthew, Winthrop's challenge was to be "the light of the world,"
to inspire humanity with the power of our example. Winthrop was
the first to articulate the idea that America was a unique and special
place. For him, that place was elevated: We bore higher responsibilities because of it; all humankind would look to this city on the hill
for inspiration. In recent years, the far right has seized on his challenge as a shallow slogan justifying a highly militaristic policy

Winthrop could never have imagined. Today, "American exceptional-ism" has become an excuse for *lowering* our moral standards, for im-plying that we have a license to do what is forbidden to others—often, what we are simultaneously *condemning* others for doing—because we are somehow different or special.

My answer to that idea is simple: We *are* different. We *are* spe-cial. What makes us special is our historic commitment to morality and freedom, and that's exactly why our justification of torture, our support of immoral regimes when they serve our convenient inter-ests, and our maintenance of enormous stockpiles of weapons of mass destruction are such tragic and indefensible mistakes. America's greatest weapon is our moral authority, the esteem in which millions of people around the world hold us. We surrender that weapon when we exempt ourselves from the standards of moral behavior we seek to uphold and enforce in the rest of the world. In an era of in-stant and global communication, America's image—our *moral power*—is an even more important strategic asset than our military power. Even the most aggressive hawks admit that our military power can only be applied in a limited number of places at a time, whereas our moral power can be felt everywhere, all the time.

Yet the radical right has established two standards of morality, one for America and another for the rest of the world. The State Department issues human rights reports every year condemning na-tions that use torture, yet Vice President Cheney, in what must be one of the most sorrowful spectacles in American politics in recent years or ever, fought all-out against a proposed law banning the United States from torturing terrorist suspects overseas. That the debate was even necessary was a national shame; that the White House actually took the wrong side, morally as well as militarily, was doubly so. We lecture other countries about freedom, yet bankroll some of the most authoritarian regimes on earth. From India and Pakistan to Iran and North Korea, we condemn the rest of the world for procuring nuclear weapons, a veritable speck in their eyes while the log of our own massive stockpile protrudes from ours.

The response from the far right will surely be swift and severe: There is a difference between the United States having nuclear weapons and Iran having them. I happen to agree. But imagine how condescending that reasoning must sound to an ordinary citizen in Tehran: "We may have thousands of nuclear warheads, while you cannot make even one, because God has a special plan for us but not for you, because we are strong and you are weak, because we are morally pure while you are morally inferior." Put yourself in the place of a citizen of a corrupt regime supported by the United States and ask whether you would find this line of reasoning defensible: "We stand for freedom and the rule of law, but you cannot have them because America is special, and serving our interests is more important than working for your freedom." Consider what a survivor of one of Saddam Hussein's prisons must think of the implicit argument that the United States is so morally upright we can be trusted to decide when torture is acceptable, but no one else can.

Suppose, as many demographers and historians predict, China or India someday overtakes the United States as the world's wealthiest or most militarily powerful nation. Would we accept such hypocrisy from them? Would we allow them to say their freedom matters more than ours or that their moral stature so exceeds our own that they can do the very same things about which they lecture us?

We wouldn't, of course, nor should we. It's possible to believe, as I do, that God has a special mission for Americans without denying the idea that every other one of God's creations, whether born in a high-tech hospital in London or a village in Africa, is special too. Our special mission can be precisely what Winthrop imagined: being, in those beautiful words of Matthew, "the light of the world." If America aspires to be an enduring global power and a beacon of democracy, we need to say to the people of the world: "We value your freedom so much we will sacrifice our own interests to support you. We deplore torture so strongly we will never use it. We love peace so much that we will give up our own nuclear weapons, weapons we do not need to defend ourselves and would never use anyway, so that we can make a morally coherent argument against others' acquiring them."

That would be a prophetic message. It would also be an exercise of the leadership that President Bush constantly claims to possess. Simply doing what is expedient is convenience, not leadership. Moral leadership recognizes that what makes America special is not a coincidence of geography—our location on a resource-rich continent shielded by oceans—and what makes Americans unique is not an accident of birth. We are exceptional when we make the conscious human choice to behave morally even when it is not easy. We are exceptional when we support the aspirations of all people to be free, not with the force of arms, but with the overwhelming power of our example. America is exceptional when we heed Jesus' call: "In everything do to others as you would have them do to you; for this is the law and the prophets." According to the Arizona InterFaith Movement, no fewer than twenty-six of the world's faith traditions teach some variation of the Golden Rule. "Love your neighbor as yourself," the Torah commands. "Hurt no others in ways that you yourself would find hurtful," a Buddhist text explains. "No one of you is a believer until you desire for another that which you desire for yourself," according to a Muslim saying. Each of these statements is as unique as the faith that produced it, but they share a common human aspiration. And not one of them contains an exemption for nations that regard themselves as special or unique.

If we want America to be special—as I believe we are and must always be—then we must be a light unto the world. Yet we are dimming that light at precisely the time the world needs it most. Nowhere do we do this more than in the national shame that is the detention center at Guantánamo Bay, Cuba.

## "I Was In Prison and You Visited Me": It's a Good Thing Jesus Wasn't Detained at Guantánamo

Camp Delta at Guantánamo Bay is where more than five hundred human beings—many unsavory, all of them our brothers and sisters in God—have been held for as long as four years in small cages without access to trials, lawyers, family, clergy, or even, despite our claims that we are prosecuting a "war" against terrorism, the rights to which prisoners of war are entitled under the Geneva Conventions. The United States routinely excoriates other countries for holding prisoners under exactly those conditions. Many have become so desperate, so completely devoid of any hope they might ever be freed, that reports have emerged of rampant suicide attempts and widespread hunger strikes. Interrogations have reportedly taken place in facilities where the Red Cross was not allowed, in rooms equipped with metal chairs and a steel ring on the floor. The Bush Administration has actually argued that the Supreme Court would not have the right to question any of its actions there, even accusations of torture.

"I was in prison and you visited me," Jesus says in Matthew 25:36. The detainees at Guantánamo are not permitted visitors. I wish I could tell you their condition. But when the National Council of Churches attempted to organize an interfaith humanitarian mission to inspect the spiritual and physical well-being of the detainees—not to make a statement, not to intervene on their behalf, but simply to see how they were being treated as children of God— we were denied permission to visit by our government. When we asked for permission again, we were turned down once more. I harbor no illusions about who may be at that prison. There are doubtless many horrible people among the inmates. Yet that is exactly the point: If we are going to preach to the world about democracy, if we are going to claim that spreading freedom combats terrorism, which I believe, then perhaps we ought not to allow the threat of terrorism to undermine our *own* commitment to democracy. Why not show the world that the rule of law works? Why not give the detainees lawyers, put them on trial, and if they are convicted, lock them up forever? But if they are innocent, why not set them free?

President Bush has rebuffed any criticism of the prison camp at Guantánamo with the claim that everyone there is guilty. We know that is false, of course, for some inmates have suffered horrible travails there and then, when we learned that there was no basis on which to hold them, we freed them without so much as a hint of humility even though they had been wrongly imprisoned. But if so many *are* guilty, there is every reason to put them on trial and then lock them up legitimately. Without a trial governed by the rule of law, we are left with the only assurance of their guilt that is available, and the only one President Bush has offered. I can summarize it in two words: Trust me. I would like to believe I could, for I believe President Bush to be a good man. But he is just that—a man, a human being, a fallible human being, which is why we have institutions of law rather than the rule of a king. America trusted him when he told us that Saddam Hussein had weapons of mass destruction. I am willing to give President Bush the benefit of all doubt and assume he believed it when he said it. But if that is true, it proves simply that no one person is so powerful and infallible that he or she should be trusted with powers that are subject to no outside checks. The arrogance of proclaiming hundreds of God's people guilty with a wave of the hand and reacting indignantly to any request for a shred of proof is breathtaking to me. Yet over and over, arrogance has become the official policy of the United States in the "war" on terror. I prefer Luke 14:11. "For all who exalt themselves will be humbled, and those who humble themselves will be exalted."

The secrecy surrounding Guantánamo allows us to hide from the consequences of our actions as a nation. It allows the "bad" people there—whether they are actual terrorist masterminds or hapless souls who were trapped in the wrong place at the wrong time and loaded into the cages with everyone else—to be faceless caricatures rather than our brothers and sisters as fellow children of God. We do not acknowledge, much less confront, their humanity. But we must ask ourselves: What would we do if some other country, China, perhaps, or North Korea or Iran, were hiding hundreds of prisoners, maybe some of them Americans, in a secret island prison camp with no access to lawyers or visitors and no hope even of trial, much less release? Would we accept their assurances of the inmates' guilt, or would we demand proof and respect for the rule of law? I do not doubt that the indignant reply will come quickly from the far right once more: We are America. We are not China, North Korea, or Iran. To which my reply, once again, is: *Exactly*, and it is time to act like it. America is not special because we have the God-given right to declare people's guilt and hold them without trial. We are special because our values tell us never to do so.

Yet even the most resolute of human values are challenged by the dangerous concept of the "other." We must have the courage to be honest with ourselves. The people at Guantánamo Bay do not look like most of us, they do not pray like many of us, they remind us— no matter who they are or how innocent or guilty they may be—of people who frighten us. So perhaps it would help to hear the testimony of a man who looks like us, whose faith is more familiar to many Americans, an Anglican envoy named Terry Waite. During the 1980s, Terry was a courageous soul who went to Lebanon to negotiate the release of American hostages on behalf of the Anglican Church, ignoring warnings that his own safety was in jeopardy. Terry was kidnapped himself and spent 1,760 horrific days in captivity before his release. In March 2004, I joined him as well as the family members of some of the Guantánamo detainees in a rally outside the Supreme Court, which was considering one of the inmates' cases. These family members all happened to be British, as were the detainees. They were typical, loving, quiet people who wanted nothing but to know the fates of their children. Afterward, Terry described why he identified with the prisoners at Guantánamo:

Many years ago when I was acting as a hostage negotiator, I was captured . . . and accused—of being an agent of government. I wasn't. I was a humanitarian negotiator. But I was held under suspicion of that. I was blindfolded and shackled. I was kept in detention for four years in solitary confinement, five years in all. I was denied due process. I had no legal access whatsoever. I faced execution and had I not been able to convince my captors that I was a humanitarian and not a secret agent, I would certainly have died and I wouldn't be here with this conversation now. Now my conditions were fairly harsh. But I maintain that the way in which I was treated: captured on suspicion, detained, no due process, and no contact with my family was very, very similar to the process under which those in Guantánamo Bay have been detained. And they have been denied legal process. They have been—they are being held in contravention of international human rights law and, in fact, in so doing, the state seems to me to have adopted the tactics of the terrorists.

This is the statement I made at the Supreme Court:

Today the U.S. government is holding hundreds of prisoners at Guantánamo Bay who have not been charged with crimes and who have been denied access to U.S. courts. Almost completely isolated, they are probably unaware that their case has brought us here to stand in front of the Supreme Court. We have not been able to learn much about them either. We certainly don't know who among them may be innocent, who may be guilty.

But we are not here to make any claims about their guilt or innocence. We are here because the principle of due process under the law also is being held prisoner on Guantánamo. We are determined to protect and defend this fundamental right. Without it, no one can be assured of fair treatment under the law. Without it, anyone could be arbitrarily stripped of the human dignity that God confers on all people. . . .

The National Council of Churches has said that the denial[s] of rights that inhere in the worth of human beings before God are not only a crime against humanity. They are a sin against God. All faiths share this basic teaching, a fact that is reflected in the broad interfaith nature of a series of events that will be held in Washington and New York City over the next few days and that are aimed at securing the right of due process for prisoners on Guantánamo. All persons are connected in the family of God. My rights, your rights, and the rights of the detainees are inseparable.

I am not accusing the United States of being the moral equivalent of terrorists. Neither was Terry Waite. Quite the opposite: He argued, as I passionately feel, that America represents something so special, inspiring, and unique that we must never allow the terrorists to drive us to act as anything other than what we, deep in our hearts and at our very best, aspire to be. And when it comes to the detainees at Guantánamo, that aspiration is summarized in Deuteronomy 16:20: "Justice, and only justice, you shall pursue . . ." There is no exception provided to that commandment, no footnote indicating "only when it is convenient" or "unless you perceive a threat." We must pursue justice not because of who the detainees are but because of who we aspire to be.

The America I love is not the one that tortured and humiliated our brothers and sisters at Abu Ghraib. Those images haunt our national conscience. The one that is forever seared into my memory is that of a frightened man perched precariously atop a box, his head hooded in black, an image so reminiscent of a KKK lynching that it is difficult to believe our government was responsible for it. Yet we were. Buck privates and lowly sergeants paid the price for that tragedy, yet not a single suit-wearing civilian was called to account. The White House appeared to operate on the fantasy that we could

convince the world the events of Abu Ghraib were, in the deeply offensive characterization of Rush Limbaugh, the equivalent of a fraternity prank pulled by rogue soldiers blowing off steam. To their
credit, several leaders of the religious right condemned the abuse but
somehow blamed it on the availability of pornography on military
bases.

For the record, I do not believe we can or should ban pornography, but I also do not believe the U.S. military should be in the business of selling it to our soldiers. But that was not the problem at Abu
Ghraib. The evidence is everywhere that such tactics were either
openly approved or tacitly endorsed at the highest levels of the Pentagon. And they cannot be meaningfully separated from the policies
the White House has endorsed. The Justice Department produced a
bone-chilling memo outlining in clinical detail just how close to the
line American interrogators could edge before their actions could
legally be considered torture. Under this standard, Americans could
inflict bodily pain as long as it was not as severe as that accompany-
ing organ failure. One apparent result was the sanctioning of "water-
boarding," the technique of wrapping an inmate's face, strapping him
to a table, and submerging him in water almost to the point of
drowning. Defense Secretary Donald Rumsfeld personally approved
a list of extraordinary interrogation techniques. Yet when the public
outcry ensued from millions of faithful Americans and millions
more in the international community, these self-styled "leaders" were
quick to blame all abuses on enlisted men and women.

When the pictures of Abu Ghraib were released, that explana-
tion was not enough for me. Like millions of other people of faith, I
am an American and I was ashamed as an American, for I believe the
responsibility for what our government does lies with us all. And this
belief is why www.faithfulamerica.org aired an advertisement across
the Arab world featuring American clergy members—a Protestant
minister, a Catholic nun, a Jewish rabbi, and a Muslim imam—expressing regret over the horror of Abu Ghraib.

The response was overwhelming. From Middle Church, it was overwhelmingly positive. From the far right, it was ferocious. We were accused of giving comfort to the enemy. But far from it: The most important force in world politics today is public opinion. Allowing the impression to stand that the horrific events at Abu Ghraib had the approval of all Americans would have seeded fertile ground for terrorists.

Even as he carefully shielded anyone of significant rank from accountability, President Bush, too, said he was appalled by Abu Ghraib. But two years later, the lessons appeared unlearned when the world witnessed the utterly immoral and abhorrent spectacle of the president of the United States threatening to veto a bill because it contained Senator John McCain's amendment banning torture. It was not so long ago that it would have been unthinkable even to need such a requirement. The fact that we believe those we torture are evil is no excuse. Almost all experts agree that torture produces useless information because its victims will say anything to make the suffering stop. But even if it *did* work, torture is an absolute evil. I agree with Senator McCain: This is not about who *they* are. It is about who *we* are.

Surely who we aspire to be is not the nation some of our leaders want us to become, the nation into which they are already transforming us. Surely we, of all nations, do not want to be the one that spies on our own citizens. Surely we, of all nations, do not want to be the one that operates a secret network of prison camps in some of the darkest corners of Europe and other parts of the world. Surely we, of all nations, do not want to be the nation that kidnaps suspects on the street, whisks them away in the trunks of cars, and in a despicable act of moral cowardice ships them to foreign countries that we pay off to torture them for us. One official involved in such renditions, as they are called, told the *Washington Post*, "We don't kick the [expletive] out of them. We send them to other countries so they can kick the [expletive] out of them." A recent State Department human rights report spoke critically of Egypt: "The security forces continued to mistreat and torture prisoners, arbitrarily arrest and detain persons, hold detainees in prolonged pretrial detention, and occasionally engage in mass arrests." It made no mention of the fact that our own country has allegedly shipped terrorist suspects to Egypt precisely so they can be tortured. This report evidenced no shame at the fact that arbitrary arrests and prolonged detentions are official American policy at Guantánamo Bay.

In his 2003 State of the Union Address, President Bush said with his trademark swagger and to thunderous applause: "All told, more than three thousand suspected terrorists have been arrested in many countries. Many others have met a different fate. Let's put it this way—they are no longer a problem to the United States and our friends and allies." Given all that we know about such practices as extraordinary rendition—including the kidnapping of suspects, their transfer to secret prisons, and their torture for weeks and months on end—this claim, the coldness with which it was delivered, and the enthusiastic and apparently unthinking applause that followed must be regarded as one of the most chilling and harrowing statements every made by a president of the United States. *Suspected*, he said. *Suspected terrorists.* It would be bad enough if they had all been convicted, yet President Bush, who has not been shy about declaring people's guilt with a wave of his hand, did not even bother to proclaim them all guilty. We must be willing to step out of our national arrogance long enough to ask whether we would tolerate, for a single moment under any circumstances at all, the intelligence services of any country, friend or foe, descending on an American city, kidnapping an American, and whisking him or her off to a secret prison to be tortured. To say nothing of a foreign leader *boasting*, not with sorrow but with swaggering pride, that *suspects* may have been killed at his discretion. This is being done in our name—yours and mine—and, what is worse, in the name of the faith we cherish. And what is worst of all, *we are silent.* The outcries from our pulpits have been scarce, and when they occur, they are far too often shrouded in politeness rather than moral exhortation.

When our government behaves in this way, we surrender a weapon more powerful against terrorism than all the bombs we could drop: our moral authority. What can we say to Robert Mugabe, the violent dictator of Zimbabwe, when he rounds up dissidents, throws them in jail without trials, and excuses it all on the very same grounds we use: that they are all terrorists? How can we challenge Russia to explore peaceful solutions with Chechnya when we defied the world and invaded Iraq? America is still a special place; the difference is that fewer and fewer people recognize us for it. "You will know we are Christians by our love," to paraphrase the apostle Paul. And I would amend that statement to accommodate Middle Church, Middle Synagogue, Middle Mosque, and mainstream Americans of all faiths: You will know we are *Americans* by our love.

To be sure, there are evil people in the world who will not allow their hearts to be penetrated no matter how much love we offer. But that does not excuse us from responsibility for our own actions and our own souls. Our hearts do not belong to the terrorists; they belong to us. And most important, the hearts of millions of young people who live without hope, hearts that will be inspired by us or captured by the terrorists, are at stake. They are hungry for the America they thought we were. So am I.

## America's Weapons of Mass Destruction: The Log in Our Eye

In the 1980s, during my tenure in Congress, a powerful and heavily armed country announced its intention to resume production of nerve gas and other chemical weapons. It hid behind the language of necessity: Its enemies had chemical weapons, so this country had to have them too. Never mind that it possessed ample strength to defend itself by other means. This country's leaders were impervious to the outcry of moral protest from the overwhelming majority of the civilized world. Instead, they claimed they had no choice, that their moral decisions had to be reduced to the lowest common denominator of their adversaries, and—in an especially Orwellian turn of phrase—that they wanted to manufacture nerve gas in order to advance the cause of peace.

That country was the United States. In 1985, during my time in the House of Representatives, the Pentagon asked Congress for more than $124.5 million to manufacture chemical weapons, whose production President Nixon had suspended in 1969. I supported a proposal by a moderate Republican congressman from Illinois, John Porter, to deny the funds. (Yes, you read that correctly, he was a Republican. Things were a little different back then.) Supporters of resuming production of nerve gas said we needed chemical weapons to deter the Soviet Union—the code phrase often used to cloak the arms race in the rhetoric of peace—an argument that struck me as wholly unpersuasive given that we already had enough nuclear weapons to destroy every inch of Soviet territory several times over. Building missiles capped with chemical warheads would have been, to say the very least and with no gruesome pun intended, overkill. Moreover, we already *had* ample chemical weapons left over from before 1969. And both the United States and the Soviet Union had spent millions of dollars to equip soldiers with protective gear in the event of a chemical attack, so the people most likely to be killed by these weapons were civilians.

The moral as well as the military arguments seemed to me to be clear. Still, I decided to listen carefully to the arguments of both sides. The arguments of the supporters seemed to me to be descending to lower and lower depths of absurdity when Democrat Tommy Robinson of Arkansas (yes, you read that correctly, too; as I said, things were different then) topped them all. "I wish you would look at the facts and not get involved in all the emotional arguments," he said, "because we need binary nerve gas." The idea that we needed nerve gas when we already had thousands of nuclear warheads seemed thoroughly wrongheaded to me. But I objected even more strongly to the idea that emotion had no place in a discussion that involved our most closely held moral beliefs. Later that day, I rose in the House to speak:

> One of my colleagues stood in this well and said, "Do not get emotional about this issue." Well, I think we can get emotional about issues relating to our national security and national defense. Both sides do. I fall on the side of those who get emotional about this Nation and its interest in providing world leadership toward an international treaty to stop the production and use of chemical weapons all over the planet. I do not think we set a good example by moving, for the first time in sixteen years, to the production of chemical weapons.
>
> I get emotional when I think about my children, three sons, and their children, living in a world that is stockpiling nuclear weapons to the point that our arsenal alone can destroy this planet and its civilians many times over.
>
> I get emotional when I think of the possible use of these chemical weapons, which lead to warfare that will end up more tragic than anyone can imagine. And as I have pointed out, that emotional reaction is backed up by the facts.

That was twenty years ago. Today, we live in times that are, in many ways, more dangerous than the Cold War, and the United States still maintains enormous stockpiles of weapons of mass destruction in the form of nuclear warheads that vastly exceed what we could possibly need to destroy any nation we choose. Just like two decades ago, the far right is advocating that we make even more weapons. This time the fantasy is of "limited" nuclear weapons like bunker-buster bombs. Once more, the arguments are familiar: The race for war somehow maintains peace and our moral choices are dictated by how our enemies behave. But there is one especially dangerous and indefensible addition: The undercurrent of the argument that the United States should build more nuclear weapons at the same time we are preaching against them to the rest of the world rests on the not-so-thinly veiled claim that it is permissible, even indispensable, for us to have them because we are better, militarily and morally, than everyone else. And just as in 1985, it is time for Americans of all faiths who care about the sanity of our world and the safety of our children to "get emotional."

There was an argument for massive nuclear stockpiles during the Cold War. It wasn't an argument with which I fully agreed, but at least it was coherent: Neither the United States nor the Soviet Union would ever start a nuclear war because each knew the other had enough weapons to retaliate in kind. This was the policy of mutual assured destruction. It triggered a nightmarish arms race when each side concluded it needed not just enough warheads to destroy the world but *more* warheads than the other had. Even so, at least it provided *some* rationale for our thousands of nuclear weapons.

Now, that argument has not simply vanished; it has been turned on its head. The United States no longer needs nuclear weapons to keep us safe. Nuclear weapons are only useful in a war with another nation, if they are useful at all, and with a defense budget at least as large as the military spending of the next eighteen countries *combined* we already have ample conventional forces to defend ourselves against any country. In fiscal year 2003, our defense budget was around ten times the size of China's and roughly seven times larger than Russia's. The real nuclear threat today is that a lone terrorist armed with a knapsack will detonate a nuclear bomb inside our country or that an unstable regime like North Korea's will become a major nuclear power. Our nuclear arsenal cannot defend against those threats; on the contrary, it is making them worse.

When the United States maintains far more nuclear warheads than we could possibly use, we make other governments, like Russia and China, feel that they must do the same. We turn nuclear weapons into a flashy symbol of international prestige and power. We send a signal to other nations, especially those that already resent our power, that the way to be as influential and impressive as America is to obtain nuclear weapons. And the more that rogue regimes, like North Korea and Iran, dabble in the nuclear trade, the likelier it becomes that nuclear materials will slip into the hands of terrorists. Indeed, many international experts believe the single largest and least reported threat of our time is nuclear weapons in the hands of Russian officers who have not been able to feed their families.

Most of all, we have completely deprived ourselves of the right to be taken seriously when we lecture other countries about nuclear proliferation. I happen to agree that it is far more dangerous for Iran or North Korea to have nuclear weapons than for the United States to have them. But we must also try to see ourselves as others see us. From the perspective of an Iranian, North Korean, or Pakistani, the American position sounds very much like: "It's OK for us to have nuclear weapons, even to develop new and more advanced nuclear weapons like bunker busters, because we're America and you're not." Far from being persuasive, that argument simply deepens the resentment others already feel. We are lecturing others about a speck in their eye and asking them to ignore the log in ours.

Rather than delivering sermons from on high while refusing to change our own behavior, the United States could take a bold and faithful step for peace by drastically reducing our nuclear arsenals as part of a worldwide disarmament effort. Such a step would not weaken us: We would still maintain vastly more strength than we need to destroy any nation on earth. Leadership is an act of self-confidence and strength. And self-confidence can be contagious: If we signal the world that we are confident enough in our strength to reduce our nuclear arsenals, Russia might feel safe in joining us. Countries like Iran and North Korea, which, far from being pariahs, are heroes in much of the developing world because their nuclear programs are seen as exposing the hypocrisy of the United States, would lose their single-biggest excuse for proliferation. That does not mean nuclear proliferation would stop or that terrorists would no longer seek to obtain nuclear weapons. But even if Iran or North Korea retained a small number of nuclear warheads, we would still be in a position to destroy them with our conventional forces. We would not diminish our defenses at all by reducing our nuclear arsenal. On the contrary, we would add an even more potent weapon: moral authority. And if Middle Church, Middle Synagogue, and Middle Mosque, if mainstream people of faith, are not willing to "get emotional" about our moral authority, no one else will.

Some on the far right say nuclear weapons are now a fact, that, in their preferred phrase, "the nuclear genie can't be put back in the bottle." Perhaps not; certainly the threat of nuclear weapons will always be with us. But it remains for us to decide whether to alleviate that threat or make it worse. In the early 1980s, at the apex of the Cold War, I read an article on the nuclear threat by a Presbyterian minister named Kermit Johnson. Like many Americans, he was concerned that the arms race was spiraling out of control. What made him different was the rank before his name: major general. General Johnson was a combat veteran and West Point graduate who finally came to the conclusion that the nuclear arms race was both moral madness and a strategic miscalculation. And, addressing those who say humanity cannot recover from the nuclear "fall," that once these weapons have been introduced the United States has no choice but to have more of them than anyone, he quoted the French Christian philosopher Jacques Ellul:

People think that they have no right to judge a fact—all they have to do is accept it. . . . A striking example of this religious authority of the fact is provided for us by the atomic bomb. Confronted by this discovery, by this instrument of death, it was quite possible for man to refuse to use it, to refuse to accept this fact. But this question was never even raised. Mankind was confronted by a fact, and it felt obliged to accept it.

We can still strive against this fact, but General Johnson correctly identified the central challenge:

> History, if there is to be a history at all, must not repeat itself. But the only guarantors of this history are the American people themselves. . . . "[T]he average person" must overcome a passive feeling of inferiority which blindly blesses government policy, and is content to "leave it to the experts." The question is not whether we trust our leaders but whether our leaders can be made to trust the American people and bring them into their confidence.

The average people to whom General Johnson refers are, of course, not ordinary at all. They are the millions of faithful Americans whose hearts are open to the prophetic voice of Paul or other voices within their own traditions. "Live in harmony with one another," Paul wrote in Romans. "Do not be haughty, but associate with the lowly; do not claim to be wiser than you are. Do not repay anyone evil for evil, but take thought for what is noble in the sight of all" (Rom. 12:16–17). It is the essence of haughtiness for America to condemn other nations for pursuing nuclear weapons when we retain so many. Giving up what we do not need would be a wonderful and prophetic act of leadership to advance what is noble for all.

## "To Let the Oppressed Go Free":
## Choosing—and Challenging—Our Friends

*We who are strong ought to put up with the failings of the weak, and not to please ourselves. Each of us must please our neighbor for the good purpose of building up the neighbor.*
—ROMANS 15:1–2

St. Paul called on us to have the courage to criticize our friends constructively, not so that we could feel superior to them, but as an act of love. Yet when it comes to choosing our allies, the U.S. government seems to follow a distorted version of Paul's teaching: We who are strong ought to exploit—or overlook—the failings of the weak. By supporting horrible and abusive regimes because they are momentarily useful to us, we have engendered the resentment of their people, and it should not surprise us that they resent us for it. That is why a foreign policy based on expedience is the most inexpedient policy of all, and why a foreign policy that chooses, and challenges, our friends based on principle would be the best and most realistic strategy for our safety.

The most recent version of a foreign policy grounded in expediency rather than principle is the alliances we have chosen to protect our supply of oil. Throughout the Middle East, we have formed friendships with corrupt and authoritarian regimes that bask in luxury while their people are out of work. The people of Saudi Arabia, for example, endure mass unemployment and virtually no political liberties despite sitting on top of a quarter of the entire world's petroleum reserves. This oil lines the already deep pockets of the royal family, among our closest political allies. The Saudi people cannot be blamed for forming the impression that our only interest in their country is sucking their oil out of the ground and consuming it for our own purposes. The sad reality is that we have not shown any interest in their prosperity or their freedom. And we have made similar alliances of convenience with other abusive regimes, such as Egypt, where political dissidents are often arrested and tortured, and Pakistan, where a military dictator rules.

There is a "practical" defense for expedient foreign policy: that we are engaged in a global war, and we must sometimes work with unsavory allies. Perhaps there is some truth to that. But whatever else might be said of this policy—a policy that exempts from criticism the most abusive regimes as long as they pledge their support to us—it is decidedly not practical. It simply trades off the hatred of these country's populations for the momentary concessions of their leaders. This was the policy we pursued throughout the Cold War. It made enemies then, and it will now.

I know. I was there. In December 1980, four American Catholic women—three nuns and one lay relief worker of the Maryknoll order—were kidnapped, raped, and murdered in El Salvador by death squads linked to a government the United States supported. Their crime was to have ministered to and cared for the poor of Central America. For this, they were regarded as communists. And because the regime running El Salvador was anticommunist, we were willing to look the other way.

I visited the Central American region the next month, on the eve of Ronald Reagan's inauguration, with Barbara Mikulski and Gerry Studds, two other members of Congress. We visited refugee camps that housed thirty-five thousand people fleeing the fighting. We listened as government and U.S. officials stonewalled our requests for updates on the investigation into the killings of the four women. But there was no denying what we saw with our own eyes and heard with our own ears: The Salvadoran army was using U.S. government funds to wage a systematic campaign of terror against villagers in the rugged mountains along the Honduran border not because they were rebels, even if a few may have been, but because they were ordinary people caught in the wrong place at a very bad time. Crops were being burned, women were being raped, innocents were being tortured, and men, women, and children alike were simply vanishing.

As my colleagues explored neighboring countries, I went up into the hills of Honduras, on the border of El Salvador, with a tape recorder and a translator to take the testimony of ordinary people. The mountains were supposed to be thick with rebels. Perhaps they were. All I met were ordinary peasants living in the most horrible poverty. And it is only with sadness that I state the truth: They hated the American government because they knew we were propping up a regime that was killing their families, all in the name of a geopolitical game they did not understand and in which they had no desire to be involved. I recall in particular one elderly woman who told me in gushing tears how the death squads had killed her husband and son. Not having realized until afterward that this trip might not have been safe, I returned with a tape recorder full of stories that plainly demonstrated we were supporting the most horrifically un-American policies one could imagine. We wrote letters to President Reagan begging him to reconsider United States policies. "In the name of justice and humanity, and to further the long-term best interests of the United States, we appeal to you . . . to halt immediately military aid to El Salvador."

Reagan did reconsider the policy: He made it worse, flooding Central America with military funds that were used to inflict persecution, death, and torture on innocents. Congress imposed a hollow requirement permitting the aid as long as Reagan certified that the governments or groups we supported were making progress on human rights, certifications he routinely signed despite harrowing evidence to the contrary. And once more the same excuses came: We had to support anticommunists at all costs. The circularity of the reasoning was maddening: We opposed communism because communism was evil, and so it was necessary to support evil regimes because they were anticommunist.

The murder of the four churchwomen touched off a wave of protest by church leaders. One interfaith group, the InterReligious Task Force on Central America, issued an ecumenical letter signed by several Catholic bishops, Protestant clergy, and rabbis. "As citizens of the United States we are particularly sensitive to the responsibility that our Government bears in the oppression and violence in Central America," they wrote. "[O]ur government is embarked on a course which we believe will only increase the bloodshed and violation of people's rights and dignity, as well as increase the danger of regional war. We deplore our Government's role in the militarization of Central America, including the slow but steady increase of U.S. military advisers in El Salvador, Honduras, and Guatemala." Their pleas were ignored by the very same administration that claimed to speak for values and morality. That was more than two decades ago. Today, in another war, we return to the same theme and the same result: that those who claim most loudly to speak for faith ignore the pleas of millions of faithful Americans.

Later in the Reagan Administration, I returned to Central America with another congressional delegation. Bipartisan, it was comprised of supporters and opponents of our policy in the region alike. I asked Reverend William Sloane Coffin, my old mentor and a legendary peace activist, to join me. One night, the congressional delegation attended a formal dinner at the U.S. embassy in Nicaragua. Republican Congressman Dan Burton of Indiana, who had spent part of the day taking helicopter rides and boasted to me of shooting machine guns as though he were playing in an arcade, was there, as were other die-hard Reagan supporters. I doubted we would receive a full and honest accounting from our ambassador in such a partisan setting. Bill Coffin and I pulled the ambassador aside in a quiet moment and asked him whether we might stay for a confidential briefing afterward. He agreed.

After the others left, we were shown to a sitting room, where Bill sat at a piano and began playing. When the ambassador, a Yale alumnus, entered the room, Bill, a former chaplain at Yale, began belting out the Yale fight song. That cracked the ice, literally, since soon the ambassador was pouring scotch over it. We talked late into the night, the ambassador struggling as best he could to do his job, which was to defend an administration policy Bill and I felt passionately was indefensible. As the evening wound down, Bill broke through the fog.

"There's just one more question," he said. "Why does U.S. policy always end up hurting the poor people of the world?" (His actual language was a little saltier than "hurt," but I'll leave to your imagination the word a man of Bill's passion might have said in a moment of such frustration.) The ambassador had no answer to this question, for he was a good man caught in an impossible situation. But it is a question Middle Church must answer.

In late 2005, I returned to El Salvador to mark the twenty-fifth anniversary of the murders that first brought me to the region. We prayed with the Maryknoll nuns who, in a wonderful ministry of hope and courage, still care for the poor despite the tragedy that befell their sisters. We visited the site where the women were murdered, and we returned to many of the poor regions of the country that I had visited a quarter-century before. The government is no longer shooting bullets in El Salvador. But the bullets the people face today are just as deadly. They are economic and environmental.

Americans wield even more influence around the world now than we did during the Cold War, and we must make a choice: We can use our power to stand with those who yearn for just a taste of the prosperity and freedom we enjoy, or we can use and manipulate the world's most vulnerable people for our momentary advantage. Surely the moral choice is obvious and the strategic one is as well. It does not make Americans safer to give hundreds of millions of people around the world reasons to resent us. We are safer when we behave in a way that earns their respect. Like Paul, we must be courageous and constructive in choosing and challenging our friends.

But there is another lesson Paul can teach: Middle Church, Middle Synagogue, and Middle Mosque cannot wait for the government to act. Paul was a Roman citizen who enjoyed all the benefits of being a citizen of the world's only superpower. He might easily have lived in relative comfort and security, but after his conversion, he roamed the world spreading the Gospel. One of his most important teachings was that Gentiles need not undergo the rituals of conversion to become Christians; they only need accept Christ into their hearts. We need a foreign policy based on a similar ideal, one that says to every person: You do not have to be an American to deserve freedom, sustenance, and shelter; you need only be a human being.

In the age of terrorism, America must not succumb to fear. Rather, we must reach out in a spirit of love. This much we must do because God calls us to do no less, but we must also do it because there is no surer strategy for protecting our safety. America must not become the modern-day version of the Pharisees whose hypocrisy Jesus constantly condemned. Yes, these are difficult times, but we must not allow the terrorists to set the standard for our behavior. America has ideals to which we must adhere no matter how low the terrorists stoop. God, too, gives us standards by which to live, and there is no exemption for times of uncertainty or danger. On the contrary, in moments of danger, God's calling is the rock to which we must cling. And we must have enough faith to believe God would not have challenged us to love our brothers and sisters if doing so was as dangerous as the radical right would have us believe.

Our challenge is not to spread a particular religious faith, but to engage in the world and extend a hand of friendship to its most oppressed peoples. We can make it known through our words and our actions that our government does not always speak for each of us, that faithful Americans uphold the dignity of each life no matter where it began or where it is lived. And most of all, we can demand that our government reflect our values. To do this, we need not like Paul be struck blind on the road to Damascus. We need only open our eyes to the needs of our brothers and sisters around the world.

## CHAPTER 6

# Reconciling Abraham's Children: Toward Peace in the Middle East

*His sons Isaac and Ishmael buried him in the cave of Mach-pelah, in the field of Ephron son of Zohar the Hittite, east of Mamre, the field that Abraham purchased from the Hittites. There Abraham was buried, with his wife Sarah.*
—GENESIS 25:9–10

*He was dividing God's land, and I would say, "Woe unto any prime minister of Israel who takes a similar course to appease the [European Union], the United Nations or the United States of America."*
—PAT ROBERTSON, AS ISRAELI PRIME MINISTER ARIEL SHARON LAY IN A COMA AFTER SUFFERING A MASSIVE STROKE

The summer of 1968 was a challenging time to be assigned to the East Falls United Methodist Church in urban Philadelphia. Racial tensions were at their peak following the assassination of Martin Luther King, Jr. Cities across the nation were on fire, and North Philadelphia was no exception. The neighborhood where the church was located—just a block and a half away from the Old Academy Players Theater, where Grace Kelly got her start as an actress—was changing. Poor whites and poor blacks, who had far more in common than they realized, resented one another's presence. African-American children had to walk through a gauntlet of white people's houses to get to school, and stories of them being chased by dogs were not uncommon.

I arrived at East Falls in June 1968, all of twenty-five years old, and moved into the parsonage. One night that summer, I thought I heard yelling outside. This was not a terribly unusual event, but that night it seemed closer than usual. I opened the front door and saw rival gangs of about fifteen or twenty black and white youth, kids maybe thirteen or fourteen years old, fighting in front of the parsonage. They were beating one another with baseball bats, throwing fists, and shouting threats. In those days, more young people carried knives than guns, but hatred armed with any weapon can kill. I rushed into the crowd and started screaming in both directions: "Stop it! Stop it!" Before I knew it, I was standing in the middle of the two gangs. The black children fled immediately, and I stood there facing the white children, one of whom was brandishing a baseball bat studded with nails. I looked him the eye, reached out, and took it away. I still have that bat in my attic.

I've been told that was brave, but there's a pretty fine line between brave and dumb, and I was probably closer to the latter than the former. Bravery is what you do when you know the risks and push ahead anyway. I never stopped to think about what I was doing. It was pure instinct, and arguably not the brightest thing for a young father to get himself into. But I thank God that instinct took over before my brain could engage, because that night taught me one of the most important lessons of my life: It's a lot easier to hate, and therefore to hurt, someone you don't know. Definitely for the white children that night—and probably for many of the black children, too—they were simply fighting a faceless other whom they could hate because they were utterly unaware of each other's humanity. If people are objects, it's a lot easier to hate them.

After that incident, our church helped form the East Falls Human Relations Committee, which sought to soothe racial tensions less through complex negotiations than through the simplest of human interactions, like social gatherings in the church and basketball games on the court around the corner from the parsonage. From those quiet moments of daily lives, people learned something no amount of pastoral sermons or political speeches could convey: They began to see each other as human beings. Once they became people rather than objects, once the other became a face and a person with his or her own unique story, hardships, and dreams, friendship took hold, and respect followed soon afterward.

This story isn't a fairy tale, and it doesn't have a magical ending. There is still racial tension in North Philadelphia, as there is across our country. Some politicians, therefore, might be quick to dismiss me as naïve or unrealistic. But anyone who has lived in an urban area or led an urban ministry knows the *only* realistic means of overcoming hatred is recognizing one another's common humanity. It is not a panacea; there are never panaceas. That's not my point. It's this: Seeing your enemy as a human being may not solve all problems, but there isn't a single problem that can be solved without taking that first step.

And whether the scene is East Falls or the Middle East, whether the conflict is between teenage gangs or ancient peoples, embracing our common humanity is the only hope for peace. There is no more realistic foreign policy than this one, and nowhere more than in one of the oldest conflicts on earth: the long-running sibling feud between the descendants of the two sons of Abraham, the Israelis and the Arabs.

I first visited the Middle East in April 1977 on a trip with Merle as well as our friends Bob and Helen Dee, a Jewish couple from my congressional district. We spent five days in Israel, where our driver and guide, David Suarez, was a veteran of the 1967 war, a nice and amiable man who turned harsh and bitter when he confronted Arabs, especially when he perceived an offense in their driving. We were not directly exposed to similar hatred from Arabs toward Israelis, but it was palpable on both sides. David was a perfectly nice and decent person; it was hatred of the anonymous other that evoked vitriol in him. The same was true of every Arab we met. It was difficult to reconcile the gentleness we saw in individuals with the hatred that we knew permeated the region on all sides. It was only in faceless, nameless interactions, moments when the enemy ceased being a human being and became the other instead, that the bitterness arose. In human interactions, when Israelis and Arabs looked into one another's eyes and saw one another as parents and children and full people with simple needs, understanding was possible.

We experienced one such interaction while we toured the pyramids. Somehow, President Anwar Sadat of Egypt found out that a young American congressman was visiting the region, and we soon found ourselves in an armored limousine on the way to his summer retreat in Alexandria. The four of us—Merle, the Dees, and I—waited in a grove of banyan trees until we were escorted into a sitting room. Bob and Helen looked as Jewish as they were, yet no one even bothered to search Bob's briefcase. ("I can't believe it!" Bob, a staunch pro-Israeli hawk, said afterward. "I'm Jewish and they didn't even ask to see what was in my briefcase!") Sadat's butler greeted us with traditional hot tea served in handleless hourglass-shaped juice glasses. The glasses were so hot we could barely hold them, but not knowing whether asking for a cold drink might violate some cultural norm, we thought it polite to stay quiet. Then Sadat came in, plopped down in a chair, and asked the butler for a Pepsi with ice.

He spoke frankly, apparently under the misimpression that a second-term congressman wielded some serious influence in Washington. It was plain to me that he saw accommodation with Israel as the only realistic military or diplomatic option, but he felt trapped by political and economic circumstances.

"God blessed all the Arab countries with oil except Egypt," he said. "In any one of them, you drill a hole in the ground and oil pops up. Here, you drill a hole and all you get is sand. All I have is a large army. The other countries use us to fight Israel while they bask in their wealth."

Tensions between Israel and Egypt were rising once again—as

they often had—and Sadat surprised me with his assessment. "I wish," he said wistfully, "the old woman was back."

That was Golda Meir, the former prime minister, who was now retired and whom Sadat had fought in the Yom Kippur War just four years earlier. Meir was tough and resolute, Sadat said, but he could work with her. Six months later, Sadat visited Israel and sat down with his old enemy. Meir is reported to have greeted him with: "What took you so long?" The two of them sat on a sofa and talked—not about geopolitics or treaties or military strategy but about their grandchildren. When I read about that meeting and thought back to that gang fight in North Philadelphia a decade earlier, I knew then what I believe every bit as passionately today: that peace in the Middle East is possible—indeed, it is *only* possible—if people look at each other face to face and see what they have in common. They have the same hopes, they love their children and grandchildren, no matter their ancient animosities, they are bound together by their common needs for food, water, shelter, and security.

Most discussion of the Israeli-Arab conflict deals with which side is to blame. But blame in that part of the world is not a scarce commodity. We do not need to argue over who deserves more of it; there is a surplus to go around. The important question is not who did what to whom in the past, but how we can move forward for tomorrow. The parties in the region are so bound to old memories that the only hope for peace is for an outside mediator to help them see their common needs. The United States is the only nation in a position to play that role constructively, if only because all parties to the conflict depend on our support.

We have played that role effectively before, most famously at the Camp David talks that resulted in peace between Israel and Egypt. The Camp David Accords were a towering success, yet history has forgotten that by offering himself as a mediator between two parties whose animosity reached literally into the millennia, President Carter took a monumental risk of failure. Indeed, the talks seemed

likely to fail even before they began. In January 1978, Carter visited
Sadat in Egypt in an attempt to persuade him to join talks. Sadat,
who felt constrained by his dependence on his wealthy Arab neighbors as well as Islamic extremists in his own country, was reluctant to
join unless Carter pledged support for a Palestinian state, which
would, in turn, have made it impossible to bring Israelis to the table.
Reports indicated Carter had exhausted all his options and was
poised to return to Washington, where he would doubtless be met
with a chorus of critics accusing him of having gambled his credibility and failed. I phoned my friend Senator Paul Tsongas, a future
presidential candidate.

"Paul, this is exactly the kind of risk presidents should be willing
to take," I said. "He deserves our support no matter how it turns out.
Why don't we organize some people to meet his plane when he arrives?"

Paul readily agreed, and we began working the phones to drum
up at least a small cadre of supporters to show Carter we supported
his courageous act of risk taking no matter its outcome. But at the
last hour, Carter and Sadat reached an agreement, and what was intended as an act of consolation became a victory rally. When Air
Force One landed at Andrews Air Force Base around 3 A.M., Paul
and I and our wives were at the bottom of the steps as a jubilant
Carter bounded down into a crowd of supporters three thousand
five hundred strong. Early the next year, Merle and I watched on the
White House lawn as Sadat and Israeli Prime Minister Menachem
Begin signed a peace treaty that endures to this day.

Yet since then, with the exception of President Clinton, American presidents have been so afraid of failure that they have been unwilling to assume serious or personal roles in brokering peace. All
they need risk is momentary popularity. Sadat paid for peace with
his life when he was assassinated on a parade stand in early 1981.
Thirteen years later, Yitzhak Rabin was shot to death by an Israeli
fundamentalist. They stand in a long tradition of peacemakers, from

Gandhi to King, who met violent ends, and their sacrifices should put the political fears of American presidents into perspective.

Yet here at home, domestic politics get in the way of constructive dialogue about the Middle East. The far religious right has staked out a position in ardent support of Israel, but far too many of their leaders think of the Jewish state the same way they do of global warming. For them it is a temporary necessity, useful for fulfilling apocalyptic prophecies that Jews will gather in Israel before the End of Days. But this treatment of our Jewish brothers and sisters is not an expression of love; it is an act of exploitation that becomes immediately clear once the literal prophecy is extended to its conclusion. That is, Jews, having served their instrumental purpose in bringing about the Second Coming, will be consumed in the Rapture unless they convert. "The Jews need conversion," Kay Arthur, a far religious right supporter of Israel, told CBS. "They need to know that the Messiah is coming. And the Bible tells us what's going to happen."

What's going to happen, if we take the extremist reading of prophecy literally, is hardly tolerance and love for Judaism. Consider this exchange on Bill Moyers' television program *Now* with Ray and Sharon Sanders, a Christian Zionist couple who moved to Israel so they would be prepared for the Rapture:

> SANDERS: According to the prophetic word of God the Third Temple will be built by the Jewish people. But at some point in time, the False Messiah will move into that Temple, declare himself to be God, and the wrath of God will be poured upon the nations.

> SHARON SANDERS: And so judgment will fall. It will fall on Israel in a way because Israel has walked away from God in many ways. And He wants Israel to return to him. But Israel will be saved out of it.

> NARRATOR: So, the False Messiah will be an Israeli? Or . . .

SANDERS: Most probably will be Jewish. Whether he's Israeli . . . maybe not, maybe not Israeli. But certainly Jewish.

I do not know Mr. and Mrs. Sanders, and I would not question
their sincerity. What I can say with complete conviction is this: I
have three Jewish grandchildren, and I find it profoundly offensive
and condescending to believe that their purpose on this earth is to be
the pawns of Christian prophecy. Neither my grandchildren nor any
other Jewish person is here to serve my needs or those of any other
Christian. We are all here to serve God and one another. Anyone
who believes that some on the fringes of the far right support Israel
out of altruistic love for Jewish people need only look at their reac-
tion when Israelis have declined to live out this narrow vision of
apocalyptic prophecy. They have turned on them with a vengeance.
When Ariel Sharon, of whose militarism I have been critical, proposed a modest land-for-peace plan, for example, the excoriation
from some corners of the far religious right in America was at least
as vicious as any criticism he faced in his own society, for he had the
audacity to depart from the script in order to serve the peaceful
needs of his own people. If former generals like Yitzhak Rabin and
Ariel Sharon can see the need for peace, why can't the extreme right
in America? The lives of the Israeli people are at stake, and their
leaders have concluded that peace is their best hope. Here in America, all that is at stake is a radical theological ideology. Gershom
Gorenberg, a Jewish writer, captured well the hypocrisy of some on
the very far religious right: "They don't love real Jewish people. They
love us as characters in their story, in their play, and that's not who
we are, and we never auditioned for that part, and the play is not one
that ends up good for us. If you listen to the drama they're describ-
ing, essentially it's a five-act play in which the Jews disappear in the
fourth act."

I don't believe most American Christians feel about Jews as some
on the radical right do. I suspect the vast majority of Middle Church,

like me, strongly supports Israel's right to exist and the Palestinians' right to live in equal security. We do not need to appeal to prophecy to defend Israel's existence. The dreadful historical persecution of the Jewish people, culminating in the horrific atrocities of the Holocaust, is the only justification Israel needs. The Jewish people need a secure state of their own where they do not have to depend on the goodwill of those who have abused them for millennia, and Israel, their spiritual and ancestral home, is the appropriate place for it to be. I supported Israel strongly as a member of Congress. I voted repeatedly to move the U.S. embassy from Tel Aviv to Jerusalem as recognition of Israel's permanence, something no U.S. president, not Ronald Reagan and not George W. Bush, has agreed to do. My admiration for Israel as an oasis of democracy in the region and a survivor surrounded by hostile neighbors is profound.

I will never forget one of my first visits to Israel, when I stayed in the town of Kiryat Shmonah, where missiles launched from terrorist outposts in southern Lebanon had killed innocent schoolchildren. The night we arrived, I could still hear missiles exploding in the distance. A drive along the Mediterranean coast is a sobering reminder that Israel is a tiny and vulnerable speck of land about the size of New Jersey. I have stood on the Golan Heights, from which Israel, Lebanon, and Syria are all visible, a sight that reminded me of the gang turf wars in North Philadelphia, where you can walk a single block and unknowingly cross from one gang's territory into another's. This is not a region of the world where simplistic solutions work. But militarism unaccompanied by any attempt to build real human understanding is the most simplistic and unrealistic solution of all.

Were Israel being created again, perhaps there are things I would do differently. If God were to ask my geopolitical counsel, I might suggest a statute of limitations on the Holy Land. Or better yet, a command that every inch of God's creation be considered equally holy and equally deserving of human stewardship and respect. But we are not going to relive 1948, and God doesn't need my advice.

Palestinians can no more reclaim everything they lost a half century ago than Cuban expatriates in Miami can expect to regain ownership of the casinos that Castro nationalized in 1959. History is history, and reality is reality. If all we seek to do is refight old battles and relive old memories time and time again, then a time will come when the bloodshed stops only because we have run out of blood to spill. The past is not what matters most. We have to build a new and peaceful tomorrow on the basis of how we live and what we need today. If Christianity has a theological lesson to contribute to Middle East peace, it is not to endorse endless division or to embrace bloodshed until the End of Days arrives. It is instead Christ's simplest and most powerful lesson: the power of forgiveness. For until all sides can forgive one another for the offenses each has felt, peace cannot be possible.

Nor can we allow the Palestinian people to become in our own minds what the African-American youth were in North Philadelphia: an unidentified, anonymous other, an object whose humanity we do not acknowledge and whose human needs we therefore do not feel. Thousands of Palestinians now live in refugee camps that are actually dilapidated cities three or four generations old. Neither side has made meaningful strides toward investing in their future, for Israel has feared the creation of a Palestinian state, while many Palestinian extremists have sought to keep alive the fiction that these camps are temporary because someday their old land within Israel's borders will be reclaimed.

If the Palestinian people are to live a decent life with the full rights of human beings, then simply proclaiming our desire for them to have a state—a goal I fully support—is not enough. We must invest in their economy as well as their infrastructure. The Palestinian people with whom I have spoken during my visits to the region feel hopeless and defenseless. Yes, there are terrorists and criminals among them, but most are good people who want nothing more than life's basic needs. There has been scandalously little investment in the basic infrastructure of life for Palestinians—schools, hospitals, housing, and other facilities. Critics of Israel in the United States have called for divestment. I have been a critic of Israel on many occasions, but I would rather those on all sides shift our focus toward *invest*ment in peace. Peace, of course, requires conditions of security and strength. But it also requires the building of human understanding in the small moments of life, the kind of understanding built in exchange programs that enable Israelis and Palestinians to encounter one another as human beings. We can do for the Palestinian people what America has so justifiably done for Israel and what the children of Ishmael deserve no less—help to build a secure and prosperous state.

Yet all that has been built in Israel is a wall, a security fence dividing Israel and Palestinian territories and, more tragically, separating Palestinian workers from their jobs, farmers from their land, even children from their schools. Rather than adhering strictly to the Green Line that officially drew Israel's borders after her war for independence in 1948, Israeli authorities built this new wall in no small part on Palestinian land. I understand the concern about terrorism that led to its construction; perhaps, were it an effective barrier, it might be more justifiable. But on the saddest visit I have ever made to the Middle East, I inspected the wall myself. It is so porous in some places that I was able to sneak across it at night with no effort, and if someone at my age can pull off that feat simply by taking an evening stroll, it seems pretty safe to assume it will not stop a determined and youthful terrorist undertaking a carefully planned mission. The wall does not stop bombers. All it does is divide.

As those on the far religious right claim to speak for all Christians in their defense of militaristic policies, another tragedy is occurring on the ground: the exodus of Christians from Israel. Christians once accounted for nearly a quarter of the population there; now they are roughly 2 percent. They understandably feel caught in the middle of a war being fought by other people and other faiths. Yet this land is holy to them too, and we cannot leave them trapped in a crossfire until the only Christians left in Israel are clergy serving as caretakers of holy sites and museums.

If there is to be peace, true peace, for Israelis and Palestinians, we must have enough love in our hearts and enough trust in our friendship to speak the truth to one another. Friends are honest with each other, so when we disagree with either side, we should have the courage to say so. On my visits to the region, I have always made a practice of meeting with public officials and ordinary people on all sides of the conflict. I try to confine my comments to what I see with my own eyes rather than what propagandists on either side claim. Too much discussion of the Middle East—both in America and around the world—is not discussion at all. It is ideological camps shouting at one another across a vast divide that neither is seriously attempting to bridge. They either support anything Israel does without paying attention to her policies or criticize her every action without respect for the extraordinarily difficult circumstances in which the Jewish state exists. It is time for peaceful minds on both sides to realize they cannot survive without one another. We must return in our hearts to that poignant passage in Genesis 25 in which Abraham's two sons, Isaac and Ishmael, join together to bury their father. Today, their descendants must join together lest an endless stream of senseless burials continue.

The "realists" will disagree with all this. They will say love cannot overcome hatreds this ancient; but if they are too deep to be overcome with love, surely they are also too persistent to be contained with weapons. They will say meaningful peace cannot be built on the simple basis of human interaction; I insist only that it cannot be built without it. They will say peace with security and understanding and mutual respect is unrealistic. I stand with Yitzhak Rabin, an old general who fought many a hard battle before giving his own life not for war but for the cause of peace, in replying that perpetual conflict is the least realistic solution of all. If peace is naïve, then so are the faiths of billions—Christian, Jewish, and Muslim alike—whose traditions counsel forgiveness and love. For my faith, I reply simply that Jesus' teachings changed history as well as hearts. If his vision was naïve and unrealistic, it is precisely the kind of innocent hope our world so desperately needs. If Jesus taught us anything, if other faiths teach their adherents anything, it is that nothing is more realistic than hope.

CHAPTER 7

Compassion, Not Contempt:
Hearing God's Call to Love the Poor

*Speak out, judge righteously, defend the rights of the poor
and the needy.*
—PROVERBS 31:9

*[Welfare is] for deadbeats that can work but won't work.*
—TEXAS TELEVISION PREACHER AND REPUBLICAN SUP-
PORTER JOHN HAGEE

In today's America, the free market has achieved demigod status,
wealth is lionized as a blessing from on high, and poverty carries
the stigma of laziness, failure, and moral corruption. I have to think
the last thing you'd want to be in today's America is a young, homeless, pregnant, and destitute woman. Yet that is precisely the kind of
person God chose to bring Jesus into the world. There was a message
in that choice and it was neither that Mary was a shiftless welfare
queen nor that her poverty was a God-given punishment for an errant lifestyle. It was that love for the poor is the greatest moral imperative, one that calls for compassion, not condemnation.

Hubert Humphrey, who served in the Senate while I was in the
House, echoed Christ's message is one of his most famous speeches:
"It was once said that the moral test of Government is how that

Government treats those who are in the dawn of life, the children; those who are in the twilight of life, the elderly; and those who are in the shadows of life, the sick, the needy, and the handicapped." We are flunking that test today. Poverty in America is a moral catastrophe, one made all the worse by both its persistence in the midst of such abundant wealth and the fact that government policy has gradually shifted from compassion for the poor to cold indifference to, finally, outright contempt. Poverty is also one of the most complicated moral challenges we face, one with far too many facets for me to cover in a single chapter. The pages I devote to it in this book reflect both the moral urgency and economic complexity of poverty.

The most recent Census Bureau statistics say thirty-seven million of our neighbors, thirteen million of them children, live in poverty, a scandalous figure in and of itself, but one that also drastically understates the actual human need in which people live. The official poverty line for a family of five is just over $23,000 in annual income, a figure insufficient to pay for even substandard housing in many parts of the country, to say nothing of food, clothing, utilities, and other needs. Even more shameful, children, those who are most innocent and defenseless, are among the poorest segments of American society. At 17.8 percent, the poverty rate for children exceeds that for both adults and senior citizens. And the problem is growing worse: 1.1 million more Americans were poor in 2004 than in 2003. To these figures, we must add other measures of injustice. More than forty-five million Americans have no health insurance. More than two million live in dilapidated housing. More than thirteen million households have difficulty obtaining enough food to eat.

These Americans do not fit the stereotypes of the lazy or morally unfit poor person. Increasingly, they work. A decade ago Congress passed and President Clinton signed a massive welfare reform law intended to move people from welfare to work. It has succeeded in that narrow goal; its utter and ongoing failure was in alleviating poverty. In 2001, five years after welfare reform, I met with the national commander of the Salvation Army, John Busby, who has since retired.

"Bob, we're facing a crisis," he said. "Half the people who are showing up at our food kitchens and homeless shelters are working full-time."

The reason is that our policies punish idleness without rewarding work. Our country is filled with good and gentle people who are working two, even three, jobs yet barely scrape by. Getting a job often means losing Medicaid and bringing home less money than welfare paid. Children, as they always do, are paying the heaviest price. Welfare reform has not included any consistent support for child care, trapping working parents and their children between a political rock and an economic hard place.

The radical right's philosophy, one in which too many moderates unfortunately have unthinkingly joined, is that poverty would go away if only we made it more miserable.

But while I do not doubt some behave foolishly or carelessly, I do not believe there has ever been a teenage girl or young woman who consciously has a child just to rake in the stingy welfare benefits our society pays. I believe there are young mothers whose lives are so filled with despair they have no hope for a better life. I believe there are young women who have been denied access to family planning services by exactly the same politicians who would then deny them support if they have children. And most of all, I do not believe there is anyone living in poverty who chooses to be there because the benefits are somehow so attractive. The poorest Americans today work the hardest.

I have met them and ministered to them. During the spring of 1962, during my freshman year in college, my father told me there was no money left to help pay my tuition, so I called the local Methodist bishop and asked to be assigned to a church. That summer, two weeks after my nineteenth birthday, I arrived at Gilberton Methodist Church, a congregation of one hundred fifty people in the coal region of Pennsylvania. The coal companies were strip-mining then, and enormous, horrendous piles of slag marred the countryside where entire mountainsides had been taken down. I had never been to a funeral before; the first one I attended was one at which I was officiating. There were too many funerals then, and too many widows and orphans left behind. Black-lung disease made otherwise strong, healthy men old in their fifties, leaving them gasping for air on respirators before dying too young.

In many ways, these miners were the very picture of the working poor today. The coal companies owned the local grocery store, inflated the prices, and kept families locked into a life of near-slavery from which they could never quite break free. Every time they seemed just close enough to breaking through to a better life, a new bill would arrive in the mail, an illness would be diagnosed, wages would be cut, or prices at the store would rise. They were running on the hamster wheel of economic life, spinning faster and faster just to keep up. They had every reason to be bitter. Instead, the mining families were generous, kind, filled with decency and love. I attended school during the week and commuted to the parish on the weekends. When I arrived on Friday nights, exhausted from a week's studies and the long drive, there was often a bag of groceries—groceries they could barely afford for themselves—waiting on the front porch of the parsonage.

In the late 1960s and early 1970s, my ministry in Philadelphia exposed me to urban poverty, first at East Falls United Methodist Church in a working-class white neighborhood sandwiched between two predominantly African-American housing projects, then as Protestant chaplain at Drexel University. The cities were aflame then, and there were two Philadelphias, the city of brotherly love that most visitors saw during the day and the city of violence that erupted after the sun went down. Riding with the Police Clergy Unit, which often arrived on the scene during fights or after tragedies, I met people living in conditions of despair that we prefer to believe do not exist in America. Just like the coal miners, most were hard-working people who seemed permanently at the edge of escaping poverty, only to face some setback that sent them plummeting back into the cycle.

One hot Friday evening, the police lieutenant with whom I was riding was called to a Schuylkill Falls housing project. Like most urban projects, it was a high-rise where the elevators were invariably broken and the stairwells became crime scenes where a few thugs preyed on the law-abiding majority. The children often played on top of the elevators, and that night, a boy had fallen down the shaft and been crushed to death. I had just met that child earlier that day at his elementary school, where I volunteered in a reading program. That evening I sat with his mother and other extended relatives and attempted to offer the small comfort of holding their hands and praying as they expressed their agony. Her son had been doing well in school; he had been the bearer of all their hopes that the family might someday climb out of poverty.

Lives like these were rarely noticed by the white, middle-class majority. Even the scant services that were available shut down at 5 P.M. on Fridays. If someone's oil burner failed in the bitter cold of winter, and they had no money to turn it back on, if they were thrown on the street for failure to pay rent or beaten in a domestic quarrel, there was nothing to do but find a way to hang on until 9 A.M. Monday. There were a couple of shelters for men in Philadelphia then, but none for women or children. I began meeting with other clergy and social workers in the area to ask what services we could provide. Inevitably, the response was excuses rather than answers: It would be too much of a hassle to get the proper licenses. It cost too much money. The city inspections would be too much trouble.

I was less interested in complying with bureaucratic codes than with following Edgar's Iron Law of Getting Things Done: It's easier to ask forgiveness than ask permission. I teamed up with a friend of mine, Jim Hallam, a United Methodist minister and the Protestant chaplain at the University of Pennsylvania. We opened up his church, the Asbury United Methodist Church, located between the University of Pennsylvania and Drexel University, as a weekend homeless shelter, with cots set up in the halls and the kitchen used to prepare food. We didn't ask for permits, attend hearings, or fill out forms; we just did it. Jim and I visited suburban churches that had ample poor funds but no poor people and persuaded them to part with some of their money. We met a disaster trainer at the Red Cross and convinced him to use his skills to train students and other people in the community to volunteer. That was the birth of the People's Emergency Center (PEC). On Friday, July 1, 1972, the church opened its weekend shelter at 5 P.M. taking in all comers and staying with them until we could refer them to social services agencies on Monday morning. We never asked questions about why people needed help; we simply took down their names, gave them a place to sleep, and prepared meals to eat.

The People's Emergency Center began as a mom-and-pop operation. Jim and I alternated our stays at the shelter on weekends, with lots of active volunteers, and I brought the linen home with me on Monday mornings for Merle to wash. She was a perfectly good sport about it until we found a mouse in one of the bags of sheets. By our second year in operation, we had installed men's and women's showers, served more than two thousand people, and—again, see Edgar's Iron Law of Getting Things Done—persuaded the city to give us the requisite permits because we were already there anyway and weren't going away. In time, the People's Emergency Center moved to its own facility in West Philadelphia. It's still there; in fact, it was recently honored as the city's social services agency of the year.

For me, this work was one of the most joyous experiences of my life. It taught me—as did my ministry with the coal miners and their families, and my later work helping Jimmy Carter to build houses through Habitat for Humanity—that it's possible to make a difference, and that people have an enormous capacity for goodness even in the midst of the most terrible conditions. Not one of the poor people I met deserved their difficulties, whether they were emerging gritty from the mines at the end of the week, showing up at the People's Emergency Center for the weekend, or driving nails into their first home at a Habitat for Humanity build. None of them was perfect, and neither am I. But they were among the most decent people I have ever known. Of this much I am certain: The only difference between them and me is a little bit of bad luck and a few dollars in our paychecks.

No one who has met any of the poor people I have known would entertain, even for a moment, the idea that punitive policies bear the slightest relation to the reality of poor people's lives. Not one of them needed to be punished; each deserved only to be loved. They are no less moral than the rest of us; often they are more so. They work no less than you or I; typically, they work much harder. They are separated from you or me only by hard luck and chance. The idea of punishing the poor is bad policy and bad faith.

While apathy toward the plight of the poor has hardened into hostility under President Bush's callous administration, neither political party is free of blame. For the better part of a decade, ever since President Clinton's pledge to "end welfare as we know it"—note, again, that no one promised (or attempted) to end *poverty* as we know it—Democrats have approached the poor from a posture of apology, accepting as gospel fact the idea that the programs of the Great Society were a terrible failure from which our nation must retreat. My response? Hogwash. Medicare, Medicaid, Head Start, food stamps, the Older Americans Act, nutrition programs, and other efforts were monumental achievements that placed food in empty stomachs and enabled millions to obtain medical care. Of course they had flaws. Of course they needed reform. They were the products of human beings and government, two annoyingly imperfect groups. But there is a difference between mistakes of love and sins of

indifference. Rather than apologizing for their proud legacy of compassion and joining the stampede to punish the poor, Democrats
should have recalled the words of Franklin Roosevelt: "Governments
can err, presidents do make mistakes, but the immortal Dante tells
us that Divine justice weighs the sins of the cold-blooded and the
sins of the warm-hearted on different scales. Better the occasional
faults of a government that lives in a spirit of charity than the consistent omissions of a government frozen in the ice of its own indifference."

Compassion for the poor is a moral imperative; there is no reason it cannot also be a political winner. On this issue as on so many
others, Democrats have consistently underestimated the fundamental goodness of the American people. During the 2004 presidential
campaign, John Edwards was the only candidate who spoke openly
about poverty in front of white audiences. The other presidential
candidates were wrapped up in hand-wringing over the travails of
the middle class. I'm not saying middle-class, bread-and-butter issues don't matter, but just once, I'd like to see a national candidate
challenge all of us in the faithful religious center to set aside our self-
indulgence long enough to see that our problems, however serious,
are nothing compared to those of a hungry child. I have enough confidence in the moral decency of Americans to believe we would respond to that challenge; I only wish Democrats shared that faith.
Democrats held a two-generation majority when they were the party
of compassion; they had to abandon their core principles before the
far right could ascend. It now falls to mainstream Americans of both
parties and all faiths to restore our society's tradition of concern for
the least fortunate and to heed God's call, in whatever form and
through whatever tradition we may hear it, to love the poor.

So it is ironic, and outrageous, that the voice most obstructing
that call emanates from those on the far religious right who seek to
co-opt faithful values as their own. They have cloaked free-market
ideology in a tragically flawed theology that paints God as an unfet-

tered capitalist whose presence is felt in our lives not through love, but through the distribution and withholding of material rewards. They call it the "Prosperity Gospel." First popularized by Oral Roberts, the televangelist who once warned that God planned to call him home if his supporters did not contribute $8 million by a specified deadline, the Prosperity Gospel began as a fund-raising tool. The pitch was enticing: Send fifty dollars to a ministry, preachers would say, and God will reward your generosity with one hundred dollars or more. Personally, I don't care for hucksters and scam artists no matter what form they come in, and I especially don't like it when they try to hide behind God. But in the last several years, the Prosperity Gospel mutated from a televangelist con game into a broader theological position that treats material prosperity as a blessing bestowed by the Almighty. Here is how the *Los Angeles Times*, reporting on the massive, and massively profitable, Trinity Broadcasting Network, summarized the idea:

> The prosperity gospel is rooted in the idea that God wants Christians to prosper and that believers have the right to ask him for financial gifts. TBN has woven this notion into its round-the-clock programming as well as the thousands of fund-raising letters it mails every day.
>
> During one telethon, [TBN chief Paul] Crouch, 70, told viewers that if they did their part to advance the Kingdom of God— such as by donating money to TBN—they should not be shy about asking God for a reward.
>
> "If my heart really, honestly desires a nice Cadillac . . . would there be something terribly wrong with me saying, 'Lord, it is the desire of my heart to have a nice car . . . and I'll use it for your glory'?" Crouch asked. "I think I could do that and in time, as I walked in obedience with God, I believe I'd have it."
>
> Other preachers who appear on the network offer variations on the theme that God appreciates wealth and likes to share it. One of

them, John Avanzini, once told viewers that Jesus, despite his humble image, was a man of means.

"John 19 tells us that Jesus wore designer clothes," Avanzini said, referring to the purple robe that Christ's tormentors wrapped around him before the Crucifixion. "I mean, you didn't get the stuff he wore off the rack. . . . No, this was custom stuff. It was the kind of garment that kings and rich merchants wore."

Houston television preacher Joel Osteen has taken these notions as far as saying that welcoming God's blessings in your life can—and, no, I am not making this up—get a hostess to seat you in a crowded restaurant. Now, maybe I don't fully appreciate the Prosperity Gospel because Cadillac sedans and designer clothes aren't my bag. My favorite restaurants are greasy-spoon diners, and when they're full, I don't mind waiting for a table. Don't get me wrong: I'm not a monk, and I haven't taken a vow of poverty. I make a perfectly good living, drive a four-door automobile, and own my own home. I've just never worried about money much, maybe because my tastes—like fishing for trout and eating cheeseburgers—aren't that exotic.

I don't look down on people who are more concerned about money than I am. I think that's just fine. And while I do object to the use of God's name to extract donations from single parents, elderly widows, and welfare recipients to support the extravagant lifestyles of some televangelists, I'm not losing sleep over the fact that some megachurches are paying their ministers megasalaries. It's not my style, and if the purpose of those salaries is to do God's work in this world, I can think of a lot of better ways to use the money. Still, I can also think of a lot of bigger issues for me to worry about than how much money some of these ministers are getting paid.

But there *is* a decidedly uglier side to the Prosperity Gospel: Once you arrive at the idea that material wealth is a blessing from God, it's a small leap—one many on the radical religious right seem to have taken—to believing poverty is a punishment from heaven.

And that is a profoundly unfaithful idea whose real-world consequences have been terribly damaging. There is no basis in the Bible, not one single word when understood in context rather than wrenched out of place, for believing that God punishes sin with poverty. The Bible explicitly rejects the notion that wealth is a reward. "No one can serve two masters; for a slave will either hate the one and love the other, or be devoted to the one and despise the other. You cannot serve God and wealth," Jesus says in Matthew 6:24. In the book of Revelation, a book many of the purveyors of the prosperity gospel otherwise treat as though it trumps the rest of the Bible, the writer states: "For you say, 'I am rich, I have prospered, and I need nothing.' You do not realize that you are wretched, pitiable, poor, blind, and naked" (Rev. 3:17).

Those words, incidentally, are preceded by a fine bit of political advice for political moderates who have joined the war on the poor rather than fighting it: "I know your works; you are neither cold nor hot. I wish that you were either cold or hot. So, because you are lukewarm, and neither cold nor hot, I am about to spit you out of my mouth" (Rev. 3:15–16). I'd hire Jesus as a campaign consultant over any of the overpriced crowd advising Democrats today. And those words are excellent advice for Middle Church, too. It's time for us to stop being lukewarm about poverty, and it's equally time for us to stop crowing about our wealth or whining about our troubles. There are children in our midst who do not have enough to eat, sick people working two full-time jobs who nonetheless cannot afford to go to the doctor, and elderly people for whom a full life's work is rewarded by economic desperation in old age. Whatever problems I may have are nothing by comparison.

Poverty in America was laid bare, stripped open for all to see and none to deny, by Hurricane Katrina. And like all tragedies, we can rescue hope from this one, if we summon the will. For Katrina presents us with a choice. We can rebuild New Orleans as though it were a Disneyland on the Mississippi, with monorails that transport tourists from one casino to the next without ever seeing the suffering on the ground; we can tear down the wreckage of the Ninth Ward's homes and replace them with luxury condominiums that only the privileged can afford; we can make Mardi Gras a year-round festival and build a city given over to indulgence alone, one so blinded by celebration that the desperation that has persisted there for decades is obscured.

Or we can make New Orleans the model for addressing poverty with the honesty and urgency it demands. We can show ourselves and the world that it is possible to rebuild in a stronger and more environmentally sound way. Rather than suspending worker protections and decent wages for the rebuilding, we can strengthen them. We can harness the urgency of this moment to establish for New Orleans—for our entire nation—what the United Nations has set for the world: clear, achievable, and *accountable* bench marks for overcoming poverty. We can promise ourselves and one another to cut the number of children living in poverty in half by 2015 and eliminate childhood poverty entirely by 2030. We can promise to cut the number of children in substandard schools in half by 2015 and give every child a decent education by 2030. We can ensure that every worker earns enough to meet his or her basic needs. And this is a goal we do not need a decade, or even an hour, to meet. We can do all this with the urgency of what poverty is: a moral and spiritual imperative.

Many on the religious right are also embracing poverty as a defining moral issue. As with the environment, justice for the poor offers opportunities to build alliances on the ground of faith, even with those with whom we otherwise disagree. In early 2005, Ron Sider, president of Evangelicals for Social Action and a conservative, led two hundred evangelical leaders in sending this challenge to President Bush (excerpts below):

January 17, 2005
The Honorable George W. Bush
The White House
1600 Pennsylvania Avenue, NW
Washington, DC 20500

Dear Mr. President:

We write as evangelical leaders to urge a strengthened, expanded emphasis on overcoming hunger and poverty both here and abroad in the next four years. Precisely the commitment to moral values (including the sanctity of human life) that shapes all our political activity compels us to insist that as a nation we must do more to end starvation and hunger and strengthen the capacity of poor people to create wealth and care for their families. . . .

In 2000, virtually every nation on the planet approved the Millennium Development Goals that included a commitment to halve global poverty by 2015. But adequate funds to meet these goals are not being given, and the U.S. ranks absolutely last (as a percentage of GNP) among all developed nations in its governmental assistance to overcome global poverty. Our nations has fallen far short of the increases in health and development assistance that you proposed. The richest nation in history can and must grasp the opportunity to lead.

Poverty in our own nation has increased in the last several years and millions more working poor lack health insurance.

We agree with you that there is a poverty of the soul and a poverty of the wallet and that government should not try to solve the first. We pledge to you to strengthen the armies of compassion in order to do more through our faith-based organizations to overcome the poverty of the soul.

But our faith-based social service agencies cannot by themselves solve the problem of poverty of the wallet. As you have often said, government can and should help solve this problem. Tragically, millions of Americans today work full time and still fall below the poverty level. The moral values that shape our lives tell us this is wrong. We believe our rich nation should agree that everyone who works full time responsibly will be able to earn enough to rise above the poverty level and enjoy health insurance . . .

We call on you, Mr. President, to declare, in your Inaugural or State of the Union address, that it is the policy of your administration to make the necessary improvements in the next four years so that all Americans who work full time responsibly will be able to escape poverty and enjoy health insurance.

Ron and these other evangelicals realized that God's command to care for the poor trumps economic ideology. All of Middle Church must join them in challenging the orthodoxy of far-right economics. The last generation has seen the destruction of communism and the triumph of capitalism as the last and only viable economic system, but capitalism is not a god; it is simply an idea, a way of organizing our labor and wealth. It's an idea that works pretty well most of the time, but we might entertain the idea that capitalism is not perfect. No economic system based on having half the world's population living in wretched poverty could be. Many on the far religious right point to scripture to paint God as a capitalist. Thus the Eighth Commandment, "you shall not steal," becomes the vow pronounced over the heavenly marriage of Moses and Adam Smith, a sacred blessing over the idol of private property.

I don't especially disagree with the obvious fact that the prohibition on stealing presupposes private property. Nor, for that matter, do I know of anyone who seriously believes in an economic system that doesn't include private property. I don't know whether Jesus was a capitalist. I suppose his carpentry was a small business, but I haven't found any references in the Gospels to Jesus paying his dues to the chamber of commerce or objecting to workplace safety standards. I always had the sense God was working at a higher level and on some bigger problems than economic policy. But what I *am* certain of is this: God is *not* calling us to worship unfettered capitalism. On the contrary, God is calling us to challenge its weaknesses, smooth its rougher edges, and, in Jesus' words, bring good news to the poor.

It's time to do for capitalism what the National Council of Churches did for the Bible: produce a New Revised Standard Version. Capitalism NRSV must recognize that every person deserves the dignity of a decent wage, affordable health care, and the hope of a secure retirement. This in turn means a living wage, universal health care, and portable pensions. A creative critique of capitalism must begin with the notion that economic growth is not the end-all, be-all of social life. There are other values that matter too, even—perish the thought—some that just might matter more. When we talk about policies like the minimum wage, pensions, or access to health care, the conversation on both sides inevitably revolves around economic growth: The far right warns that these initiatives would impede growth; the left responds that they would enhance prosperity.

For the record, I happen to fall into the latter camp. In my various adventures in life, I've managed large groups of colleagues, and I have invariably found they were more productive and loyal when they were compensated fairly and treated well. When I was president of the Claremont School of Theology, we implemented a program that helped the faculty purchase homes by making investments from our endowment. The faculty began staying with us longer, and the endowment earned a healthy return. I also understand that leadership requires tough economic choices. When I came to the National Council of Churches, we faced a financial crisis that compelled us to reduce our staff by 50 percent. It was a heart-wrenching effort, but we also made sure to use the opportunity to raise the salaries of everyone we were able to keep, and I believe we get more bang for our buck as a result. And I might add that if the Prosperity Gospel is true and God rewards those who live by the Bible's precepts, then we might expect the hand of heaven to come down and stimulate the economy every time we raise the minimum wage or broaden access to affordable health care.

But in a larger sense, these debates over economic right and wrong obscure the greater point: moral right and wrong. The simple fact of the matter is that I'm willing to pay $1.25 rather than ninety-nine cents for a hamburger at a fast-food restaurant if it means the person frying it can have health care and a living wage. As I said, I don't believe that would be the economic catastrophe the far right always claims, but even in the unlikely event it *did* reduce our economic output slightly, even if the stock market edged down just a point or two, we must still do what is right. God calls us to love the poor. The command is clear, it is unequivocal, and those who are constantly warning against moral relativism should not be implying that the rule does not apply if it might inhibit economic growth. We have enough wealth in our country to ensure that every child eats, every sick person is treated, and every worker has adequate housing. I have little doubt that doing so would actually increase our material wealth. I have even less doubt that wealth is not the point and that arguing only in those terms cedes the moral high ground that we must claim for the least of these, our brothers and sisters.

This critique and fine-tuning of capitalism demands the courageous voices of Middle Church, Middle Synagogue, and Middle Mosque. It requires us to reject the new McCarthyism that derides as socialist anyone who dares to question the perfection of unbridled capitalism. ("Mostly pink" was the label one Republican used when he opposed me for reelection. I'm not sure whether I objected more strongly to the idea that I was socialist or the implication that I believe "mostly" rather than "passionately" in my principles.) When I chaired the Congressional Clearinghouse on the Future during the 1980s, Jonas Salk, the discoverer of the polio vaccine, told us he envisioned two epochs for the world. One emerged after World War II, when we assumed a competitive economic system would always make life better for everyone. "I have a vision for another epoch that's breaking out in the world," I recall him saying. He called it Epoch B, a time that would replace competition with cooperation and collaboration and that would honor quality of life rather than only the quantity of economic output. Someone asked, "How do you get from Epoch A to Epoch B?" Salk thought for a moment and then replied: "In every change in human society there are mutations. And what we need today are intellectual mutants. Those are people like you—average, ordinary, common people who are a mutation, who are willing to bridge the gap between where we are and where we ought to be."

Capitalism is the best economic system available to us. But it is not perfect. And to spread good news to the poor, we need the courage to critique and fine-tune it. We urgently need intellectual mutants, modern day prophets, to take on this important challenge.

CHAPTER 8

# A Living Wage: Washington's Callous Antipathy to the Least of These

*Remain in the same house, eating and drinking whatever they provide, for the laborer deserves to be paid.*
—LUKE 10:7

*Woe to him who builds his house by unrighteousness, and his upper rooms by injustice; who makes his neighbors work for nothing, and does not give them their wages.*
—JEREMIAH 22:13

*Minimum wage is not a biblical issue, that's a union issue.*
—VANCE LACKORE, CHRISTIAN COALITION OF PINELLAS COUNTY, FLORIDA

In 1964, just weeks after he took office, President Lyndon Johnson declared unconditional war on poverty. The years immediately following that call produced some of the most important social and economic legislation in American history, from Head Start to Medicare and Medicaid. It was a war fought on many fronts, one that recognized that poverty has many causes and many consequences, and while it did not succeed in every goal it was a noble undertaking that spoke to the deepest spiritual beliefs of the American people. Since then, the war on poverty has gradually mutated into a war against the poor, a punitive approach that places increasing pressure on the least of these, our brothers and sisters. Today we need a twenty-first-century version of the War on Poverty, a partnership between government and private organizations that takes on the many manifestations of poverty at the dawn of the millennium. From the minimum wage to health care reform to education that unlocks the potential in every young person's mind, we must prevent poverty before it starts and deal with it aggressively when it arises, and we must do so in the spirit of the forty-first Psalm: "Happy are those who consider the poor; the Lord delivers them in the day of trouble" (Ps. 41:1).

## A Living Wage

"But let justice roll down like waters," the prophet Amos said, "and righteousness like an ever-flowing stream" (Amos 5:24). But where is the justice for those among us whose hard and productive labor is rewarded only with poverty? An individual working full time at the minimum wage will earn the less-than-grand total of $10,712 in an entire year: less than the cost of family health coverage, which went for $10,800 in 2005, less even than the poverty line for a single parent and a single child. Two parents working full-time at that wage will earn well below the poverty line for a family of five—not enough for food, clothing, and shelter, to say nothing of such necessities as child care or such distant dreams as saving for college.

Far from getting ahead, minimum wage workers are steadily falling behind. Adjusted for inflation, the minimum wage today is worth less than it was in 1950; as of 2005, it had not been adjusted since 1997, meaning it was steadily losing value for eight straight years. During the same time, pay for members of Congress soared from $133,600 to $162,000, with the increase alone amounting to nearly double the entire annual income of a full-time minimum wage worker. Tom DeLay, an ardent opponent of increasing the minimum wage, once made this heartfelt plea for increasing Congressional pay (read it while imagining mournful violins playing in the background):

Mr. Speaker, I will tell you something: Members of this House have families. They have two homes, in most cases. Some members are living in their offices, because they cannot afford a second residence . . . I am not making excuses or apologizing, it is difficult to raise a family and serve in Congress under these conditions . . . [My] wife and my children sacrifice enough.

That's true, of course; members of Congress do have families. I'm all for paying congress people an adequate salary. But home-health aides have families as well. Fast-food workers cannot afford even one home, much less two, and many sleep in quarters far worse than the comparatively comfortable confines of a Congressional office. The spouses and children of day-care attendants do far more than "sacrifice enough." I bear members of Congress no ill will; I was one, and I value their service. But they and their sufferings are unlikely to make anyone's Top Ten list of America's most disadvantaged groups. By all means, pay them what they deserve, but do not deny the same fair treatment to any other American.

Perhaps—and only perhaps—if corporate America had been suffering all these years, the stagnation of the minimum wage might be justified. But both corporate profits and worker productivity are rising. According to an excellent report compiled by my colleagues Holly Sklar and Reverend Paul Sherry, who lead the National Council of Churches "Let Justice Roll" campaign to increase the minimum wage, inequality is surging. In 1980, the average CEO earned as much as ninety-seven minimum wage workers; by 2004, it took 952 people earning the minimum wage to account for one CEO's pay. (By the way, you can read that report—and I encourage you to—at www.letjusticeroll.org.)

This erosion of the minimum wage is neither an accident nor the product of apathy alone. It is the result of a deliberate successful policy choice by the far right. The *Wall Street Journal* explained that choice in a 2001 article:

"If we would have had our druthers," acknowledges Murray Weidenbaum, the chairman of Mr. Reagan's first Council of Economic Advisers, "we would have eliminated [the minimum wage]." However, because that would have been such a "painful political process," Mr. Weidenbaum says that he and other officials were content to let inflation turn the minimum wage into "an effective dead letter."

The far right has built its campaign against the minimum wage on myths. Two of their favorite arguments—try to overlook the crashing contradiction between them—are first, that increasing the minimum wage would destroy millions of jobs, and second, that nobody actually earns it. The minimum wage is derided as a teenager's pay; adults, they claim, actually earn more. That's factually wrong. Millions of Americans earn the minimum wage, and for millions more, the minimum wage sets a floor that determines their pay. Those working at or below the minimum wage take care of some of the most important jobs in our society. They are home-health aides caring for senior citizens and day-care workers whom we entrust with our children. They cook our food, clean our hotel rooms, and check our groceries. They work every bit as hard as the rest of us, often far harder. They should not be exempted from Jesus' command—a command equally present in Judaism, Islam, and many other faiths—that laborers deserve to be paid. We see them every day; they smile, and we smile back, and the heartache and struggles they face when they get home are invisible to us.

I leave it to people smarter than I am to debate the economic impact of raising the minimum wage. Many economists and businesspeople reject the assumption that doing so destroys jobs: On the contrary, they believe paying a fair wage increases productivity and makes it easier to retain workers. Based on my experience as a manager, I agree, but it is my vocation as a minister that matters more. For the simple fact is that rewarding work with poverty is a moral abomination, plain and simple. It is a violation of faith. Not just mine, but nearly every major faith tradition of which I am aware.

Poverty cannot be eliminated as long as working traps people in poverty rather than helps them climb out of it. We know that lifting the minimum wage to seven dollars an hour would help more than seven million workers; if it tops nine dollars, millions will be lifted out of poverty. A moral minimum wage must also be a living wage, one that reflects the cost of housing, food, and other needs in each individual market. It does not mean the same thing to earn seven dollars an hour in rural Nebraska as it does to earn seven dollars an hour in Boston, New York, or Los Angeles. Despite the stalemate on the minimum wage in Washington, many voters have successfully led living-wage campaigns at the state and local level, passing statutes and ordinances that set minimum pay rates higher than what Washington requires. And these efforts have been led by grassroots activists who have found broad support in the mainstream.

We in Middle Church, Middle Synagogue, and Middle Mosque must add our voices to theirs, and we must bring the critical and decisive component of morality and faith to the debate. Polls show widespread support for increasing the minimum wage; state ballot initiatives to raise minimum wages have passed by overwhelming margins. What we have not yet done is make the living wage a values issue. No other issue so clearly and closely touches on the values of so many different faiths. No other issue could give more meaning to President Bush's still-hollow pledge of "compassionate conservatism."

## Unfaithful Priorities

Here's one for you: An evangelical, a Presbyterian, a Methodist, and a Jew are walking through the U.S. Capitol. No, that's not the start of a bad joke, although I have plenty of them. But this topic is no joke. In 2005, along with Reverend Jim Wallis, Reverend Elenora Giddings

Ivory, and Rabbi David Saperstein, I was one of that small gang, and we were on our way to the Capitol Rotunda. We were on our way to pray that Congress would reconsider what must be regarded as one of the most immoral and unfaithful measures it has ever considered: a budget containing some $50 billion in cuts to aid for the poor, including food stamps, Medicaid, welfare benefits, and early childhood education programs, while extracting not one dime from the very wealthy whose taxes had been cut by hundreds of billions of dollars. This budget was simply the latest and most egregious installment in a decade-long attack on programs for the least of these. Lyndon Johnson's War on Poverty, a noble effort that saved countless lives, was well in the nation's rear-view mirror by this point: Washington was now waging a war on the poor, one made all the more outrageous by the fact that politicians had done so much to ease the "plight" of the privileged. When the shape of the budget became clear, I joined nineteen religious leaders in sending a letter to every member of Congress. Among other points, we wrote that we watched as members of Congress vowed to help rebuild the Gulf Coast. Yet despite those pledges, members of Congress stood ready to cut $50 billion in essential programs, a moral disaster of monumental proportion, and one that was avoidable.

Wallis, Giddings Ivory, Saperstein, and I held our press conference at the Capitol as part of a last-ditch effort to reach members of Congress with a prophetic voice that reflected the values of Middle Church, Middle Synagogue, and Middle Mosque. After the press conference, we went to pray in the Capitol Rotunda. As it happened, I knew some shortcuts from my old days in the House, and because I still carried a photo ID card identifying me as a former member, I was able to get our little crowd around all the security checkpoints and through all the back ways. Just as we were rounding the corner hallway behind the Senate chamber, we spotted Speaker of the House J. Dennis Hastert bounding out of Majority Leader Bill Frist's office. Since we figured God was available to listen to us 24–7 while a meeting with the Speaker of the House was a little tougher to come by, we took the opportunity to corner him.

"Denny! Denny!" I called. In one of those events I like to call a "Godcidence"—not quite a miracle, but a little more than a coincidence too—we caught up with him under the Capitol dome on the exact spot on which Rosa Parks had lain in state just a few days before. I could feel the spiritual power of her presence, the moral power of her courage with us. I have always approached everyone with whom I speak, including politicians and even those as far to my right as Hastert, with the assumption that their hearts, as well as mine, are open and that each of us can reach one another. After all, I come from a tradition based on conversion, a religion in which a Roman citizen who had participated in stonings of Christians was struck by the light of God on the road to Damascus and became a saint. If it worked for Paul, it can work for any of us. I wanted to speak forcefully but also respectfully and in a voice someone who disagreed with me would be able to hear.

"Denny," I said, "we're concerned about what's happening with the budget, and we hope you'll rethink it. The budget is a moral document, and what Congress is doing is immoral."

Hastert looked startled, and his response was gracious but also a touch defensive.

"Well, there's waste in government, and we've got to set priorities," he offered, which was exactly true. Congress *did* need to set priorities, and there *was* waste in government, and that's precisely where I suggested Hastert start.

"We ought to rethink the issue of enormous tax cuts for the wealthy," I answered. "We ought not to balance the budget on the backs of the poor."

Wallis, Saperstein, and Giddings Ivory added their voices, and Hastert parried each of their pleas with defensive protestations about making hard decisions. We parted by promising to keep him in our prayers. We did, but while God may have been attentive to our words, Hastert was not. In an especially callous display, the House voted to pass the budget just six days before Christmas. Once again, politicians who pride themselves on values were on the opposite side from millions of mainstream Americans of faith. I was as outraged by the content of the House's vote as I was by its timing, and in a statement later that day, I noted the irony of the decidedly un-glad tidings being delivered to the poor in the season of Christ's birth:

> The story of Jesus' birth recounts the treasured gifts that the wise men brought to Mary and Joseph—gifts of gold, frankincense, and myrrh. Today, by passing this abysmal budget, the House has delivered hunger, hardship, and suffering to millions of American families. The book of James addresses this issue of favoring the rich over the poor: "But you have dishonored the poor. . . . You do well if you really fulfill the royal law according to the scripture, 'You shall love your neighbor as yourself.' But if you show partiality [to the rich], you commit sin and are convicted by the law as transgressors" (James 2:6a; 8–9).

President Bush's voice of compassion, which had risen when his poll numbers were suffering in the wake of Katrina, was suddenly silenced. He issued a perfunctory statement thanking the House for meeting "national priorities" and urging the Senate to pass the bill quickly. But whose priorities were these? Perhaps they were the priorities of sincere adherents of supply-side economics, maybe they were the priorities of those who believe government should play no role in helping the poor. But whatever else might be said for them, they were surely not God's priorities, not if the teachings of Christianity, Judaism, or Islam are to be believed.

The voices of the far religious right were silent too, except to ignore or pour derision on our efforts to raise a prophetic voice for the poor.

The Christian Coalition, whose 2004 congressional scorecard rated how members voted on several tax breaks but didn't rate any votes on issues affecting the poor, had little criticism when the House voted to heap added misery on people in poverty. James Dobson's Focus on the Family told the *Washington Post* that issues like abortion (which merits not a single word in the Bible) and homosexuality (which is mentioned twice) were more important than help for the poor, which the Bible commands literally dozens upon dozens of times. Tony Perkins of the Family Research Council conjured up a biblical division of labor between the government and the church, one that must have escaped Jesus' notice, for he never once mentioned it: "There is a [biblical] mandate to take care of the poor. There is no dispute of that fact. But it does not say the government should do it. That's a shifting of responsibility." And in perhaps the most offensive statement of the lot, Janice Crouse of Concerned Women for America flatly declared that "the government is not really capable of love."

But in one very limited sense, Perkins had a point. The Bible does not say government should help the poor. For that matter, it doesn't say churches should, either. It simply says *people* should, and I do not know of any individual or institution exempted from that highest of all commands. Government is not the only means we have for making a difference, and for many of my adventures, such as the People's Emergency Center, it has not been the means that I chose. But government is how we express ourselves and our values as a people. It is often the single largest lever we have for moving large amounts of resources when circumstances call for them. It is the only institution capable of compelling corporations and individuals to observe the rules of fair play in the marketplace. And simply to write the government off, to concoct some false distinction by which the Bible deprives it of jurisdiction or relieves it of responsibility, is to surrender an important and often powerful means of helping the poor while letting politicians off the hook.

To say government can do many things is not to say government can or should do everything. There are enough problems in our world not to ration responsibility for them. There is no need for turf wars between government, businesses, religious institutions, and other nonprofits. All can be part of the solution, and each must give all it can for there to be any hope of overcoming some of the most horrific injustices in our world. Churches, synagogues, and mosques are absolutely indispensable deliverers of social services. One study by the National Council of Churches found there are actually more children in church on Monday mornings, attending programs like Head Start, than there are on Sunday mornings. Churches can play a vital role in dealing with many problems, including the critical lack of quality day care for many working parents. But the faith community alone cannot handle the vast scale of poverty in the United States. We and government must be partners in the cause of love, in the monumental task of caring for our brothers and sisters.

The faith community can offer an important advantage: Unlike writing a check to a distant charity or paying taxes to the government, we can provide opportunities to engage personally, in human terms, with those who need our help. Such engagement defeats poverty's greatest ally: the anonymity of the other. Among the many reasons I love Habitat for Humanity is that the recipients of homes help the volunteers build them. It's as important for those who give as it is for those who receive. For when we see the least of these as human beings, when we look into their eyes and see their struggles and hear their dreams, we can no longer entertain the fantasy that they are different from us, that they somehow deserve their difficulties. Instead we are confronted with the reality that each of us is no more than a twist of fate—a diagnosis, a factory closing—away from poverty. And when we unburden ourselves of the baggage of judgment, our spirits—every bit as much as those of the people we help—can soar.

There are also times when partnerships between government and religious institutions may with very careful safeguards make sense. I do not object in principle to the idea of President Bush's faith-based initiative. Churches, synagogues, and mosques often have intimate familiarity with their communities and expertise in delivering social services from which government can benefit. But such partnerships must be undertaken with great care to preserve religious freedom. Just after President Bush took office, Jerry Falwell urged that faith-based funding be withheld from Muslim groups: "The Muslim faith teaches hate," he falsely (one might even say "hatefully") declared. Others on the far religious right began warning with horror that cults might be eligible for funds. Such fear-mongering shows the ease with which a financial relationship between government and religious institutions can slide into government favoring of some religions over others. And when religious institutions are the *only* available source of social services, the temptation to use these supports as intimidating or coercive tools for proselytizing may be overwhelming, however sincere one's intentions.

Perhaps these difficulties can be adequately addressed. But a far larger difficulty looms: As long as government practices outright hostility to the poor with the tacit approval of the far religious right, no private efforts, no matter how heroic, will be able to alleviate the misery that remains all too prevalent in our society. And when it comes to balancing the budget on the backs of the poor, I am far less concerned about the approval of the religious right than I am about the apathy of the religious center. Whatever else the faults of the radical religious right may be, you have to admire the fear and respect they strike in the hearts of elected officials, many of whom dread nothing more than ending up on the wrong side of a Christian Coalition congressional scorecard. But Middle Church is faithful too, and our numbers are even stronger. Until we are willing to raise our prophetic voices with the same force with which the far right speaks, we must expect Washington to continue giving short shrift to our values.

### Reaping What We Sow: Investing in People's Lives

When Paul warned the Galatians that "you reap whatever you sow," he was not dispensing agricultural advice. He meant that our actions, spiritual or otherwise, in any given moment have consequences and, conversely, that outcomes we do not like are often the result of efforts we did not make. "So," he says in Galatians 6:9, "let us not grow weary in doing what is right, for we will reap at harvest time, if we do not give up." It was an epistle of spiritual redemption; Galatians would serve equally well as a platform for human development. For we cannot expect to reap a harvest of productive and peaceful lives if we do not sow the seeds of each individual's potential.

Suppose, rather than balancing the budget on the backs of the poor, government built our future on their shoulders? Modest investments in education and crime prevention would pay dividends several times over, and the moral returns would far exceed the monetary ones. Yet public education is struggling under the weight of constant neglect and occasional assault. One reason is that the proliferation of religious schools that accelerated after the *Brown v. Board of Education* decision as a means of dodging desegregation has triggered a movement for vouchers that drain resources out of the public schools. I have nothing against religious schools; I know many parents who have sent their children to them, and many very fine young people who have graduated from them. Merle and I sent our own children to public school, and we believe they benefited from, and were broadened by, exposure to a wide and diverse circle of peers who were not from the same socioeconomic group. Still, whatever one thinks of private schools, it was churches that first led the charge for public education back in the nineteenth century, and we must once more offer a prophetic voice to say public schools need more support, not less. Yet in this area as in so many others, the voice of Middle Church is all too hushed. Of the National Council of Churches' thirty-five member communions, only one—the United

Church of Christ—employs a full-time staff person whose primary responsibility is encouraging support for public education.

Public schools have also suffered from declining political support as populations have aged. Senior citizens who now commonly live into their eighties, nineties, and beyond are often resentful of the property taxes they must pay to finance public education. Some of these complaints come from seniors living on thinly stretched and highly fixed incomes, who genuinely cannot afford the bills, and they need and deserve protection from rising taxes. Others come from more comfortable retirees whom we must confront with a moral challenge. The most effective strategy both educationally and politically is building bridges between the old and the young, two segments of our most vulnerable populations, by getting retirees involved in schools. This retiree involvement is a growing trend of which I learned on a recent trip to visit my elderly mother in New Jersey.

"Mom, do you need to run any errands?" I asked.

"Yeah," she replied. "I need to drop off this book for a little girl at the school."

Mom Edgar, it turned out, was mentoring a kindergartner at the elementary school right behind the senior center that she attends daily. I drove her up to the door, and my eighty-one-year-old mother, who earned her GED in her fifties, climbed out of the car, walked up to the front door, asked for a pass, and visited the girl's classroom. The fastest-growing segment of our population is people over age one hundred, the next fastest are those over the age of eighty-five. As Americans live longer, often spending literally decades in retirement, they both desire and benefit from a vocation. Working with young people may be the very best thing for both groups, and that is a connection that institutions of faith can facilitate.

Even where property taxes enjoy broad support, widespread inequities in property values often leave the disadvantaged students who most desperately need education stranded in the least funded schools. They attend schools that are falling down around them, study from books that are often years out of date, and are taught by educators who, while often doing a heroic job under terribly difficult circumstances, are paid less than their peers in wealthier districts. These same students must then compete for jobs, scholarships, and scarce college admissions slots with other young people who have attended public schools with high-tech computers, fully equipped labs, up-to-date books, and many of the most sought-after teachers. Personally, I would prefer that schools be funded with a source of money entirely different from property taxes, but at a minimum, state, federal, and other funds must help to balance the inequities. Here, too, churches, synagogues, and mosques can be catalysts for change, as the National Council of Churches was in supporting Good Schools Pennsylvania, a statewide campaign that has successfully pushed for reforms in school financing.

Education is one of many strategies that might divert young people from crime. Punishment is often the most appropriate response to crime, but it is also almost always the most expensive means of protecting society. Early intervention in young people's lives, helping those who do go astray to put their lives back together, rather than consigning them forever to the most troubled corners of our society, is far cheaper, and far more moral, than putting them in prison for the rest of their lives. As a young minister, one of my duties was serving as the chaplain at the federal penitentiary in Lewisburg, Pennsylvania. I ran a Bible study group there each week. There were few angels in the bunch, and many who fully deserved to be there. But there were others desperate to salvage their lives, and many who had been driven to crime only by desperation. I remember one young man who robbed a bank and then made a deliberately slow getaway in a yellow convertible—not exactly the kind of car likely to pass unnoticed—in a deliberate attempt to get caught. Life in prison seemed more secure than the desperate existence he endured on the outside. But surely incarcerating him for fifteen years was neither the moral nor the expedient thing for society to do. We could have reached him—just as we can turn around many other young lives—much earlier.

Today's tough-on-crime political climate is neither good policy nor an accurate reflection of a religion built on the concept of redemption. Jesus bestowed the blessing of forgiveness on the criminals who were crucified alongside him on Golgotha. There is an excellent case to be made that he would counsel mercy to us, but there can be no doubt he would prefer that we invest in young lives before crime ever becomes an option. Politicians are fond of declaring their loyalty to the "three strikes and you're out" policy, but it seems far more sensible and faithful to me to focus on preventing the first strike. We also know that crime, like poverty, can become a cycle in which entire families are trapped for generations. There are some two million young people who have a parent in prison, and statistics indicate 75 percent of them will someday be in prison themselves. Minister and former Philadelphia mayor Wilson Goode's Amachi program, which mentors children of prisoners using both federal funds and charitable contributions, is an excellent example of the kind of partnership between the faith community and government. Reverend Goode is salvaging lives and, I have no doubt, saving money, too.

Any strategy for investing in people's lives and achieving economic justice must also include affordable health care as a basic human right. Forty-five million Americans—a number growing by as much as a million a year—have no health insurance, and like the poor, they are largely those who work. In Matthew 10, Jesus summons the apostles and gives them the authority to heal the sick. Can we not see ourselves as their heirs, those whom God is calling to care for the sick, not with miracles but with the far easier resource of modern medicine? That includes diseases of the mind as well as the body, for addiction and mental illness are physiological ailments, too, and can be every bit as devastating as any other illness. I know, for

my nephew, who suffers from bipolar disorder, has been in and out of
clinics as often as he is in and out of homes and on and off the streets
of San Diego. He lives in the netherworld between health conditions
for which society has sympathy and others of which we are scared.
But that is a false and primitive distinction of which science has long
since disabused us.

Businesses have always howled that universal health care will cost
jobs and money. Once more, I reply that in any version of faith, no
matter where one worships, what is right must supersede what is
economically expedient, especially when the human right to health
care is pitted against the profits of corporate hospitals and drug companies. Moreover, dependable, universal health care, like portable
pensions that workers can take from job to job, also enables people to
be more productive, mobile, and entrepreneurial rather than feeling
trapped in a job for fear of losing their benefits. The economic fact is
that affordable health care pays. The spiritual fact, the more relevant
fact, is that some things are more important than money. There
comes a time when the relentless proliferation of new drugs is mean-
ingless when so many people cannot afford the ones that already
exist. The profits of corporate hospitals do not outweigh the rights of
a sick person whose illness is treatable but who cannot afford to go to
the doctor.

None of these are cure-alls; there are no easy fixes for poverty. To
be sure, all these efforts—education, crime prevention, health care,
and others—cost money, and if you cannot reap what you do not
sow, you also cannot sow seeds you cannot afford. But the question is
not simply whether we can afford to invest in better lives, it is
whether we can afford not to. No nation in history has ever been as
wealthy as the United States, and many societies far less rich than
ours provide outstanding education and universal health care. The
United States could reduce defense programs by two-thirds, invest
that $300 billion in education and health care, and still spend more
on our military than any other nation on earth. I am not suggesting

we should necessarily do this; I use the illustration to point out the indisputable fact that our government's priorities are the product of our choices, and it is time our choices reflected our values. What we lack is not money. It is simply the will to act.

## Voting with our Pocketbooks:
## Supporting Those Who Support the Least of These

The government may have hundreds of billions of dollars to spend, but each faithful American has a resource that can also make a significant difference: the dollars in our own pockets. I don't mean personal charity, although that's certainly important. I mean leveraging our dollars into widespread social change by supporting companies that support our values, especially standing with the least of these, our brothers and sisters. And therein lies an inspiring story that begins with the unlikeliest of products: pickles.

We rarely think of it when we fish a pickle out of the jar and crunch down on it, but these refugees from the relish tray are actually a massive industry. This business sometimes thrives on the backs of one of the most abused segments of the labor force: farm workers. Farm workers are already exempted from many of the federal wage and labor standards that protect other workers, and when they are migrants, as is often the case, they feel even more vulnerable. The slightest complaint, much less an effort to organize, often means being branded a troublemaker, having one's visa or work permit revoked, and being deported back to a life of poverty that makes even the most deplorable working conditions here seem preferable by comparison.

In the late 1990s, the National Farm Worker Ministry received reports detailing the unsafe and unsanitary conditions in the camps and fields in which workers, most of them legal migrants from Mexico, toiled on farms that supplied the Mt. Olive Pickle Company in North Carolina. When the National Council of Churches became involved, I visited the area myself. Most of the workers had arrived from Mexico by bus, carrying H-2 visas, and been dumped at a farm with little idea of their rights. They lived in ramshackle, barracks-style housing, often putrid and barely heated. Some had only one toilet, which was either broken or filthy. The lucky ones had a single refrigerator to share. Workers suffered disabling injuries and frequently lacked access to medical treatment. Because they were paid by the bushel rather than by the hour, many earned far less than the minimum wage—often as little as fifty-five cents for picking a thirty-three-pound bucket of cucumbers—and it was not uncommon for farm workers not to receive even their meager pay for work already performed. Farmers often charged rent for their dilapidated living quarters, reducing their take home pay to barely over one hundred dollars a month.

Yet they were trapped: They were living in squalor, but the misery in which their families in Mexico lived was worse, and they were willing to endure the travails of the farms to squeeze out a few extra dollars to send home. And they knew that complaining often meant a fast ticket home and the end of what little hope their families entertained for a better life.

It was a despicable cycle of exploitation that recalled the story of 1 Kings 12, when the Israelites ask Rehoboam, Solomon's son, to lighten the heavy load the latter had placed upon them. "Your father made our yoke heavy," they complain. "Now therefore lighten the hard service of your father and his heavy yoke that he placed on us, and we will serve you." Rehoboam asks the counsel of his father's elderly attendants, and they answer sensibly: "If you will be a servant to this people today and serve them, and speak good words to them when you answer them, then they will be your servants forever." But Rehoboam insists on following the callous advice of his young and impetuous advisors, attempting to discipline the Israelites rather than partnering with them: "My father made your yoke heavy, but I will add to your yoke; my father disciplined you with whips, but I will discipline you with scorpions." Within two verses, Rehoboam's taskmaster has been stoned and the king has been forced to flee.

Fortunately, the courageous farmworkers who formed an organizing committee despite the risks they knew they faced were intent on more peaceful means than stoning. They tried persuasion and bargaining first; when that failed, they called for a consumer boycott that the National Council of Churches endorsed. The farmers in North Carolina and the corporate leadership of Mt. Olive Pickles were a long way from Rehoboam and his taskmaster, but the lesson was applicable: Had they treated the workers with dignity, the migrants would have been more loyal and more productive. Exploiting them was both morally wrong and economically unwise. I felt that the corporate executives, like the Israeli king, could use a touch of gray-haired counsel, so along with several other religious leaders of many denominations, both Protestant and Catholic, I went to lobby them and their suppliers.

The CEO of Mt. Olive is a fellow named Bill Bryan, a down-to-earth, decent, and genetically nice man who seemed to get a little more irritated every time I patted his arm and told him so. "You're so nice," I'd say. "Why don't you help these workers and try to solve this problem?" Bill was a fellow United Methodist, and the fact that the name of his company was so similar to the Mount of Olives, near the Garden of Gethsemane, where Christ, the greatest labor organizer of all time, prayed before his arrest, added moral power to our appeal. Most of those in authority I met were nice people who invariably had good excuses for their exploitative labor practices. The pickle company blamed the farmers, the farmers blamed the pickle company, and the carousel of finger-pointing spun around and around. They, too, reminded me of a valuable lesson: Just as each of us is only a step removed from poverty, each of us is also only a step removed from immoral behavior, a step all mortals take from time to time. Sometimes, as Jesus reminded us, we get so focused on the speck in someone else's eye that we can't see the log in our own. North Carolina farmers, corporate chieftains, and Washington politicians are rarely ever evil sorts playing the part of a movie villain. More often than not, they are good people who like all of us have enormous powers of self-justification for bad behavior.

But it was less moral persuasion than the simple power of the purse that changed their minds. A boycott encompassing the forty-five million Christians belonging to National Council of Churches member communions as well as the many other people reached by the organizers was too much of an economic strain for Mt. Olive and the pickle growers to bear. They signed an agreement guaranteeing the eight thousand migrant farm workers in North Carolina the right to organize and file grievances. Mt. Olive agreed to pay more for pickles and give farmers financial incentives to provide better pay and benefits. In an especially inspiring moment, the signing ceremony was presided over by religious leaders, a stirring testament to the power of faith and the true essence of spiritual values.

Suppose people of faith were to take similar approaches to other large corporations that exploit workers? What if we were to say to Wal-Mart, just as we said to Mt. Olive, that the faithful religious center is comprised of tens of millions of people who are willing to pay just a little bit more for products so those who make and sell them can live a decent and dignified existence that accords with our spiritual values? And, conversely, that we are prepared to boycott those products rather than subsidize and reward exploitation? The experience with Mt. Olive suggests we have the power to make a difference if only we are willing to use it. The boycott proved what Rehoboam learned the hard way, that treating people with dignity is cheaper than dealing with them harshly. It also demonstrated a lesson equally applicable to politics: When we leverage our prophetic voices with courage, values, and, when need be, our wallets, Middle Church, Middle Synagogue, and Middle Mosque are a force to rival any other in America today.

CHAPTER 9

# The Poverty That Kills:
# Hunger, Injustice, and AIDS:
# Our Global Moral Crisis

*When Jesus had come down from the mountain, great
crowds followed him; and there was a leper who came to him
and knelt before him, saying, "Lord, if you choose, you can
make me clean." He stretched out his hand and touched him,
saying, "I do choose. Be made clean!" Immediately his leprosy was cleansed.*
—MATTHEW 8:1–3

*AIDS could be God's judgment against a nation that chooses
to live immorally.*
—JERRY FALWELL

The first time I saw the poverty that kills, poverty so wrenching
and steeped in misery that it claims lives in addition to hope, I
was eighteen years old. It was also the first time I saw the possibilities of faith, the profound and life-saving results that occur when we
match spiritual values with worldly action. The time was July 1961,
and I was a naïve young man of eighteen whose only exposure to
poverty had been distant glimpses of deteriorating neighborhoods
out the window of the Chester bus. My world, the world I saw at
church and school and on our suburban street, was clean and white
and overwhelmingly middle class, or at least close enough to it for me
to believe just about everybody lived in similar comfort.

Just after I graduated from high school, I traveled to Europe as a youth delegate to the Tenth World Methodist Conference in Oslo, Norway. Seventeen girls and around half a dozen boys formed the delegation (an excellent ratio, I thought), and we traveled to eleven European countries, visiting missions, seeing sights, and feeling for all the world like globe-trotting diplomats visiting distant lands. But no tourist or historic sight we visited prepared me for what I saw out the window of our bus as we drove through Naples, Italy, one morning. I looked out at the most horrendous slum you could imagine, not a run-down housing project with boarded windows and sirens in the background but genuine hovels. Shacks made of tin and cardboard were piled one on top of the other, and the only sign of modernity was the aerial television antennas that occasionally jutted out from the crumbling roofs and walls. The stench was overwhelming. Children who were barely clothed and completely dirty were playing in slime and filth.

The slum went on for block after block until the bus pulled up to a gate on a street called Corso Garibaldi. On the other side lay the villa where we would stay overnight, a beautiful stucco estate once owned by the prince of Monaco. The buildings were a subtle red, the shutters on the windows behind the balconies a vivid green. The grounds teemed with well-kempt children, neatly washed and groomed, dressed in clean, Western-looking clothes. They chattered and sang, and attentive caregivers followed their every move. This was the orphanage of Casa Materna. Founded a half-century earlier, its operation interrupted only for a brief period during World War II when the German command occupied the grounds, the orphanage was run by Methodist ministers and deaconesses. All that separated the children on the inside from those huddled under cardboard boxes within shouting distance from the gate was luck—and love. It was a day of stark contrasts and stirring inspiration, the first time I fully contemplated the tremendous impact people of faith could make on their world, and it cemented my decision to enter the ministry.

Nearly a half-century has passed since then. Unfortunately, Casa Materna closed a few years ago due to lack of resources. I have not been back to Naples since, and I suspect the tin-and-cardboard slums have long since been cleaned up. But the poverty that kills is with us every bit as much as it was in 1961. I have traveled to even farther corners of the world, and from Kenya to Korea, there is hardly a place where I have not seen it. The National Council of Churches operates a humanitarian relief organization called Church World Service whose work allows us access to corners of the world that are normally shielded from view. When we traveled to North and South Korea on a humanitarian mission in November 2003, even the poverty in the south would have seemed luxurious in the north. Having barely survived a famine, the people of North Korea still endured some of the harshest poverty on earth. North and South Korea are part of the same peninsula and arose from the same ancient culture. Yet flying overhead in a small plane, I could see that the difference between the two countries was striking and evident even from the air. In the south, the scenery was green and lush; in North Korea, even the countryside looked as barren and torn-up as a construction site. Anything that grows had been either eaten for food or burned for fuel. Vast hillsides were completely stripped of vegetation. The people in the south wore vibrant, colorful clothes, drove cars, and had plenty to eat. In the north, the clothing was drab and tattered, nearly all the people looked gaunt, and as we looked out the window of our bus, we saw farmers plowing their fields with oxen. There was hardly a car in sight, and not a single piece of mechanized farm equipment. I felt as though we had been jettisoned back to 1910.

The poverty that kills is a moral blight on all humanity. Every day—*every day*—twenty thousand people die of poverty-related causes such as malnutrition, poor sanitation, and the simplest of diseases, ailments like diarrhea that are easily treated with over-the-counter medications in the developed world. More than one billion of the world's people, each of them created in God's image, and entrusted to our care as our brothers and sisters, are attempting to survive on one dollar a day. More than 800 million people are so malnourished they cannot meet their daily energy needs. Hunger in early childhood, when the brain and body are developing and starved for nutrients, is a particular tragedy whose effects are felt throughout life, yet the very young are one of the world's most malnourished groups.

But the greatest moral blight is not the poverty itself, but the wealth amid which it exists and, even worse, the ease with which it could be cured. If the world's wealthiest nations devoted just 0.7 percent of their income—less than one dollar out of every one hundred—we could cut in half the poverty that kills within a decade. Yet the United States gives less than one half of one percent of our national income to help the world's poorest countries. The poverty that kills is a massive problem but not a complicated one. It is not the result of complicated social problems; it is poverty in the simplest, textbook sense, the kind that arises solely from lack of money. People in the developing world die of malaria because they cannot afford mosquito nets for their beds; they die of dysentery because their communities cannot build or repair their sewer systems; they die of hunger because they cannot purchase food. And this is one of those very few areas where simply spending money can, all by itself, save millions of lives.

The financial needs are modest. Still, meeting them will require the Casa Materna within each of our hearts and each of our communities—the commitment to unconditional, biblical love in the midst of misery and squalor. More than any other, this is a crisis that demands Middle Church, Middle Synagogue, and Middle Mosque. One of the most prophetic voices being raised on the poverty that kills is that of Jeffrey Sachs, a Columbia University economist with whom I have had the pleasure to work. He is a brilliant man whose eyes contain both the memory of all the misery he has seen around the world and the optimism of a man who knows it can be cured.

Sachs came up with the idea of the Millennium Development Challenge Goals, eight simple goals, each matched with specific policies and targets, for cutting in half the poverty that kills by 2015:

+ Goal 1: Eradicate Extreme Poverty and Hunger—by halving the proportion of people living on less than one dollar a day and the proportion of people who suffer from hunger.

+ Goal 2: Achieve universal primary education.

+ Goal 3: Promote gender equality—by eliminating the pervasive practice of gender discrimination in schools.

+ Goal 4: Reduce child mortality—by cutting the under-five mortality rate by two-thirds.

+ Goal 5: Improve maternal health—by reducing the ratio of mothers killed in childbirth by three-quarters.

+ Goal 6: Combat AIDS, malaria, and other diseases—by cutting their incidence in half and reversing their spread.

+ Goal 7: Ensure environmental sustainability—including cutting the proportion of people without sustainable access to safe drinking water by half, significantly improving the living conditions of at least one hundred million slum dwellers, and reversing the loss of environmental resources.

+ Goal 8: Develop a global partnership for development—one that brings the public, private, and non-governmental organization sectors together to address global issues like free trade, debt of developing countries, and access to pharmaceuticals and technology.

Imagine someone handing you a one-hundred-dollar bill and saying that if you gave seventy cents back, you could achieve every goal on that list, every last one, transforming the lives of more than one billion of the least of these. We can! The tiniest fraction of the wealthiest nations' income could accomplish all this through steps as simple as purchasing mosquito nets to protect residents of tropical areas from malaria while they sleep. Sachs has proven himself to be as adept at diplomacy and activism as he is at economics, for his vision has captivated the world and its most prominent leaders. The United Nations is leading a global effort to implement the Millennium Development Goals, and most developed nations, including the United States, have promised to do their part.

But promises do not save lives—only money can—and we are neither keeping all our promises nor doing all that we can. The United States spends less than twenty cents of every one hundred dollars in national income on development for the poor, and many nations that have pledged their support are faring little better. The results are clear in the spotty progress humanity has made toward these goals. In sub-Saharan Africa, the proportion of people living on less than a dollar a day has actually *grown*, from 44.6 to 46.4 percent. We have seen malnutrition get better, but progress has slowed in recent years, and nearly all the progress has now been wiped out by deterioration. Declines in the number of women who die in childbirth have escaped those parts of the world that suffered from the most intense problems. Perhaps most disturbing, AIDS is surging. Fully seven out of every one hundred people in sub-Saharan Africa is now infected, a toll so stunning and heart-breaking our imaginations can hardly accommodate it. Every region of the developing world has endured large increases in the incidence of AIDS. In Southern Asia, its prevalence has skyrocketed nearly ten times over. We know that all these problems are exacerbated by conflict and that the persistence of such misery, in turn, inflames conflict, whether it is disputes over scarce resources, ethnic violence, or fanatical terrorism.

And yet, as much as these figures must shock the world out of its apathy, there is also reason for that most faithful of attributes: hope. Across the developing world, the total proportion of people living on less than a dollar a day is actually falling. Remarkable strides in gender equity, especially in elementary and secondary schools, have been made. Sanitation has been improved for millions upon millions of people. We know—we absolutely *know*, with no doubt at all—that every Millennium Development Goal is achievable. These goals are the Beatitudes, the Ten Commandments, of our day; each of them is that sacred, for I cannot imagine anything being more important to God.

Anytime I begin to feel despair, to entertain the notion that these problems might be too vast to be solved, I remember a nun named Sister Peggy Healy. I met Sister Peggy in 1981 on my congressional trip to Central America, where she was the Maryknoll order's representative. A nurse practitioner who had given over her life to ministering to the barrios of Managua, where wretched poverty persisted, Sister Peggy showed me through the slums and told me about the December day the year before when she drove two of her colleagues to the airport for a mission to El Salvador. Hours after they landed, they were met by two other religious women. As they drove from the airport, all four were kidnapped and brutally murdered. They were her sisters both religiously and figuratively, colleagues who had shared her love for the poor and filled her life and the barrios of Managua with hope. Suddenly, one day, they were gone. Yet there was not a trace of bitterness or despair in Sister Peggy's voice. There was the most profound sorrow, to be sure, but her sadness was overcome by the joy she brought to the barrios. Hers was a life of commitment and hope that transcended a tragedy the rest of us can only imagine. And if she did not surrender to despair, neither must we.

We must both give from our own hearts and wallets and speak with prophetic and insistent voices for dramatic increases in government funds. The increases must be dramatic because we invest so little today, but the entire amount needed to implement the Millennium Development Goals would barely dent our economy.

Our policies, not simply our pocketbooks, must change, especially when it comes to battling the AIDS epidemic. While there is growing recognition of the crisis, especially the full-blown catastrophe that is engulfing Africa, our response is still inhibited by domestic politics, especially the far religious right's ongoing and irresponsible opposition to the use of condoms. The insistence of such groups as the Family Research Council on funding only abstinence-based AIDS programs in the developing world is as naïve as it is deadly. Personally, I would just as soon that everyone practice responsible sexual behavior; we Americans, living in a society saturated with both the practice and encouragement of casual sex, are in no moral position to lecture the rest of the world about abstinence. As for safe sex, I do not know what God thinks of condoms, but I am confident the God in whom I have placed my faith does not want an entire continent of our brothers and sisters destroyed in a dispute over their use.

The far religious right's opposition to condoms and the insistence on abstinence-only programs carries—perhaps unintentionally and certainly, I hope and believe, not maliciously—the distant echoes of those early days of the epidemic when Jerry Falwell and others openly described the disease as a vengeful God's just punishment for errant behavior. AIDS in many ways has become for some in our world what leprosy was in Jesus' time, the disease of outcasts, one the fortunate and healthy were content to deride as a heavenly punishment. Today we must heed Jesus' example and go into the houses of the lepers, heal their bodies with our medicines, and touch their hearts with our love.

President Bush raised a courageous and prophetic voice in this effort when he pledged $15 billion over five years to fight AIDS in Africa. But the promise was empty: The first budget his own administration submitted to Congress after he made that pledge asked for less than half a billion dollars. When I joined a group of faith leaders meeting with then National Security Advisor Condoleezza Rice to discuss the administration's AIDS initiative, she was full of excuses for the lack of funds. A program that large could not, in her phrase, be "ramped up" quickly. Local governments were corrupt and might steal some of the money if we gave it to them. But while I believe in Dr. Rice's sincerity—she was one of the officials who persuaded Bush that AIDS must be a priority—her excuses were as empty as his promises. There were religious institutions in every one of those countries through whom the funding could have been targeted. It is difficult for me not to speculate that the administration trimmed its sails rather than incur the wrath of the radical religious right. Even if it did not bow to the far right, the White House certainly failed to hear the voices and values of Middle Church, Middle Synagogue, and Middle Mosque.

AIDS, like each of the Millennium Development Goals, demands an absolute and unrelenting effort led personally by the president. He was willing to brandish his veto pen when Congress threatened to limit his authority to torture terrorist suspects; he should show as much commitment to eliminating the poverty that kills. How refreshing it would be to read that President Bush has promised to veto any congressional budget that does not include full funding—every last cent—for both his AIDS initiative and the Millenium Development Goals. Politicians should be equally aggressive in courting corporate contributions, whether they come in the form of money or products and services. They know how to work CEOs for campaign contributions; surely they can apply the same skills to extracting resources for reducing the poverty that kills.

Despite the relative ease with which we could make such tremendous progress toward those goals, the plight of the world's poorest people, those who are dying from their poverty and our indifference, remains largely outside the orbit of Americans' attention. The victims of poverty live in conditions that so exceed our imagination that we must challenge ourselves not to consign them to the role of the faceless other whose lives we neither see nor save. That we are Americans is but a geographic coincidence. There is not a soul in any of us that could not just as easily have been breathed into the body of a newborn baby in Africa or Asia for whom a case of diarrhea can be a death sentence, an ear infection can mean going deaf, or a vitamin deficiency can cause blindness. If we wish to call our citizenship the divine providence of God, perhaps that is fine, but we must not indulge the arrogance that implies God values the life of any other person, anywhere, any less.

In the international arena even more than at home, we need the courage to subject capitalism to a mid-course correction. Peasants in countries like China work in nearly slave-like conditions so that we can buy and sell cheaper products. We exploit the limited and non-renewable natural resources of other countries—precious metals from Africa, oil from South America and the Middle East, and more—so that we can pay less for our consumer goods. We promote free trade, a policy I fully agree is the very best hope for helping the people of the developing world to help themselves, but resist international labor standards that create a truly level playing field and protect those we seek to help from exploitation. We have helped to hook some of the world's poorest countries on debt they can never repay. The inequality between the prosperity we enjoy and the wrenching poverty of the global labor force that makes it possible is too crushing, too wide, too immoral to escape our notice.

It is time for a New Revised Standard Version of international capitalism, and it must begin with the simple proposition that each of God's children deserves love equally. That does not mean all incomes must be equal; least of all does it mean wages in Phuket must equal those in Philadelphia or that a factory worker in Nairobi must make the same as his or her counterpart in New York. But we can make economic life more equal without making it fully or literally equal; we can say we value the life and labor of an African no less than those of an American. The world is calling faithful Americans in words similar to those Jesus spoke to his disciples: "Just as you did it to one of the least of these who are members of my family, you did to me." They need resources, and we must share them; above all, they need hope, and God is calling us to be the hope-givers. The world cries out to us in the words of 1 Chronicles 29:15: "For we are aliens and transients before you, as were all our ancestors; our days on the earth are like a shadow, and there is no hope." And we must answer in the aspiration of Psalm 9: "For the needy shall not always be forgotten, nor the hope of the poor perish for ever."

## CHAPTER 10

# Changing Our Beatitudes: Guideposts for Deep-Water Citizenship

*Blessed are those who are persecuted for righteousness' sake...*
—MATTHEW 5:10

*Discrimination against people of faith, particularly Christians, has become an epidemic in this country.*
—MATHEW D. STAVER, PRESIDENT AND FOUNDER OF LIBERTY COUNSEL, A GROUP PROVIDING LEGAL SUPPORT TO FAR RELIGIOUS RIGHT CAUSES

If only it were true.

If only Christians and other Americans of faith were so appalled at poverty, war, and environmental degradation that we rose up and protested our government's policies with a voice so passionate that we were persecuted for righteousness' sake. But persecution is not our problem. Indifference is, for we are so caught up in the daily challenges of our lives that we have allowed our faith and our government along with it to be stolen from under us. The prophetic voices are silent only because the faithful majority of Middle Church, Middle Synagogue, and Middle Mosque have not yet chosen to raise them. And if we are to reclaim our nation, as I believe we must and, in equal measure, I know that we *can*, we must shake ourselves from our complacency and connect the values of the faith we share with the policies of the nation we cherish.

The voice of faith in American politics today comes primarily from the far religious right, and it is a version of faith so at odds with mine, so contrary to the central teachings of Christianity, Judaism, and Islam, that it condones poverty, condemns peace, and contributes to the despoiling of God's creation. As I write these words, the extreme religious right and those who share or submit to their worldview control both the White House and the Congress. They have answered their success with a newfound cry: We are persecuted. The claim reached its wildest height—or, from my point of view, depth—with the 2005 campaign to "save" Christmas, which, from what I was able to ascertain in my own exposure to shopping malls, was never in mortal danger. John Gibson of the Fox News Channel published an entire book titled—and I had to double-check this to make sure it wasn't a joke—*The War on Christmas*. (Memo to Fox Television: Quit stealing Dr. Seuss's ideas. America isn't Whoville and non-Christians aren't the Grinch.) Speaker of the House Denny Hastert ordered that the National *Holiday* Tree on the Capitol lawn be restored to its previous glory as the National *Christmas* Tree. Jerry Falwell called for a boycott of stores that employ the phrase "Happy Holidays" rather than "Merry Christmas" in their marketing. Many on the far religious right even excoriated the White House for inscribing its Christmas cards with "Happy Holidays."

I suppose I should say for the record that a big spruce tree with shiny lights, ornaments, and an angel on top looks a lot like a Christmas tree to me, and I don't have any particular objection to calling it one, nor, as far as I know, do any of my Jewish or Muslim friends. I hadn't noticed an insidious campaign to banish Christmas from our department stores. If anything, I'd be pleased if they'd ease up a bit on the whole buy-things-for-Christ's-sake routine. Nor am I aware of any Jews, Muslims, or people of other faiths taking offense to the phrase "Merry Christmas." But if it would salve some fragile spiritual psyches for stores to greet shoppers with "Merry Christmas" rather than "Happy Holidays," that's fine with me, too. And I hope they'll throw in a "Happy Hanukkah," "Blessed Ramadan," or other appropriate greetings for the other special days their customers observe. The bottom line is that when the earthly issues about which God is concerned are tallied up, I admit to harboring some healthy skepticism about whether "the war on Christmas" is going to make the top of the list. I'm a lot more concerned with getting Christ back into our debates over going to war than with getting Christ into our holiday cards.

The "war on Christmas" was part of a broader pattern of radical right-wingers claiming that America is out to get Christians. Such was the claim of the Justice Sunday events at which far religious right leaders converged to bemoan on theological grounds the fact that Democrats had approved almost all, but not every last one, of President Bush's judicial nominations. Just Us Sunday seemed more like it to me; the events seemed to leave little room for mainstream people of faith. As they saw it, you were with the far religious right or against Christianity. There were no telecasts about poverty or peace, only a pervasive sense of persecution because other people declined to agree with the totality of their agenda.

It hardly needs to be stated that people disagree with one another all the time. As long as we have a democracy, it's going to be pretty hard to avoid that. If I'd gotten discouraged, much less indignant, every time I was on the losing end of some political effort, I would have hung it up a long time ago. When I ran for the United States Senate in 1986, the people of Pennsylvania disagreed with me. As Mo Udall, with whom I had the privilege to serve in Congress, famously said after his failed presidential campaign, "The people have spoken, the bastards." I would have rather won than lost, of course, but the last thing that occurred to me was that anyone was out to get me for being Christian. Most of the people I know in Pennsylvania are pretty nice folks, and they just wanted somebody else to be their senator. On election night, I walked over to the headquarters of my

Republican opponent, Senator Arlen Specter, shook his hand, and wished him well. Then I went back to address my own supporters. I told them not to feel bad for me; I'd had twelve exciting years in Congress, and if God had other plans for me, I'd go figure out what they were. On the way out, Mom Edgar looked over my way. "Bob," she said, "I still think you're a neat kid." That was good enough for me. In politics as in life, you take your lumps and your losses.

It's just plain silly to claim that judicial filibusters and banners proclaiming "Happy Holidays" at shopping malls add up to a campaign of discrimination against Christians. Christians are persecuted in Sudan. In ancient Rome, they were thrown to the lions. In the United States, the radical religious right runs the government, and it's a pretty far cry from the trials of the early Christians to the halls of power in Washington. Never since Jesus walked the earth have Christians been as powerful and comfortable as we are today. That may be exactly the problem. Gene Winkler, a United Methodist minister in Chicago, now retired, identified the heart of the matter in a sermon a few years ago: "Christians today are not persecuted; we are ignored. We are not ridiculed; we are faced with indifference. We don't lose our jobs or our heads because of our faith; we lose our courage to talk about our faith." It's time for faithful Americans to regain that courage. Not simply to talk about our faith, but to vote it; not just to go to church or to the synagogue or mosque but to reach into our communities. For all around us, opportunities for making a difference abound.

I do not believe making a difference is so very difficult. But even if it were, there comes a time when what is right must take precedence over what is easy, even over what is possible. That time is upon us. God's creation is getting warmer. Wars are maiming and killing thousands upon thousands of God's children. Poverty is depriving our brothers and sisters of hope and stealing the possibilities that are otherwise spread out before us. These are affronts to God, and there is no affront more abominable than apathy and indifference. After all, if Jesus was willing to die on the cross for righteousness' sake, is it too much to ask that we give up a Sunday afternoon of televised football to reach into our communities, much less take a couple of hours on one Tuesday out of the year to cast our votes?

"If a man hasn't discovered something that he will die for," Martin Luther King, Jr. said, "he isn't fit to live." None of us is being asked for our lives, only our hearts and our time. And the difficulty of the tasks ahead is no excuse not to try. I do not believe the odds are so very long, for most of the issues I have discussed in this book lie at the heart and in the lifeblood of faith traditions espoused by vast electoral majorities. But in a sense, our chances of success are not the point. We are closer to God when we try to do what is right than when we surrender to helplessness, and we are truer to our values when we act as though they were important enough to risk just a little bit, especially when the harshest risk is the gentle chance of losing an election. (Trust me, I've tried it, and it's not that bad.) When discouragement, the serpent of political life, dangles temptation before us, let's recall that one person can always make a difference.

A couple of thousand years ago, it took only one person surrounded by a small yet courageous band of twelve to change the world. One of those twelve, a fellow named Matthew, recorded their leader's core beliefs in a passage called the Beatitudes. Delivered in the Sermon on the Mount, the Beatitudes were a series of statements designed to surprise Jesus' listeners, to challenge their assumptions and provoke them to think about the world in a radical new way. Each of these statements declares that a different character trait is blessed. Over the centuries, they have become an ideal of behavior toward which Christians strive, which is why we preachers sometimes call them be-*attitudes.*

We need to return to what Jesus, in the Gospel of Luke, called the "deep waters." And so I propose—with a little less poetry and a lot fewer credentials than the original author—seven beatitudes for deep-water citizenship, a simple plan, if you will, for changing the world.

### 1. Blessed Are the Faithful Risk Takers

My father worked the very same job (testing electrical relays) on the very same shift (3 P.M. to 1 A.M.) at the very same desk at the very same plant (General Electric's facility on Elmwood Avenue outside Philadelphia) for thirty-seven years. He made twenty-six dollars a week when my parents married, and when he died in 1976, he was earning the not-so-princely sum of nine thousand dollars a year. His extravagances were few: taking the trolley car to go fishing on the weekends, occasional family trips to the New Jersey shore. On the salary he made, in the precarious financial balance in which our family hung, the one luxury my father could least afford was taking a stand. Yet that was a luxury he indulged with courage, conviction, and generosity.

In 1946, my father was one of thousands of workers who went on strike against General Electric, seeking their modest share of the postwar economic boom, a dollar or two a day in extra wages. Management was furious, and the company enlisted the local police force in an attempt to intimidate the workers. Many of these workers were returning veterans and others who had contributed to the war effort by accepting wage controls throughout those lean and hard years. Police on horseback and motorcycle stormed through the crowd swinging billy clubs. One day during the strike, my mother took my brother and me to visit our grandmother, who lived near the plant. I was a tender young sprout at the time, but in my memory, I can still hear the pounding of the hoofbeats and feel the fear as we passed through the crowd and the police chased us up onto the sidewalks and then onto the porches of row houses along the picket line.

My parents, who were already living hand-to-mouth even when the plant was operating, must have felt an equally imminent threat:

surviving with no income. The easiest thing for my father and his coworkers to do would have been to take their meager wages and stay quiet. We may each be thankful that silence was not the course they chose, for without the labor movement, children would still work in factories, the forty-hour work week would still be a distant dream, and people like my father would still be begging for pennies on the hour. The leaders of organized labor risked everything precisely when—precisely *because*—they had nothing.

Today, we have more than they could have ever dreamed yet we are paralyzed by fear, our values seemingly less important than the dread of losing a small portion of our disposable incomes. The fierce urgency of now demands that we risk our comfort, that we share our happiness, and that we listen to the prophetic voice calling upon us to urge our world forward rather than simply conserving old gains. We cannot live up to God's standards from the comfort of our daily lives. In our time as in Jesus', the biggest fish are in the deepest waters, in the currents where it seems just a little rougher, a touch riskier, to sail our vessels.

Risk demands that we push ourselves beyond our comfort zones. That might mean the courage of a peace activist visiting a war zone, or the commitment of a Sister Peggy Healy ministering in the slums of Managua. Whistle-blowers at corporations that pollute are prophetic risk takers; so were those who told the American people, at the peril of their jobs and even their freedom, about the Bush Administration's illegal and invasive practice of eavesdropping inside the United States without warrants. My friend Peter Edelman, who resigned from the Clinton Administration to protest a cold-hearted dismantling of social-welfare programs, took a courageous risk. But the reality is that for most of us, risk requires simply that we stand by our values and that we be willing to place our comfort on the line. More often than not, the greatest risk we run is that a neighbor will disagree with us or an election will be lost or the average blood pressure in the pews will spike for a minute or two. Is that so terrible to behold? We should be so fortunate, we should believe so deeply in our values that we are willing to speak passionately on their behalf.

Yet I worry that our spiritual leaders, those who should challenge us to give the most, are themselves willing to risk the least. Most Americans are fed a steady diet of sermons that are generically nice, as sweet as the punch and cookies in the social hall, often tasty but rarely challenging. There are a few prophetic voices among our clergy today, but many others are on what I call "autopulpit"—clinging to their pulpits and hoping retirement comes quickly, taking great care never to offend. My evangelical friend Tony Campolo put it best: "I find it strange that the last place I can quote Jesus these days is in American churches. They don't want to hear 'overcome evil with good.' They don't want to hear 'those who live by the sword die by the sword.' They don't want to hear 'if your enemy hurts you, do good, feed, clothe, minister to him.' They don't want to hear 'blessed are the merciful.' They don't want to hear 'love your enemies.'"

Tony is exactly right, and if those of us in mainline denominations are afraid to preach Jesus' message from the pulpit, we should not be surprised that it is absent from politics. Say what you will about the far religious right—whatever it is, I assure you I've said worse—but they have the firmness of their convictions, and when conservative preachers ascend the pulpit, few seem to be inhibited by fears of losing their jobs. Neither are most ministers on the left. It is the voices we most urgently need to hear, the voices of the vast American center, that are silent.

What if Middle Church, Middle Synagogue, and Middle Mosque heard similar passion for *our* values? Suppose, before the war in Iraq, our institutions of faith had been filled with prayers for peace—not simply nice poetry, but passionate exhortations, not simply words to God, but (the truest prayer of all) actions by human beings? Suppose, the day before Congress voted on its latest round of appalling cuts in desperately needed social programs, every parishioner and congregant had been challenged to place a call to Capitol

Hill and speak with a prophetic voice for the poor? What if there had been an outcry of moral protest on the Sunday morning after the United States unilaterally abandoned negotiations on global warming?

Perhaps a preacher or two would have gotten into hot water with his or her board of elders or the equivalent in different religions. Of that prospect, I can only say what President Bush said of the insurgents in Iraq: Bring 'em on. I pray for the day when we read of a rash of firings at churches enmeshed in controversy because parishioners have been challenged to rise up for the poor and peace and our planet. I wish persecution on no one, but surely that would be better, and closer to God's plan, than the smiling politeness with which too many of our clergy accede to a government whose hostility to the least of these violates everything in which we believe. If clergy see one of their parishioners violating the precepts of the Sermon on the Mount or other aspects of scripture, they generally speak out; when we see a government representing three hundred million of us doing exactly the same thing, we somehow feel obligated to remain *silent*. One reason is that our seminaries offer exquisite preparation for the nineteenth century: They teach the Bible and theology and pastoral care, yet place far too little emphasis on bringing these lessons to life in the real world that spiritual leaders confront. But another reason, perhaps a more powerful one, is that it is more pleasant to affirm than it is to challenge, and safer to tell people what they *want* to hear than what they *need* to do.

Already, I can hear the first protest from the folks who attend church on a regular basis: I don't want to hear about politics in church, a sentiment I am sure is equally expressed in synagogues and mosques. But if all we want is to hear what we already think, to have our backs spiritually patted and our tickets spiritually punched, there is another place to go on Saturday and Sunday mornings: our living rooms. We come to church and other places of faith because we seek something more, because we want to be challenged, because we want our minds and our hearts stretched beyond where they already were. And we do all this because the greatest risk of all is to confine our souls to the prison of compromised values and baseless fears. But there is no joy more liberating than being true to ourselves.

Let us raise our voices in prayerful thanks to God that Martin Luther King, Jr., was not as polite as many of us in the ministry feel a need to be today, for his pulpit was a place from which a nation was called to its conscience and politics was understood to be what it was: a moral laboratory for doing justice. Without politics in the pulpit, slavery would never have been abolished, women would never have gotten the vote, and segregation would never have been demolished. I think often of the contrast between the risks that Dr. King took and what is, by comparison, the very minimal price the rest of us must pay to speak for our values. When he was jailed in Birmingham for leading a campaign of nonviolent civil disobedience, he did not know when or whether he would see daylight again. A group of mainstream clergy members met his sacrifice with a statement calling for order and characterizing Dr. King's activities as unwise. It bore all the hallmarks of the polite moderation we see in modern pulpits. His reply became the famous "Letter from a Birmingham Jail." Forty years later, I was arrested in front of the Sudanese embassy in Washington during a protest of the genocide in Darfur. There was not a fire hose or a vicious police dog in sight; on the contrary, the arresting officers treated me with the utmost respect. "Watch your head, Reverend," they said while gently easing me into the back of a paddy wagon. I was in and out of jail inside of ninety minutes. Dr. King wrote a letter during his imprisonment; I barely would have had time to scribble a Post-it note.

The risks we must run today are nothing next to what Dr. King and his contemporaries faced, and our odds of success are much greater. All we need is their courage, and if we can harness it, we will also find what they knew: the joy of truth, a joy that far exceeds whatever material comforts we feel a need to protect. We do not need popularity; we need the purity and passion of a prophetic voice. We need to build, inspire, and leverage what Dr. Bernard Anderson, who taught the Old Testament at Drew Theological Seminary, called the "remnant minority." And that brings me to the second beatitude for deep-water citizenship in our modern age.

## 2. Blessed Is the Courageous Remnant

Every four years, I get together with several thousand of my fellow United Methodists for our denomination's General Conference. It's an occasion I always look forward to—an opportunity to renew old friendships, contemplate Christ's teachings, and draw on the inspiration of soulful prayers. I enjoy it except for this one little thing that, every once in a while, drives me up a wall. We spend days and days sitting in front of little computer machines, pressing buttons, and doing something that neither Jesus nor his disciples nor any of the holy prophets of the Old Testament ever saw a need to attempt: *We vote.* We take some of the most pressing moral issues of the day, whether it's a question of public policy or private morality, and subject them to majority rule.

In and of itself, it's not such a bad idea, and I probably shouldn't complain about it as much as I do. I agree with my fellow United Methodists more often than not. Either way, I rarely lose sleep over the outcome of those votes, nor do I have a better idea for how to run a church. There are certainly worse strategies than listening to the majority, and I'd sooner trust the collected wisdom of a few hundred delegates than the opinions of a small number of church leaders—including me. But I also can't help wondering whether we sometimes allow our democratic ideals to trump our prophetic ideals.

The prophets, like Jesus' disciples, knew something we sometimes forget. Majorities can be wrong. That's why it's so hard to picture Amos or Hosea retreating from the street corner and calling for a referendum on the wages of sin—or the apostles focus-testing the Sermon on the Mount and trying to wave Jesus off the "blessed are the merciful" bit because it made him sound soft on crime. The prophets never took a poll, and the disciples never took a vote. That observation was the basis of what Dr. Anderson called "remnant theology," the belief that what is morally right cannot be ascertained by majority vote, and, equally powerful, the knowledge that a courageous minority can gain enough leverage to prevail.

Majorities are the best and fairest way I know to run a government. That doesn't mean they're sacrosanct. When I served in Congress, I was one of a relatively small number of clergy members in the House, and our merry little band found itself on the losing end of a great many majority votes. Majorities in Congress were, in my view, consistently wrong on the morality of nuclear proliferation. They never saw a weapons system they didn't love, even when the Pentagon didn't want it. Majorities were consistently wrong on wasteful and environmentally destructive water projects. Majorities were consistently wrong on providing adequate funding for the needs of the poor. (And just because the majority happens to include a guy wearing a clerical collar or going by the title of Reverend doesn't make it right either. I've been wrong more than once—although I remind you that we're keeping that a secret from Merle.)

We need to remember the admonition of Exodus 23:2: "You shall not follow a majority in wrongdoing . . ." The question isn't what majorities want, it's what the faithful remnant—those who stand for God's will, who believe passionately in what they know to be right— has the courage to do. Don't get me wrong. I'm not attacking majority rule. I agree with Winston Churchill about democracy: It's the worst system of government, except for all the others. Instead, I mean simply that we don't *need* majorities—we don't have to *wait* for majorities—to make a difference. Before we can build a majority, we must be true to our own beliefs.

Martin Luther King, Jr., did precisely that. The civil rights movement began with a courageous remnant, one that included, I might add, church leaders who were undeterred by the fact that most Americans surveyed in public opinion polls disagreed with them. When Rosa Parks passed away, she was eulogized by both the right and left. Liberals and conservatives alike issue proclamations for Martin Luther King, Jr., Day. What we forget, looking back in time from the present day, is that the cause of civil rights was not always lionized. Both Mrs. Parks and Dr. King—and other leaders of the early civil rights movement—rose up with the strength of a comparatively small minority of Americans. Another minority—virulent racists—opposed them. It was the vast center of Middle Church, Middle Synagogue, and Middle Mosque that was up for grabs. The courageous remnant minority gradually became a majority, but that could not have happened had the remnant minority not maintained its own integrity and the courage of its convictions.

Today, the remnant minority is too deferential to majority views. After Republican victories in the 2000 and 2002 elections, Democrats did something that was very mature, quite thoughtful, and completely self-destructive. They became *reasonable*. They decided that since majorities seemed to be siding with President Bush, their job was to accede to his agenda, perhaps moderating it here or there, but rarely opposing it outright. When he wanted enormous tax cuts, Democrats supported tax cuts that were merely large. When he wanted to go to war in Iraq, Democrats were willing to go to war, too. Just not as quickly. When he wanted to slash support for the least of these, our brothers and sisters, Democrats would support cutting welfare, too. A little bit less. We were left with three political parties in America: big Republicans, medium-sized Republicans, and little Republicans. And when voters were given a choice between Republicans who meant what they said and Democrats who mimicked what Republicans said, they understandably chose the genuine article.

Compromising core principles is always bad politics. I won election six times in one of the most Republican districts in Pennsylvania with one of the most liberal voting records in Congress, and if I had moderated my views one bit, I would have lost every time. When I voted for things like increasing the minimum wage, I went to the chamber of commerce and explained why I believed as I did. More often than not, their answer was: "Bob, we disagree with you, but we respect the fact that we know where you stand." Especially in times of rapid change and perceived dangers like those in which we live today, people gravitate toward leaders with a clear sense of purpose and vision, even when they disagree with them.

The faithful remnant must have the courage to stand for its principles no matter what, but it's often the case that the majority will agree with a clear moral vision once it sees it. Sometimes the majority needs to be led. Politics today is largely divided between firm cores on the right and left and a vast middle whose votes and voices are decisive. We are far likelier to prevail in the political arena if we begin with a courageous remnant and reach out to the faithful religious center than if we stay silent until the majority wakes up and begins to speak. A courageous remnant can form the core around which a majority is built, but if we wait for a majority to coalesce before taking a stand, we will wait forever. "Give me a lever long enough and I'll move the world," Archimedes said. Give me a remnant minority courageous enough, and we can *change* the world.

### 3. Blessed Are Those Who Love the Stranger

Let me tell you about two of the most faithful and prophetic people I have ever known. One has spent the better part of thirty years urging Congress and our nation to heed God's call to love the poor, steward the earth, and work for peace. The other has fought for the world's most vulnerable people and been an eloquent voice for reconciliation and understanding. These two fellows exemplify what I interpret as Christ's call to serve the least of these, our brothers and sisters. Each has worked as tirelessly as anyone I know on behalf of godly values on the religious right, the religious left, or the religious center. It just so happens that they share something else in common: Neither one of them believes Jesus was the Messiah. Their names are David Saperstein, a leading Reform Jewish rabbi, and Dr. Sayyid M. Syeed, the secretary general of the Islamic Society of North America.

I first got to know David when I was a member of Congress and he was just getting started with the organization he now runs, the Religious Action Center for Reform Judaism. David was then, and remains, the most effective religious lobbyist in Washington. Along with his faith, he possesses a law degree, a brilliant legal mind, a passionate devotion to the separation of church and state, and a keen sense of the balance between welcoming faithful expression into the public sphere and maintaining individual freedoms. He's also smarter than I am, but I like him anyway. David and I have ridden shotgun together on some of the most important faithful issues of the last generation, including speaking out against genocide, global warming, and budget cuts targeting the poor.

I've gotten to know Sayyid more recently. He founded the Islamic Society of North America, which is, in a manner of speaking, a Muslim equivalent of the National Council of Churches. Sayyid established his organization's headquarters in Plainfield, Indiana, right smack in the middle of Amish country, and if you saw a picture of him with his long, clean-cut, salt-and-pepper beard, you'd know he fits right in. Sayyid chose Plainfied because it was within driving distance of most of the country. That kind of organizing insight may explain how he manages to get over forty thousand people together for his annual convention, a feat I've never managed. That puts him in the same company as David, namely, smarter than I am, but I love him, too. In addition to his work on behalf of the world's poor as well as the environment, Sayyid is also a powerful and forceful voice for healthy, moderate, and faithful Islam. He is deeply committed to interfaith dialogue. No religious leader has spoken more passionately against terrorism since 9/11.

The Senate Finance Committee rewarded these efforts by demanding the Islamic Society of North America's financial records as part of an investigation into whether Islamic charities were linked with terrorists. When I heard about it, I called Sayyid and only half-jokingly told him that if he turned over his records, I was going to call the senators and threaten, on behalf of the National Council of Churches, to unload half a century's worth of NCC's financial records on them. Sayyid (remember, I said he's smarter than I am) kept a level head, cooperated, and the committee found exactly what was there, namely, nothing but a moving and inspirational record of advocacy on behalf of their fellow human beings, Muslim, Christian, and Jewish alike.

So I would just ask: If you were concerned about the future of our planet, or the cause of peace, or if, through no fault of your own, you fell on hard times and found yourself among the least of these, whom would you want on your side? For that matter, if you were looking for an exemplar of biblical values, would you choose David Saperstein or Pat Robertson, Sayyid M. Syeed or Jerry Falwell? "You shall not murder," the commandment says. It wasn't Sayyid who called on the United States to assassinate the president of a foreign country. It was Pat Robertson, talking about President Hugo Chavez of Venezuela. "You shall also love the stranger, for you were strangers in the land of Egypt," God declares in Deuteronomy 10:9. It was Jerry Falwell, not David Saperstein, who called Mohammed a terrorist.

Moreover, tell me which of these voices offered in the wake of 9/11 is faithful and which is fanatical:

> We, the undersigned Muslims, wish to state clearly that those who commit acts of terror, murder, and cruelty in the name of Islam are not only destroying innocent lives, but are also betraying the values of the faith they claim to represent. No injustice done to Muslims can ever justify the massacre of innocent people, and no

act of terror will ever serve the cause of Islam. We repudiate and dissociate ourselves from any Muslim group or individual who commits such brutal and un-Islamic acts. We refuse to allow our faith to be held hostage by the criminal actions of a tiny minority acting outside the teachings of both the Quran and the Prophet Muhammad, peace be upon him.

—STATEMENT SIGNED BY SAYYID M. SYEED AND OTHER LEADERS OF THE ISLAMIC SOCIETY OF NORTH AMERICA

I really believe that the pagans, and the abortionists, and the feminists, and the gays and the lesbians who are actively trying to make that an alternative lifestyle, the ACLU, People or the American Way, all of them who have tried to secularize America, I point the finger in their face and say: you helped this happen.

—JERRY FALWELL, INTERVIEWED SHORTLY AFTER 9/11 BY PAT ROBERTSON, WHO REPLIED, "WELL, I TOTALLY CONCUR."

I disagree with David and Sayyid on plenty of theological issues and probably even a couple of political ones, too (if you put David's views on Israel and Sayyid's on Palestine on a chart, you'd probably find me just about in the middle), but their day-to-day work comes far closer to the content of the Sermon on the Mount than the preachings of many leaders on the far religious right. I would hate to be compared with David or Sayyid in a heavenly contest to see who among us can be most faithful to God's will. I just can't believe that God has anything but love for them as human beings and awe and appreciation for what they do. And I *certainly* don't buy the idea that my God, a God of love and understanding, will answer their faith and acts with eternal fire.

Despite the religious differences among us, all three of us know that what God cares about most is our love for our fellow human beings and our commitment to meaningful acts that express that love. More important, God created human beings with free will, an annoying but unavoidable little fact that occasionally makes life harder but also renders our time on this earth more beautiful and meaningful. And he included the wondrous diversity of voices and traditions through which people express their love for God and one another.

I cannot join Pat Robertson in believing that God might refuse to listen to the people in Dover, Pennsylvania, because they decided not to teach intelligent design in school. My God hopes for positive outcomes. My God does not play tricks or predetermine outcomes. My God has enough self-confidence to be less concerned with the language in which people pray than with the fullness with which people love one another. Most important, my God does not withhold love or acceptance from a Hindu child in India, a Buddhist child in Thailand, a Jewish child in Jerusalem, or a Muslim child in Ramallah.

Of course, I'm a grown-up (you *can* tell Merle that one), and so are David and Sayyid, and I think both of them would join me in acknowledging the obvious fact that anyone who takes his or her religion seriously—as all three of us try to do—believes it's something very special. But God doesn't call us to judge one another; in fact, I seem to recall a pretty specific commandment *not* to. Nor, in my personal opinion, does God even ask us to convert those who espouse other faiths. I believe God reveals his love to different people in different ways and through different vehicles. All of those vehicles, for me, are Christ-like. But in my faith, "Christ-like" refers to Jesus' message, not whether one accepts him as the Messiah. Do we actually believe Jesus was so shallow, so insecure, that he would reject—even smite—someone whose prayers do not include his name but who fully heeds his call to love the poor and work for peace? I believe Christ is my way to understand God. He is my Messiah!

There is a wonderful teaching from David's faith that captures it for me. According to the Talmud, a gentile offered to convert to Judaism if the sage Hillel could teach the entire Torah while standing

on one foot. Hillel obliged, perching himself on one foot and ex-
plaining: "What is hateful to you, do not do to your neighbor. That is
the whole Torah. The rest is commentary. Go and learn the details."
The Golden Rule, however one states it, is all of God's will. The
rest—including the language in which we pray and the tradition in
which we believe—is details.

When we drive wedges between each other because we pray differently, we commit a twofold sin. We fail to love the stranger—a
commandment in itself—and we miss an opportunity to work together to love all of humanity. In my efforts to live by Jesus' words,
my friendship with David and Sayyid has been as valuable and powerful as any prayer. Faith can divide us by denomination or unite us
in the actual work of God's love, however we recognize it. We must
heed the words of the poet Edwin Markham:

> He drew a circle to shut me out—
> Heretic, rebel, a thing to flout.
> But Love and I had the wit to win:
> We drew a circle that took him in!

## 4. Blessed Are Those Who Read the *Whole* Bible

Stop the presses! Edgar forgot a chapter!

I must have forgotten something, right? After all, how can you
write an entire book about faith and politics and not talk about homosexuality, abortion, and stem cell research—the holy trinity of the
far religious right? Well, before deciding what to say about these
supposed "values" issues, I went back and consulted some of my favorite books. One was written by this fellow named Moses (you
know the guy—he's got a long beard and a shepherd's staff and looks
an awful lot like Charlton Heston), and there was a whole series by
these four guys called Matthew, Mark, Luke, and John. I figured if
they could get through their books without making homosexuality,

abortion, and stem cell research a central focus, I should be able to pull it off, too.

And that's the most important thing to understand about these issues: They're important. People of good will and sincere faith disagree about them, and those disagreements deserve a respectful hearing. But they are *not* the whole Bible. They wouldn't even make the executive summary. They are *not* the sole tests of whether a politician or an individual or a religious institution favors family values—not even close. In fact, two of these personal piety issues didn't even make it into Scripture at all, and the other one is mentioned only twice. Poverty and peace, you may recall, come up in the Bible more than two thousand times. If we are to be faithful to God's entire word, then Middle Church must be prepared to agree to disagree about homosexuality, abortion, and stem cell research and unite behind the far broader issues of peace, justice, poverty, racism, and the need to heal planet Earth.

My feelings on these issues of personal piety, like my feelings on *every* issue, are strongly held and passionate. They are profoundly important to me. There's ample place for discussing them in the public square. But if God didn't let these issues get in the way of all those moving and powerful words about love of neighbor, neither should we. So rather than put you to sleep with a long essay on my political views, I'd rather talk with you about an old neighbor I admire and love very much.

Gwynne Guibord is an Episcopal priest in Los Angeles, an old-fashioned family lady who's been in a faithfully committed relationship for more than twenty-seven years. A psychotherapist by training, Gwynne felt a profound and deeply spiritual call to ministry after her sister died of cancer. She was living a life of material comfort and professional success, but within two weeks, she had enrolled at Claremont School of Theology and devoted herself to God's service.

There's one more thing you should know about Gwynne, something that doesn't have one whit's worth of relevance to her qualifications as a counselor and minister of God, but that does matter in today's political climate: She's a lesbian. She and her partner, Lo Sprague, who's also a psychotherapist, are two of the most authentic Christians I've ever met. I mention their orientation only to say that the extent of one's faith is not determined by sexual preference and to challenge each of us to question how well our own adherence to Christ's teachings would stack up next to Gwynne, Lo, or any number of other gays, lesbians, or transsexuals who are good and faithful people.

If we are to condemn all homosexuals, hundreds of millions of our fellow human beings are going to have to be excluded from God's love. And that is a result I cannot accept—not as an American, not as a Christian, and certainly not as a minister.

It's my own view (and that of most scientists) that individuals don't choose their sexual orientation. The claim advanced by many on the radical right that homosexuality is just another among life's many temptations makes little sense to me, and, I suspect, to most clear-thinking heterosexuals who have never felt tempted in that way. Why anyone would flippantly or casually *choose* a life that subjects them to the kind of persecution and ostracism that homosexuals endure is beyond me. I do not believe anyone does or would make such a choice. I believe homosexuals—like heterosexuals—are what God has made them, and especially in this age of divorce and disintegrating families, I pray we can open our hearts and our minds not just to tolerate homosexuals, but to learn from them about the meaning of love.

Few are free of sin when it comes to extending the love that our homosexual brothers and sisters deserve. Certainly I am not. Not long after I became general secretary of the National Council of Churches, I was asked to join several other Christian leaders in signing a statement called "A Christian Declaration on Marriage." Marriage had worked out pretty well for me, and the statement seemed benign enough, so I put my name to it without much thought. Soon afterward, at our General Assembly, Gwynne confronted me with a mixture of tears, respect, and firmness. The statement was actually full of code words intended to disparage gays and lesbians. She wanted to know how I could lend my name to it, and she was right. The next morning, I walked up to the podium at the conference, announced that I was removing my name from the statement, and then walked to the back of the room, put my arms around Gwynne, and asked, "Can you ever forgive me for hurting you?"

It goes without saying that controversy erupted immediately, as I knew it would. The National Council of Churches' member communions hold a variety of opinions on homosexuality, and I faced a torrent of criticism from those on the left who wanted to know why I signed the statement in the first place and others on the right who were outraged that I removed my name. But the choice for me was simple enough: I decided my heart was with the people who were in tears. So, I believe, is God's.

Leviticus contains two verses banning homosexual behavior, and I find these passages—like so many in the Bible—challenging. I don't have all the answers, nor do I pretend to. It may be that we need to take the historical and social circumstances in which the Bible was written into consideration. And even those who believe the Bible to be God's literal word must grant that God's meanings are not always comprehensible to us. It's not important that all Christians agree about whether homosexuality is a sin. What matters is that we accept the indisputable Christian teaching that we are *all* sinners. Whether homosexuality is a sin against God or an innate human preference, none of us has any business casting stones. We can disagree about the morality of homosexuality without rejecting Christ's call to love one another. A call I cannot find anywhere, for example, in far religious right commentator Alan Keyes' claim that "Hitler and his supporters were Satanists and homosexuals. That's just a true statement."

People of faith must be able to conduct a respectful and open conversation about all aspects of sexuality including homosexuality. God has a lot to say on all those topics, and if we skip the listening and rush straight to the judging—an enterprise in which we're not supposed to be involved anyway—we can't hope to make serious progress in our discussion. That's why, at Claremont, I helped establish the Center for Sexuality and Christian Life, which explores a wide range of viewpoints on a broad array of biblical issues related to sex. Scholars there disagree about a great many things, but they are unified in their belief that we must study the *entire* Bible, and do so in context.

One verse in that Bible says homosexuality is a capital offense. The Old Testament also prescribes the death penalty for breaking the Sabbath, committing adultery, and cursing at one's parents. I have yet to hear of Karl Rove mounting a campaign of ballot initiatives to codify God's will when it comes to teenagers mouthing off to their mothers or fathers. (He might want to look into that one—I bet nine out of ten parents would be for it, at least as a threat.) When it comes to Old Testament capital offenses, the White House has confined its purported piety to homosexuals for a simple, cynical reason: Homosexuals in our time are what the lepers were in Jesus' time, an outcast class on whose backs they can score cheap and shameful political points.

I want to be very careful about that metaphor, because I do *not*—repeat, *not*—believe there is anything unhealthy or unclean about homosexuality or homosexual people. In biblical terms, the leper is the pariah on whom society heaps judgment and scorn. And the Bible tells us that Jesus responded to lepers not simply with tolerance but with active love. For love is God's teaching. We see it over and over and over again, and even if I cannot fully explain why the Old Testament says what it does about homosexuality, I can say with the certainty of all my faith that God does not want us to discriminate or to persecute or to treat homosexuals with anything less than the fullness of love due to every one of God's children.

And while we're on the topic of God's children, let's not forget half of them. Respect for women plays a central role in many faiths. In mine, we see the special role two women named Mary played in Jesus' life. One brought him into the world, and the other he rescued from prostitution to become one of his most faithful followers. Two days before the crucifixion, we see Jesus reciprocating the honor a woman has shown him (a scene that takes place, incidentally, in the home of a leper). In Judaism, there is a beautiful tradition on Sabbath eves of husbands reciting to their wives Solomon's words in Proverbs 31:30–31. "Charm is deceitful, and beauty is vain," the passage includes, "but a woman who fears the Lord is to be praised. Give her a share in the fruit of her hands, and let her works praise her in the city gates."

I believe women deserve an equal share, which is why I support equal pay, equal jobs, and equal rights, not just as a matter of personal politics but of biblical faith. It's also why I believe women are more qualified than legislators to make decisions about whether or not to have a child. I do not believe abortion should ever be undertaken lightly, and I have never met a woman who did so. Those I counseled as a minister understood fully the moral gravity of the choices they faced as well as the responsibilities they had to balance. And I know, too, the devastating consequences of substituting politicians' judgment for women's. During my time with the Philadelphia Police Clergy Unit in the early 1970s—before *Roe v. Wade*—I saw the tragic aftermath of botched back-alley abortions: women lying on stretchers in hospital emergency rooms, bloody, often mutilated, sometimes fighting for their lives. I cannot bear the thought that in the name of faith, we might return to that time.

But on this issue especially, I understand that many sincere people disagree. I believe their views, every bit as much as mine, have a place in this discussion. Abortion and childbearing touch on many of our most closely held values, and even those of us who believe government should not impose any one religious view should also welcome and respect the honest spiritual beliefs of those who feel differently. Many Christians who feel strongly and sincerely that abortion should be illegal have also been faithful prophets of God's word by working for the poor and for peace. My quarrel is with those on the radical religious right who would reduce the entirety of God's word to these very few narrow issues, who attempt, on that flimsy basis, to lay exclusive claim to faith despite their hostility to the poor and the planet and the cause of peace.

The values of Middle Church have an equal place in the discussion of stem cell research. Stem cell research is a highly promising field that can enable us to give meaning to Jesus' instructions to his disciples, and through them to all of us, to heal the sick. At the same time, the ethical issues involved in stem cell research are highly complex, and they begin with respect for human life that is, in the psalmist's beautiful words, "fearfully and wonderfully made." That fear and wonder are an essential part of the joy of human life, which is one among many reasons that I firmly oppose human cloning. (And here, for perhaps the only time, I agree with my former Republican colleague in Congress Dick Armey, who, upon being asked what he thought of reproduction by cloning, ventured the prediction that most people would decide to stick with the old-fashioned method.)

All of these personal piety issues are important, but no faithful reading of the Bible can possibly elevate them to the end-all, be-all of religious belief. That does not mean politicians are not entitled to their own beliefs, even passionate beliefs, about homosexuality, abortion, and stem-cell research. It does mean—it quite decisively means—that they cannot cut and paste two verses of Leviticus, ignore the rest of the Bible, and call the result a "faithful" agenda in American politics. It may be a sincere agenda; it is not a Christian one. I welcome any discussion of politics that begins with assertions of religious belief. For abortion and stem-cell research do not occupy that ground, and homosexuality traverses it only on the margins. If the radical religious right feels a need to reduce the whole of Biblical faith to a single sound bite, one litmus test, they should consult Matthew 22:34–40, where Jesus provides it:

> When the Pharisees heard that he had silenced the Sadducees, they gathered together, and one of them, a lawyer, asked him a question to test him. "Teacher, which commandment in the law is the greatest?" He said to him, "'You shall love the Lord your God with all your heart, and with all your soul, and with all your mind.' This is the greatest and first commandment. And a second is like it: 'You shall love your neighbor as yourself.' On these two commandments hang all the law and the prophets."

### 5. Blessed Are the Faithful Voters

I'm kind of new to this book-writing business, but even I know one of the most important parts of the process is editing, nipping, tucking, and cutting out all the important things you really want to say but just don't have the space for. That must be what happened to the Sermon on the Mount. Picture the scene: The crowds are dispersing, their hearts stirred and their spirits soaring, and Matthew sidles up to Jesus and says, "Hey, nice speech, boss, but I'm going to have to cut it down to the sound bites before I write it up." Lost on the floor of Matthew's cutting room were such verses as, "Blessed is the permanent extension of the $1,000-per-child tax credit," and, "You have heard it said that firearms should be registered with the federal government, but I say to you that when you propose licensing of gun owners, you have already violated the Second Amendment in your heart."

I don't recall learning about those commandments in seminary. But, on the other hand, I was a C student, and I was working full time to boot. Merle and I had small children, too, so maybe (perish the thought!) they were in an assigned reading that I neglected. But several million Americans did learn about them when the Christian Coalition distributed its voter guide for the 2004 elections. This handy pocket card informed Christians of where George W. Bush and John Kerry stood on—and I quote—"key faith and family issues."

Given that grammatical combination—a "Christian" voter guide focused on "faith and family"—you might expect at least one of the actual, published Beatitudes to have made the cut. But the Christian Coalition Voter Guide contained neither one jot nor one tittle about feeding the hungry or clothing the naked. Its fifteen "faith and family" issues included three planks on tax cuts. It's not entirely clear to me how abolition of the estate tax or, for that matter, privatizing Social Security and replacing it with investment accounts, another item in the voter guide, squares with Jesus' admonition in Matthew 6:19 not to "store up for yourselves treasures on earth." Abortion and homosexuality accounted for another five items combined. Two other planks endorse (oops—I meant to say "provide objective information on") educational vouchers (to pay for religious school tuition, I'm guessing) and federal funding for religious charities. (A friendly taxpayer alert: That funny sensation you're feeling in your hip is Pat Robertson's hand in your pocket.) And I don't have any idea how they came up with "Federal Firearms Registration," "Placing US Troops Under UN Control," or "Affirmative Action Programs that Provide Preferential Treatment" as "key faith and family issues."

That's not to say they aren't key issues. A lot of them aren't key for me. There are many political issues keeping me up at night, but the federal tax on multimillion-dollar estates isn't one of them. In fact, Merle and I have been very conscientious about ensuring that our children won't have to worry about that particular piece of paperwork after we shuffle off this mortal coil. Unless this book is optioned as a Hollywood blockbuster (with Robert Redford playing Robert Edgar, no doubt), our estate should sneak in under the limit. Still, I don't have a problem with other people caring about these issues, nor do I have any objection to the distribution of a politically conservative voter guide.

But here we need to set aside my smart-aleck remarks and get serious: To identify an agenda as "Christian" without so much as a nod to peace, poverty, and planet Earth is a shameful exploitation of faith. Christ did provide us with a voter guide. It's called the Gospels, and it is replete—chapter after chapter, verse after verse—with love for the poor and concern for peace. My own CliffsNotes version of Jesus' voter guide is borrowed from Gandhi, who identified what he called the "Seven Deadly Social Sins": wealth without work, pleasure without conscience, science without humanity, knowledge without character, commerce without morality, worship without sacrifice, and politics without principle.

That last one is my favorite, and it's where truly faithful voting for Middle Church, Middle Synagogue, and Middle Mosque must begin. Just as Jesus had to drive the moneychangers from the temple before God's presence could be felt, we must reform our political system before the voice of faithful Americans will be heard.

Congress isn't quite the "den of robbers" Jesus famously declared the Temple had become. For that matter, the sometimes rough-and-tumble arena of politics isn't supposed to be as sacrosanct as God's house. But our democratic institutions are the seat of our highest aspirations as a people, and anyone who thinks money doesn't truly matter isn't paying careful attention. I know; I was there. Back in my day, members of Congress were permitted to accept honoraria from interest groups, legal bribes not so thinly veiled as speaking fees. It took a few events like the House banking scandals to shut down honoraria. But in politics, money always has a way of finding its way back. Now the payoffs come in the form of "fact-finding" junkets, golfing outings to Scotland, conferences at Disney World, and so forth. Another round of "reforms" is sure to follow the most recent round of scandals, which booted Tom DeLay from the majority leader's office and got lobbyist Jack Abramoff a felony rap sheet. I can't predict exactly what will happen, but you don't have to be a prophet to know the end result: The money will come back until we decide to get serious about reform.

Politicians' typical approach to reforms is incremental. They'll lower the ceiling on how much a lobbyist can pay to take them to lunch, or ban free trips but not free meals, or maybe require more disclosure (as though a working family holding down several jobs has time to take field trips to Washington to troll through the voluminous disclosure forms on file there). It's as though Jesus came into the Temple and negotiated a settlement whereby the moneychangers could stay as long as they reduced the exchange rates. But Jesus' approach is exactly what we need today—knocking over the money-changers' tables and driving them out of the temple of our democracy altogether. Faithful reform can't just reduce the role of money in politics; it has to get money *out* of politics.

I'd start by banning gifts of any sort, not reducing their price or increasing disclosure. There's no need for one nickel of food, travel, cigars, trinkets, or whatever coins are being exchanged. I have a hard time buying the idea that members of Congress are financially stretched compared to families pulling down the minimum wage, but if they are, let's pay them more and do it right out in the open rather than let lobbyists do it for us. Congress should enact bipartisan ethics reforms that prohibit gifts and lengthen the amount of time required to lapse before a member of Congress can become a lobbyist.

We need the same approach to campaign reform. As long as we're focused on *fewer* campaign contributions, the cause is lost. There's too much money to be made in Washington to count on either interest groups or office-holders to abide by self-restraint. What we need is dramatic reform that expels private money from politics altogether. One of the more interesting proposals is the so-called Arizona model, developed by an organization called Public Campaign, whereby candidates get full public funding for campaigns as long as they promise not to take large private contributions. Total reform like public financing is the only way to get the moneychangers out altogether. It's also the best hope for getting some ordinary people in Congress—fewer lawyers, more teachers and nurses, and maybe even a handful who actually know what it's like to try raising a family on the minimum wage.

Personally, I'm in favor of some more dramatic reforms that break Congress—especially the House of Representatives—out of the permanent reelection mode that has seized and now dominates the entire institution. Term limits would be a powerful place to start. I served six terms in Congress and I don't think I would have been effective very far beyond that. Lifetime service in Congress is a little bit like military service in *Catch-22*: If you want to be there for life, that's irrefutable proof that you shouldn't be. Once the idea of permanent service in Congress is dangled before politicians as a temptation, each election takes on growing importance, and money becomes a greater influence.

I remember well how it worked. I'd vote with interest groups like teachers or organized labor, not because they wanted me to but because that's just where my values were, so they'd donate to my campaign. Then, soon after an election, they'd show up and remind me that I won with 50.000001 percent of the vote. (This was supposed to be a warning. For me, it was a badge of honor. It told me that people knew where I stood. I've always said it's a waste for anyone to leave office popular. Popularity gets you elected; doing the right thing is called "spending it.") Since I barely won, they'd intimate, I was going to need their support—financial and otherwise—even more the next time around, and they would be pleased to help me, and by the way, there were another ten or twelve legislative items they'd like to discuss for the upcoming session of Congress. Now, as it happened, I supported what teachers and labor organizations wanted more often than not anyway. But because I wasn't interested in staying in Congress forever, the idea of leaving an election or two earlier than I'd planned wasn't that big a deal to me. I wasn't clinging to every campaign for dear life. So in my political campaigns, I was free to take their money or leave it and evaluate their legislative ideas on the merits.

The point of term limits isn't so much that politicians turn into pumpkins after twelve years. It's that each election seems just a little less important the moment you give up the idea that you have to win every election for the rest of your life. In fact, I'd take matters even further. Let's pass a constitutional amendment to put members of the House of Representatives in office for four years instead of two so they don't have to start running for reelection the minute they're sworn in. Let's encourage them to get out and see the world—to feel it and touch it, to interact, to listen—and let's quit our griping about junkets and foot the bill so they don't have to go on the take from special interests. I'd much rather pay for a member of Congress to visit Darfur or spend a week visiting with Americans struggling with rural poverty—legitimate expenses that would enrich their understanding and deepen public policy—than save a few fractions of a penny per taxpayer so politicians can go to Scotland on private jets and play golf with lobbyists at private expense. And here's another constitutional amendment: Presidents should be limited to a single, longer term—maybe six years, perhaps eight—so they can focus on doing what they believe is right rather than heeding the advice of pollsters.

But here's the catch: Reform is an agenda, not an excuse. Corruption isn't nearly as big a threat to our democracy as corrosive cynicism—the kind that provokes faithful Americans to throw up our hands rather than rolling up our sleeves. "All have sinned and fall short of the glory of God," the Bible tells us (Rom. 3:23). None of us is pure, and we shouldn't expect our political leaders to be any saintlier than the rest of us. I accepted some speaking honoraria when I was in Congress, and many Americans have voted their personal pocketbooks but too rarely stopped to vote the pocketbooks of the poor. The vast majority of members of Congress are good people doing their best in a tough job that's a little like sitting in front of a television with five hundred stations while someone keeps flipping the channel. My lobbying advice is simple (and, I admit, plagiarized from Jesus): Do unto an elected official as you would have that elected official do unto you. Make eye contact, speak respectfully and, most important, don't get discouraged. The radical religious right has lost just as many elections as the faithful majority has, and I have yet to see them give up on the political process. We won't reclaim our democracy until we decide our values are as important to us as the far religious right's principles are to them.

I've heard every excuse there is for apathy and inaction, and I have yet to hear a good one. "But Bob," mainstream people of faith say, "politicians won't listen to us." For that problem, I have a top-secret solution guaranteed to work 100 percent of the time: Give them an award. But don't present it until the end of the meeting, after they've heard you out. You're likelier to meet a unicorn trotting up Pennsylvania Avenue than a member of Congress who won't show up at a church or synagogue to get his or her picture taken and receive a plaque. If you ask for a meeting, try holding it in your community rather than in Washington. The Capitol may be more star-studded, but it's also filled with alcoves, roll-call votes, and committee hearings that provide ready-made excuses for politicians not to show up. If you're relegated to a meeting with staff rather than the Big Guy or the Big Gal, be grateful rather than resentful, because staff members are often the quickest way to get things done. And help them learn with experiences, not just words. No lecture about the poor is as compelling or memorable as inviting your member of Congress to spend a night in a homeless shelter or a morning sitting on the floor of a Head Start center.

"But even if they show up," the reply inevitably comes, "they only care about money, and we don't have any to give them." Nonsense. The faithful center has something politicians covet even more:

votes. The member communions of the National Council of Churches include some 45 million parishioners, and if just half of them voted their faithful values, if we joined together with our brothers and sisters in Middle Synagogue and Middle Mosque, we would trigger a seismic, historic change in American politics. Politicians take us for granted only because we let them, because we allow our consciences to be bought off with a couple of tax cuts or a pork barrel project here and there. If we are to be faithful voters, politicians must be as afraid to cut welfare as they are to raise taxes, as eager to make peace as they are to start wars. Faithful voting demands that we take our consciences to the ballot box with us, that, in our hearts if not our coat pockets, we carry a little less of the Christian Coalition Voter Guide and a lot more of Micah 6:8: "He has told you, O mortal, what is good; and what does the Lord require of you but to do justice, and to love kindness, and to walk humbly with your God?"

## 6. Blessed Are Those Who Challenge Us to Work for Justice

In 2004, I flew to Los Angeles to speak at a retirement party for Cecil "Chip" Murray, the long-time pastor of the First AME Church in Los Angeles, or FAME, as it's so rightly called. I got the unenviable job of speaking right after Muhammad Ali and right before Stevie Wonder (and if you can believe this, nobody—not one single person—asked for my autograph that night). Chip grew FAME from a struggling congregation of a couple hundred parishioners to a thriving church of more than eighteen thousand, and he did it by constantly forcing every last one of them out of their comfort zones. During the tragic Los Angeles riots of 1992, Chip asked one hundred African-American men in his congregation to stand in the least comfortable place I can imagine: between the police and the rioters. He made FAME a focal point of social action in his community. Some of the most innovative programs for at-risk youth were run out of his church. He challenged, he offended, he inspired, and most of all, he grew.

Mainline churches face a choice. (And I'm guessing this applies to mainline synagogues and mosques as well.) We can provide nice places where people can sing songs and hear sermons for an hour on Sunday mornings and maybe attend club meetings during the week. It's a nice, comfortable spot at the edge of the riverbank where we're not likely to get too wet, but we aren't going to catch many fish, either. Or we can follow prophetic leaders like Chip Murray into the deep waters. Chip was on the leading edge of a well-documented trend: Whether on the right or left politically, churches that engage in social action and stand firmly on the side of issues they are passionate about are growing. Those that aren't involved—*actively* and *personally* involved—in life-changing social action are shrinking.

Mainline churches have a lot of problems today, and any minister will tell you that money is pretty close to the top of the list. I know the feeling. But churches don't have a financial problem. That's the symptom, not the illness. We have a vision problem. People don't give money and time to deficits or bland operating budgets; they donate to visions. Visions have to be clear, powerful, and unencumbered by the fear of giving offense.

Remember all those ministers who I said were on autopulpit? I hear from them all the time. "I agree with you, Bob," they'll say when I challenge them to move their parishioners out of their comfort zones and into some of the most vulnerable corners of our society. "But people don't like being lectured, and I can't afford to lose any more members." My response is equally frank: "If you want to keep getting smaller, keep doing what you're doing. Because if you don't raise a prophetic voice, if you don't give people something to believe in, you *will* lose members." Of course, nobody likes being lectured, which is why I believe in nonverbal sermons—meaningful, concrete expressions of love that change the world around us. "You will know we are Christians by our love," the hymn writer tells us.

It's not enough for Middle Church to engage in faithful voting, for we cannot drive a truck full of society's problems up to the polling place and dump the responsibility of love for neighbor at the government's doorstep. To say that *only* government is responsible for the least of these, our brothers and sisters, is no more sensible or faithful than the far right saying only private charities are responsible. Rather than ideological assertions that government is useless or government is all-powerful, we need partnerships between the public, private, and nonprofit sectors. Institutions of faith are the backbone of civil society. There are many desperately needed social action programs—drug and alcohol rehabilitation come to mind—that work better in the trusted and comfortable setting of a church, synagogue, or mosque. Other efforts, like Head Start, work just as well whether the building is secular or religious.

Most institutions of Middle Church do a great deal in the area of social action, but all could do more. Equally important, we must engage personally, not just at the arm's length of collecting donations for worthy causes. Let me give you one example. Many on the far religious right are obsessed with prayer in school. Well, as long as there are final exams, there will *always* be prayer in school, and we don't need teachers or principals to lead it or governments to demand it. What churches, synagogues, and mosques can do is open their doors *after* school, providing a safe and constructive place for young people to be during the after-school hours when they are at the greatest risk of drug use, risky sexual behavior, and other forms of troublemaking. Whether it's after-school activities for children or weekend shelters for the homeless, the resources of our churches, synagogues, and mosques can be deployed far more effectively to make love of neighbor a meaningful commitment. We owe this not simply to the least of these, our brothers and sisters, but to ourselves.

There are ample excuses, even very thoughtful and well considered reasons, for institutions of faith not to make their resources available to the community. If you take this idea to your elders or board of directors or other governing body, you'd better be prepared. Don't have the money? Raise it. Lacking in personnel? Find volunteers. Worried about damage to the building? Get over it. Logistical problems? Solve them. (Feel free to mix up these answers. It keeps everyone on their toes.) And when all else fails, recall Edgar's Iron Law of Getting Things Done: It's easier to ask forgiveness than to ask permission.

There's one other barrier to prophetic leadership from Middle Church: institutional egos. You've heard of the "Not Invented Here" syndrome, the genetic disorder that causes organizations to resist any idea that didn't originate with them? Both institutions of faith and progressive organizations generally suffer from a plague of it. We tend to be either so specialized or so layered with bureaucracy or so worried about who gets credit for what that we rarely work together. We don't form coalitions or "deep frame" issues because we are reluctant to work with anyone who does not agree with us on everything.

My friend Andrew Greenblatt, an environmental activist, describes the attitude this way: "I'm an environmentalist. I'm an environmentalist who cares about water. I'm an environmentalist who cares about water in rivers. I'm an environmentalist who cares about water in rivers, but especially estuaries. I'm an environmentalist who cares about water in rivers, but especially estuaries, but what I really want to see is land management around wetlands. I care about wildlife in wetlands. But only frogs, not lizards." Now, frogs are swell animals, and wetlands are fine places, and there's nothing wrong with being concerned about either one. But that's not exactly an attitude likely to result in a broad-based environmental movement, much less a broad-based coalition for peace, poverty, and planet Earth.

Maybe that problem exists on the far religious right, too, but from the outside, it looks as if they do exactly what Middle Church needs to do: identify a few large issues and get behind them without all the behind-the-scenes bickering that inhibits collaborative efforts.

Ask anyone from a progressive group what it's like to organize a coalition, and I guarantee you'll hear that they spend more time negotiating who gets credit for what and who stands where at the press conference and whose name comes first on the press release than they do about the substance of an issue.

I've learned at the National Council of Churches that you have to build consensus where it exists, not demand orthodoxy on everything. One of my most memorable learning experiences was the time I sent an e-mail to the offices and key staff persons within our thirty-five member communions telling them we were preparing some literature on the Millennium Development Goals and would welcome their input. I spent the next two and a half days answering irate messages from people demanding to know why I hadn't gone through the proper channels (whatever those were) and consulted the proper authorities (exactly what I was attempting to do), but not one single inquiry about the substance of the Millennium Goals.

Another friend of mine handled such a situation even more directly. He was discussing a particular point of the war in Iraq with the Washington representative of a major Protestant denomination.

"Well," this representative protested, "I can't talk to you about that because we don't have policy on it."

"Excuse me," my exasperated colleague replied, "but we have the Bible!"

Indeed we do, and all things considered, the Bible's dictates are pretty straightforward. One of them is: "Pride goes before destruction, and a haughty spirit before a fall." There's an antidote to the "Not Invented Here" syndrome. I call it "ego disarmament." The institutions of Middle Church and progressive politics need to stop focusing on pride and purity and start working together to frame issues deeply and engage in them more effectively.

We're making progress. The antiwar coalition contained a number of groups that disagreed with each other on issues ranging from the environment to the economy. Different religious denominations are working together more closely as well. Jim Wallis and I disagree on a few issues, for example, but my policy is that if he calls a press conference or organizes an event on an urgent topic—such as the immorality of balancing the budget on the backs of the poor—I'm going to be there. If somebody else wants to put their own logo on the front of a booklet prepared by the National Council of Churches, that's fine, too. What matters is the substance of our work, not whose name is attached to it.

We all have excuses, whether it's institutional ego or individual inertia, for not engaging more actively in our world. They are all serious—and solvable—problems, but I don't think they're the real reason institutions of faith have become so cautious and timid. No, I believe we are too easily intimidated by the scope of problems in our world. We do not reach out to one homeless person because we feel an obligation to rid the entire nation of homelessness. We do not feed one hungry child because we are too busy worrying about the global epidemic of hunger. What we need is a spirit that moves us to change the world we see one heart at a time. The first must be our own. What we need is the final and perhaps the most urgent beatitude for deep-water citizenship.


## 7. Blessed Are Those with a Sense of Humor and a Sense of Hope

Merle tells a story about the time when we were young and struggling a bit and Bob, Jr., was a baby (of course, maybe she'd say the same thing about Bob, Sr.). I was commuting two hundred miles each way between Lewisburg, Pennsylvania, where I was working with my friend and mentor, Reverend Ned Weller, as an assistant pastor of Beaver Memorial United Methodist Church, and Drew University, where I was finishing up my last year of seminary. We traded in our old car with thousands of miles of hard wear and tear to buy a new, green Volkswagen. It still had two years of payments on it. We were living on the third floor of an old apartment building that didn't have parking, so we left the car a couple of blocks away on the street. One afternoon, we got a call from someone at the church who said we'd better go check on the car, because it looked like someone had smashed into it.

We scooped up the baby and ran down there as quickly as we could, only to see the entire front end of our little VW crumpled up. There clearly wasn't enough to salvage. We had insurance, but with a very high deductible. On our limited salary, we had enough trouble making the payments on the car we had, and now we were looking at buying a new one. Merle was standing there, with a baby in her arms, crying and panicked. She asked aloud how in God's name were we ever going to find the money to buy a new car. I took one look at the car, shrugged my shoulders, and said not to worry about it, that we'd figure it out, and at least no one was hurt.

Merle and I are a pretty good team. She keeps me pulled down to earth, and I lift her up when the everyday concerns of life drag her a little too close to the ground. I suppose you could say I was putting on a brave face at a tough time for a fragile family, but the truth is that I don't remember contemplating the possibility that we wouldn't figure a way out of this jam. There must be a worrying chromosome that God forgot to give me.

And not having a worrying chromosome is a helpful trait these days, when the values in which you and I believe, the values that have animated my faith tradition for two thousand years, are under assault. Middle Church feels overrun and outfought and powerless, our nation is embroiled in a tragic war whose end appears distant, and the far religious right controls the White House and both houses of Congress. And yet, I'm sorry, I can't help it, *I believe.*

I believe because hope is one of the greatest moral absolutes, because it is the wondrous gift with which God repays faith, because the alternative is despair. And if hope is the highest commandment, then despair must be the greatest sin. When Dr. Jonas Salk, who invented the cure for polio, spoke before the Congressional Clearinghouse on the Future back in the 1980s, one of my colleagues asked him why he was an optimist.

I remember his reply: "It's easy to be a pessimist. All you have to do is go home at night and wait for the sky to fall. I choose to get out of bed in the morning and try to do something about it."

Ingrained in my faith is God's call to provide a flicker of light in the midst of darkness. This is not the only time in our history that dark clouds have brewed on the horizon. Neither must it be the first time we surrender to despair rather than reaching deep within ourselves for the hope and possibility and promise with which God has equipped every human soul. We are called to use our faith to give hope to others—and ourselves. Paul has charted our way. His letter to the Corinthians must now be received as a message to Middle Church: "And now faith, hope, and love abide, these three; and the greatest of these is love." I slightly disagree with Paul. They are all great! And I would add laughter, for laughter is the sustenance and nourishment of hope. "Make a joyful noise to God," the Psalm 66 invites us. To laugh and to hope and to smile is not to be blind to tragedy, for in a world of hunger and hopelessness, of war and disease, racism and intolerance, tragedy and calamity can escape our notice only if we avert our eyes. Rather, to be an optimist is to care enough to try, to have faith enough to believe that the small actions of our lives, those fleeting moments in which we raise a courageous voice or touch a stranger's heart or cast a faithful ballot will be woven together into a tapestry of meaningful and global and prophetic change. We must weep at our world, but weeping must be a prelude to action. And we cannot act from the comfort of our daily lives. We can act only in the deep waters and the fast currents, where bombs destroy and children go hungry and the air and water are foul, and we can do so only with a sense of hope.

These are the places where we are afraid to go, but I do not believe it is the disease or the despair we fear nearly so much as the prospect of failure. That fear, like all others, is one we can overcome only by confronting it squarely. I have failed plenty of times in plenty of endeavors, and I recommend it highly. Progress is what's left over when ninety-nine defeats are subtracted from a hundred victories. We move forward an inch at a time, just a bit, just enough, to change our world and sustain our faith.

I cannot countenance the agenda of the radical religious right in whatever form it is expressed, but least of all can it be permitted to speak for the faith I cherish and to which I have devoted my life. The constant clatter of the far religious right, those radical few who invoke Christ from one side of their mouths and, from the other, advocate war and environmental destruction and cuts in support desperately needed by the poor, is precisely what Paul meant when he said those who profess faith without love are a "noisy gong or clanging cymbal." It is disgraceful, but not nearly so much as the apathy that has allowed it to prevail. Middle Church cannot drown out that clanging with silence. Only a prophetic voice of genuine love can be heard.

The question Middle Church must ask, that mainstream Americans of all traditions must ask, is simple: Do we value our faith enough to reclaim it? Do we believe fervently enough in Christ's message of love—or however we hear God's word—to stand up and say we will no longer allow it to be co-opted in the service of an agenda that runs contrary to our religious teachings? Do we believe the peacemakers are blessed enough to stand up to those who make war in the name of our faith? Do we believe God's creation is sacred enough to say we will not sit by as it is despoiled by those who invoke God's name? Do we believe the poor deserve our love enough that we will not allow those who call themselves ministers of God to heap scorn and misfortune upon the least of these, our brothers and sisters? Do we believe *our* family values—peace, poverty, and planet Earth—deserve equal billing with the so-called values agenda of the far religious right?

These are the questions we must ask. And then we must ask ourselves another.

Are we foolish enough to believe and faithful enough to hope? I hope we are. After all, in a world where a kid who got 730 combined on his College Boards can grow up and be a minister and run for Congress and write a book, surely God did not intend to put anything beyond anyone's reach. It is neither the far right nor the far left on whose action or apathy the fate of our planet and its people depends. It is Middle Church, and Middle Church must awaken from a long slumber, during which what we understood for two thousand years to be Christ's message of love for all has been seized by one small sliver of the evangelical religious right. It is not the geniuses on whose shoulders our faith rests. It is the fools, those courageous and prophetic few whose hearts are sufficiently overflowing with God's love that they have a surplus to share, those, to borrow the phrase of John Wesley, the founder of Methodism, whose hearts are "strangely warmed."

I pray for the strength and faith Middle Church (the faithful center of all religions) needs in order to reclaim our nation. Yet there is no prayer more powerful than our own works, and so I leave you with exactly such a blessing, a Franciscan benediction in whose words there is enough power for authentic and passionate faith to prevail. For the answer to this prayer, like all others, must come not from God but from ourselves.

*May God bless you with* discomfort . . .
*At easy answers, half-truths, and superficial relationships,*
*So that you may live deep within your heart.*

*May God bless you with anger . . .*
*At injustice, oppression, and exploitation of people,*
*So that you may work for justice, freedom, and peace.*

*May God bless you with tears . . .*
*To shed for those who suffer from pain, rejection, starvation, and war,*

*So that you may reach out your hand to comfort them*
*And to turn their pain into joy.*

*And may God bless you with enough* foolishness . . .
*To believe that you can make a difference in this world,*
*So that you can* do *what others claim cannot be done.*

And to that prayer, in whatever language we express it, in whatever tradition it is heard, let all us all say in a joyful and faithful and prophetic voice that weds prayer with works and hope with action: Amen.

# Acknowledgments

I am enormously grateful to a large number of friends, family, and colleagues who have inspired and shaped my thinking over the years. Their dedication to justice and openness to sharing their insights with me have been greatly appreciated. To all of them I owe my deepest gratitude and I am indebted to each and every one.

I wish to especially thank Greg Weiner for his assistance in carefully writing and rewriting this text. He was the not-so-ghostlike force behind making the words match the message. While coming from two different faith traditions, we share a common faith in God. We continue to have faith in our fellow citizens to turn away from the radical right's neoconservative vision of America and toward an America that stands for justice and models itself on the highest moral standards. Rebecca, Hannah, and Jacob Weiner heeded the biblical call to "love the stranger" even when their husband and father became one while helping me with this book.

Bob Bender, our editor at Simon & Schuster and, more important, a model of both personal faith and faithful politics, conceived of this project and guided it with skill that was exceeded only by his patience. Several very creative researchers helped check important facts. Thanks to Katie Kaplun, Adam Salazar, and Amanda Rebekah Evans.

I also want to thank all those who helped get me started in ministry and taught me that God was broader and deeper than the image of an old godlike man flying around on a cloud zapping people. Pastors such as Reverend George Mamourian, Reverend Charlie Lobb, Reverend Ned Weller, Reverend Ted Loder, Reverend Bill Coffin, the Reverend Dr. Martin Luther King, Jr., and many others taught me that the church can be relevant and effective in speaking out for justice and the poor.

Let me also thank all those who taught me how to run for public office and who sustained me over my political years in Congress, putting up with my strange sense of humor and insatiable need to make a difference. People such as John Briscoe, Ed McGuire, Joan Mandel, Bonnie Hallam, Skip Powers, Richard Fuller, Audrey Bardsley, Kathy Altman, Will Robinson, Van Sheets, Gary Grobman, Walter Pierzchalla, Pricilla Skillman, the constituents of the Seventh Congressional District of Pennsylvania, and many others who taught me about the political process and enabled me to win six terms in the United States House of Representatives as a liberal Democrat in one of the most Republican congressional districts in America. Also, members of Congress who talked the talk and walked the walk with grace and honesty, such as Senator Hubert Humphrey (D-MN), Senator Paul Simon (D-IL), Senator John Heinz (R-PA), Congressman Berkley Bedell (D-IA), Congressman James Leach (R-IA), and many others who understood what it meant to be ethical public servants.

In addition, let me thank all those who had enough faith in me to select and support me as president of the Claremont School of Theology in Claremont, California. Although I had few academic credentials, we laughed and worked our way through enormous fiscal exigencies to stabilize the school and make a contribution to modern theological education. People like Roy Miller, Judge Ted Todd, Dr. Marjorie Suchocki, Reverend Jim Swenson, Spencer Bates, Reverend Don Locher, the students-faculty-trustees-donors, and many others who helped salvage and enhance a great institution.

Thanks to Dr. Lo Sprague and Dr. Gwynne Guibord, whose courage and grace have modeled for me the meaning of love in harmony with the world.

I am pleased to thank the leaders of the National Council of Churches for their willingness to explore ways to make the churches' voices clearer and more effective in confronting the major moral and church-dividing issues of our times. People like Bishop James Matthews, Bishop Mel Talbert, Reverend Cliff Kirkpatrick, Bishop Mark Hanson, Elenie Huszagh, Bishop Thomas Hoyt, Father Leonid Kishkovsky, Ambassador Andrew Young, Reverend Michael Livingston, Clare Chapman, Reverend Cheryl Wade, and many others whose faithful commitment to ecumenism has been a model for me to emulate. Also, people like Vicki Manning, Leora Landmesser, Reverend Patrice Rosner, Reverend Brenda Girton-Mitchell, Pat Pattillo, Dr. Ann Riggs, Dr. Tony Kireopoulos, Reverend Shanta Premawardhana, Dr. Eileen Lindner, Sarah Vilankulu, Reverend Leslie Tune, Cassandra Carmichael, Reverend Paul Sherry, Vince Isner, Garland Pierce, and other staff and former staff of the NCC who work hard day after day to give voice to the voiceless and hope to the hopeless. In addition, people like Jim Winkler, Gary Ferdman, Reverend Jim Wallis, Andrew Greenblatt, J. Irwin Miller, Paul Gorman, Rabbi David Saperstein, Sayyid Muhammad Syeed, Reverend Ken Bensen, Don and Peggy Shriver, and many, many others who have helped me wrestle with the art of ecumenism and the science of interfaith relations in a pluralistic world.

A special word of thanks and appreciation goes to my oldest and closest friend, Reverend Thomas Gallen. Thom has known me since my days in church youth groups, college, seminary—throughout my life. If you want the inside story on Bob Edgar, check with Thom.

Finally, let me thank my wife, Merle, my sons, Rob, David, and Andy, and my entire extended family for putting up with both my puns and my passion to help change the world. Merle has kept me grounded. My sons have kept me focused. My grandchildren have kept me hopeful. My mother, Marion, has kept me smiling. My brothers, Ralph and Richard, have kept me rooted in my love for sports and fishing. And my father's memory has kept me filled with the joy for life.

I am grateful to all those persons who have helped me along life's journey. They have been inspirational, but are not responsible for what follows. As the African proverb reminds us: "If you want to walk fast, walk alone. If you want to walk far, walk together." Thanks to all those who have walked together with me thus far.

# Notes

## Preface

Page

2   *"If by a liberal"*: John F. Kennedy, "Acceptance of the New York Liberal Party Nomination," September 14, 1960, http://www.pbs.org/wgbh/amex/presidents/35_kennedy/psources/ps_nyliberal.html.

## Introduction

Page

15   *We are now faced*: Martin Luther King, Jr., *Where Do We Go From Here: Chaos or Community* (New York: Harper & Row, 1967).

## Chapter 1:
## The Two Churches

Page

17   *If Christian people*: Alan Dershowitz, "Beware of the Stealth Candidates," *Buffalo News*, August 9, 1995, 3B.

22   *You say what's going to happen*: Garry Wills, *Under God: Religion and American Politics* (New York: Simon and Schuster, 1990), 147.

26      *"Woe unto the world"*: William Safire, *Lend Me Your Ears: Great Speeches in History* (New York: W. W. Norton & Company, 1997), 471.

29      *formulated by Marian Wright Edelman*: Marian Wright Edelman, *The Measure of Our Success: A Letter to My Children* (Boston: Beacon Press, 1992), 95.

Chapter 2:
In the Beginning, God Created the Heavens and the Earth ...
So Stop MessingThem Up!

*Page*

31      *The fact is that there is no global warming*: CNN, *Inside Politics*, November 20, 2002.

34      *If you read back in the Bible*: CNN, *Late Edition*, October 9, 2005.

35      *Forty-five senators*: Glenn Scherer, "The Godly Must Be Crazy," *Grist*, October 27, 2004, http://www.grist.org/news/maindish/2004/10/27/scherer-christian/.

35      Mother Jones *revealed*: *Mother Jones*, "Put a Tiger In Your Think Tank," May/June 2005, http://www.motherjones.com/news/featurex/2005/05/exxon_chart.html.

36      *He explained the effort*: Michael Janofsky, "When Cleaner Air Is a Biblical Obligation," *New York Times*, November 7, 2005, A18.

36      *"You can always find"*: ibid.

39      *A secular society*: Scherer, "The Godly Must Be Crazy."

40      *If today is a typical day*: David W. Orr, *Earth in Mind* (Washington, D.C.: Island Press, 1994), 7.

46      *there are around* one trillion *tons*: *Climate Change: Science—Action—2005 Conference, October 6–8, Aspen; Colorado*, workbook for Aspen Institute conference.

53      *Phyllis Schlafly, the founder*: Phyllis Schlafly, "Kyoto's Goal = Kick the U.S.," *The Phyllis Schlafly Report*. July 2001, http://www.eagleforum.org/psr/2001/july01/psrjuly01.shtml.

61      *"Join us in restoring God's Earth"*: National Council of Churches,

"God's Earth Is Sacred: An Open Letter to Church and Society in the United States," February 14, 2005, http://www.ncccusa.org/news/14.02.05theologicalstatement.html.

## Chapter 3:
## What Part of "Blessed Are the Peacemakers" Don't They Understand?

*Page*

63    *We should invade:* Ann Coulter, "This Is War," *National Review Online*, September 13, 2001, http://www.nationalreview.com/coulter/coulter.shtml.

64    *In the long run:* People for the American Way, "Talking Out of Turn: The Right's Campaign Against Dissent," *Right Wing Watch Online*, April 29, 2003, http://www.pfaw.org/pfaw/general/default.aspx ?old=10389.

64    *"why any churchman":* Jim Brown and Bill Fancher, "D. James Kennedy Questions Rationale of Church Leaders' Anti-War Attitude," Agape Press, March 26, 2003, http://headlines.agapepress .org/archive/3/262003a.asp.

64    *Pat Robertson would later accuse:* People for the American Way, "Talking Out of Turn: The Right's Campaign Against Dissent," *Right Wing Watch Online*, April 29, 2003, http://www.pfaw.org/pfaw/general/default.aspx?old=10389.

77    *Pat Robertson, for example:* Pat Robertson, "Bring It On: The War on Terror," http://www.cbn.com/700club/features/BringItOn/waron terror-index.asp#8.

77    *"Years ago, while still in seminary":* Erik Kolbell, *What Jesus Meant: The Beatitudes and a Meaningful Life* (Louisville, Kentucky: Westminster John Knox Press, 2003).

## Chapter 4:
## Deny Them Their Victory: Faith in the Age of Terrorism

*Page*

85    *If it takes ten years:* CNN, *Live Sunday,* October 24, 2004.

90    *"We're not attacking Islam":* "Hall of Shame," *Washington Post,* November 22, 2001, A46.

90    *"Conservatives saw":* Patrick D. Healy, "Rove Criticizes Liberals on 9/11," *New York Times,* June 23, 2005, A13.

98    *A 1998 report:* Dick Bell and Michael Renner, "A New Marshall Plan? Advancing Human Security and Controlling Terrorism," Worldwatch Institute, October 9, 2001, http://www.world watch.org/press/news/2001/10/09/.

99    *I think the insecurity: William Sloane Coffin: A Lover's Quarrel With America.* Old Dog Documentaries, Inc., 2003.

100   *"We will have to repent":* Martin Luther King, Jr., and James M. Washington, ed., *A Testament of Hope: The Essential Writings and Speeches of Martin Luther King, Jr.* (New York: HarperCollins, 1990), 296.

100   *"To be neutral":* Desmond Tutu, *The Rainbow People of God: The Making of a Peaceful Revolution* (New York: Doubleday, 1994).

## Chapter 5:
## We're the Good Guys—Let's Act Like It!

*Page*

101   *The United States condemns:* U.S. Department of State, *The United States' Commitment to Fight Torture,* http://www.state.gov/p/io/fs/2002/14901.htm.

101   *[Torture] must be equivalent:* Mike Allen and Dana Priest, "Memo on Torture Draws Focus to Bush," *Washington Post.* June 9, 2004, A3.

105   *Interrogations have reportedly:* Michael Ratner and Ellen Ray, *Guantánamo: What the World Should Know.* (White River Junction, VT: Chelsea Green Publishing Company, 1994), 42–43.

108   *Many years ago:* Terry Waite interview with Democracy Now!

http://www.democracynow.org/article.pl?sid=04/03/10/1537255, March 10, 2004.

110 *the equivalent of a fraternity prank:* Laura Randall, "How to Separate a Boy From His Beer Change," *New York Times*, August 1, 2004, 4A7.

111 *"We don't kick":* Dana Priest and Barton Gellman, "U.S. Decries Abuse but Defends Interrogations," *Washington Post*, December 26, 2002, A1.

112 *"The security forces continued":* U.S. Department of State, "Country Reports on Human Rights Practices, 2004," http://www.state.gov/g/drl/rls/hrrpt/2004/41586.htm, February 8, 2005.

114 *"I wish you would look at the facts":* Congressional Record, June 19, 1985.

118 *And, addressing those who say humanity:* General Kermit Johnson, "A Nuclear Reality: Beyond Niebuhr and the Just War," *Congressional Record*, December 13, 1982.

122 *"As citizens of the United States":* Charles Austin, "300 Church Leaders Protest U.S. Policies in Central America," *New York Times*, November 28, 1982, A14.

Chapter 6:
Reconciling Abraham's Children:
Toward Peace in the Middle East

*Page*

127 *He was dividing:* CNN, "Robertson Suggests God Smote Sharon," January 6, 2006, http://www.cnn.com/2006/US/01/05/robertson.sharon/.

133 *"The Jews need conversion":* 60 Minutes, June 8, 2003, http://www.cbsnews.com/stories/2002/10/03/60minutes/main524268.shtml.

133 *According to the prophetic:* Now With Bill Moyers, PBS, February 20, 2004, http://www.pbs.org/now/transcript/transcript308_full.html.

134 *"They don't love":* 60 Minutes, June 8, 2003.

## Chapter 7:
## Compassion, Not Contempt:
## Hearing God's Call to Love the Poor

*Page*

141  *[Welfare is] for deadbeats:* Patrick Jasperse, "Christian right's banner is social ills," *Milwaukee Journal Sentinel.* January 21, 1996, A1.

141  *"It was once said":* Hubert Humphrey, *Congressional Record*, November 1, 1977.

142  *The most recent Census Bureau statistics:* U.S. Census Bureau, "Poverty: 2004 Highlights," http://www.census.gov/hhes/www/poverty/poverty04/pov04hi.html.

148  *"Governments can err":* *The Columbia World of Quotations*, www.bartleby.com.

149  *The prosperity gospel is rooted:* William Lobdell, "The Prosperity Gospel," *Los Angeles Times*, September 20, 2004, A1.

150  *Houston television preacher:* Joel Osteen, *Your Best Life Now* (New York: Time Warner Book Group, 2004), 41.

## Chapter 8:
## A Living Wage: Washington's Callous
## Antipathy to the Least of These

*Page*

159  *Minimum wage is not a biblical issue:* Sharon Tubbs, "Sorting Through the Catholic Vote," *St. Petersburg Times*, October 16, 2004, http://sptimes.com/2004/10/16/Floridian/Sorting_through_the_C.shtml.

161  *Mr. Speaker:* Holly Sklar and the Rev. Dr. Paul H. Sherry, *A Just Minimum Wage: Good for Workers, Business and Our Future*, http://letjusticeroll.org/justwage.html.

162  *"If we would have had our druthers":* Sklar and Sherry, ibid.

167  *James Dobson's Focus on the Family:* Jonathan Weisman and Alan Cooperman, "A Religious Protest Largely From the Left; Conserva-

tive Christians Say Fighting Cuts in Poverty Programs Is Not a Priority," *Washington Post*, December 14, 2005, A8.

167 *"There is a [biblical] mandate"*: ibid.

167 *"the government is not"*: ibid.

169 *"The Muslim faith teaches hate"*: Don Lattin, "Bush Courts Right to Back Program; But Falwell Urges President to Withhold Social Service Funding from Islamic Groups," *San Francisco Chronicle*. March 8, 2001, http://www.sfgate.com/cgi-bin/article.cgi?file=/chronicle/archive/2001/03/08/MN220744.DTL.

## Chapter 9: The Poverty that Kills:
### Hunger, Injustice, and AIDS: Our Global Moral Crisis

*Page*

179 *AIDS could be:* "Dr. Koop Warns of Spread of AIDS," *New York Times*. January 20, 1987, C11.

182 *Yet the United States:* Organisation for Economic Co-operation and Development, *OECD in Figures—2005 Edition*, http://www.oecd.org/document/34/0,2340,en_2649_201185_2345918_1_1_1_1,00.html.

## Chapter 10: Changing our Beatitudes:
### Guideposts for Deep-Water Citizenship

*Page*

191 *Discrimination against people of faith:* National Alliance Against Christian Discrimination, http://naacd.com/support.htm.

195 *"If a man hasn't discovered":* George Seldes, *The Great Thoughts* (New York: Random House, 1985), 229.

198 *"I find it strange":* Quoted in Barbara Zielinski, "Whom shall I fear?," *Catapult*, March 11, 2005, http://www.catapultmagazine.com/be-afraid/article/whom-shall-i-fear.

206 *It was Pat Robertson: 60 Minutes.* October 6, 2002.

208 *I cannot join Pat Robertson:* " 'Intelligent Design' Vote Has Robert-

son Warning Town," *The Houston Chronicle*, November 11, 2005, A7.

212   *"Hitler and his supporters"*: People for the American Way, "Presenting Alan Keyes," *Right Wing Watch Online*, http://www.pfaw. org/pfaw/general/default.aspx?oid=16725.

# Index